Walter Coote

Wanderings, South and East

Walter Coote

Wanderings, South and East

ISBN/EAN: 9783337003814

Printed in Europe, USA, Canada, Australia, Japan

Cover: Foto ©Andreas Hilbeck / pixelio.de

More available books at **www.hansebooks.com**

WANDERINGS.

SOUTH AND EAST.

KANGAROO HUNTING, FOUR-IN-HAND.

WANDERINGS,

SOUTH AND EAST.

BY

WALTER COOTE, F.R.G.S.

WITH TWO MAPS AND FORTY-SEVEN WOOD ENGRAVINGS,

EXECUTED UNDER THE DIRECTION OF EDWARD WHYMPER, FROM SKETCHES BY THE AUTHOR, NATIVE DRAWINGS, &c.

LONDON:
SAMPSON LOW, MARSTON, SEARLE, & RIVINGTON,
CROWN BUILDINGS, 188 FLEET STREET, E.C.
1882.

[*All rights reserved.*]

LONDON:
PRINTED BY WILLIAM CLOWES AND SONS, LIMITED,
STAMFORD STREET AND CHARING CROSS.

TO

GEORGE FREDERICK POSTLETHWAITE,

This Book is Inscribed,

IN REMEMBRANCE OF THREE YEARS' TRAVEL AND UNBROKEN GOOD
FELLOWSHIP,

BY

HIS MOST AFFECTIONATE FRIEND

THE AUTHOR.

"Here you may range at large from Pole to Pole;
Trace Nature's vast expanse, survey the whole;
O'er lands remote an easy passage find;
Extend your knowledge, and delight your mind;
Travel through regions wide of space immense,
Secure from hazard, at a small expense.
No storms to combat, traveller's charge to pay,
No horse to hire, no guide to point the way,
No Alps to climb, no dreary deserts pass,
No ambuscade, no thieves to give you chase,
No bear to dread, no ravenous wolf to fight,
No flies to sting, no rattlesnake to bite,
No floods to ford, no hurricane to fear,
No savage war-whoop to alarm the ear,
No scorching suns, no chilling blasts to fly,
No thirst and hunger, and relief not nigh;
These perils, all, and horrors you may shun,
Rest when you please, and when you please go on."—*Old Preface.*

PREFACE.

A FEW lines will suffice as introduction to the present volume, which pretends only to be a descriptive record of four years' very pleasant experiences in the far South and East.

The traveller of but a few months or years cannot do more than record, with such truth and freshness as may be possible to him, his impression of the countries as he saw them. He cannot speculate, more than superficially, upon national developments, or the effects of civilisation, but by writing of the things that he has seen and from the information that he has gathered, he may hope to do a little towards dispelling the somewhat widely-spread apathy which prevails amongst his countrymen with reference to the world that lies beyond their shores.

This, however, is no mean object, for the more intimately nations become known, the more rapidly are unsound prejudices dispelled; it is therefore to be hoped that any reasonably interesting book of foreign travel may stand a chance of serving a useful purpose.

I have been indebted, in New Zealand, for much assistance in seeing the country to Sir George Grey; also, in Fiji, for kindly hospitality and valuable information to Sir Arthur Gordon; and, above all, for a prolonged and cordial reception on board the *Southern Cross* and at Norfolk Island, to Bishop Selwyn of the Melanesian Mission; nor can I allow these pages to go to press without the warmest expression of gratitude to the numerous friends in many lands, who so often welcomed me and made their homes as my own.

I have commenced my narrative with Australia, because that country is the true Southern Land. From there I have passed to the Pacific Islands, and thence to "Far Cathay," and still farther Japan. My last division has been devoted to the countries of Spanish origin in South America, and these, although generally recognised as belonging to the Western World, may, after all, by a traveller in Australia or the Orient, be considered as the legitimate "Ultima Thule" of his *Wanderings. South and East.*

London, *January,* 1882.

CONTENTS.

PART I.
THE AUSTRALASIAN COLONIES.

CHAPTER I.
QUEENSLAND.

                                                                PAGE

Departure from Singapore—Volcano of Tambora—Booby Island—Thursday Island—Kanaka pearl divers—Albany—Torres Straits—Cooktown—Whitsunday Passage—" Potting " blacks—Brisbane—Darling Downs—Queensland "bush"—Toowoomba—Climate—A Queensland Station—Kangaroo-hunting—Australian pioneers—Four-in-hand in the bush 1

CHAPTER II.
NEW SOUTH WALES AND VICTORIA.

Sydney—Its suburbs—Port Jackson—The Hawkesbury—The Blue Mountains—Govet's Leap—Solitary bushmen—Lost in the bush—Melbourne—The Yarra Yarra—The public gardens—Politics—Hobart Town—The Tasmanians—The Black's Spur—Big trees—Tree-ferns—Horse-racing—The colonies compared—New South Wales—Cultivation of land—Emigration.. 16

CHAPTER III.
NEW ZEALAND.

Land at The Bluff—The South Island—Lake Wakatipu—Dunedin—New Zealand harbours—By rail to Christchurch—Christchurch—Dinornis skeletons—Lyttleton—New Year's Day at Lyttleton—A coach journey—Hokitiki—Kumara—Public houses—A tramway—Greymouth—Nelson—Wellington—Napier—Lake Taupo

—A native conference—A war-dance—Rotomahana—The pink and white terraces—Ohinemutu—A long ride—The Maori question 31

CHAPTER IV.

NORFOLK ISLAND.

Position of Norfolk Island—Pitcairn's Island—Lord Howe's Island—A difficult landing—Hospitable reception—"The Town"—The prisons—Old convict days—The Cemetery—Norfolk Island scenery—Mr. Nobbs—Whaling—The Melanesian Mission—The College—The Patteson Memorial Chapel—Treatment of the Melanesians—Condition of the community—Invitation to make a voyage in the *Southern Cross* 50

CHAPTER V.

FIJI.

Sydney to Fiji—The Fiji Group—Levuka—Street Life in Levuka—A Native Village—A Fijian Negro—Crossing to Mbau—The Island of Mbau—Hospitality—Native Houses—Kava Drinking—Personal Experience—A Native Doctor—A Historic Spot—The Native School—Singing—Interview with Thakombau—Presents 63

CHAPTER VI.

FIJI continued—THE REWA DISTRICT.

The Rewa River—The Delta—Singular Climatic Conditions—An Evening Walk—Native Farms—Harry Smith's—English Children Canoeing—A Row up the Rewa—The Colonial Sugar Co.—The Rewa Valley—Government House, Levuka—Fijian Pottery—Suva—Fijian Resources—Wesleyan Missionaries—Safety of Englishmen in Fiji 77

PART II.
THE PACIFIC ISLANDS.

CHAPTER VII.
OAHU AND MAUI.

Honolulu—The Hotel—The Streets—Government Building—King Kalakaua—The Pali—Waikiki—A Hawaiian Steamer—Maui—Irrigation—A "ranch"—Haleakala—Ascent—View from Summit—The Crater—Telephones—Molokai 89

CHAPTER VIII.
HAWAII AND ITS VOLCANO.

Coast of Hawaii—Hilo—The Hilo River—Mauna Loa—A Long Ride—Hawaiian Liquor Law—A Drunken Guide—The Volcano House—Descent into Crater—The Lake of Fire—Spectacle by Night—Threatened Eruption—Phenomenon at Kilauea—Eruption of 1881—Professor Clerk's Theory—The Visitors' Book 97

CHAPTER IX.
HAWAII continued.

Native Travellers—Their Habits—Eating Poi—Appearance of the Coast—Natural Products—Caves—Native Canoes—Kealakeakua Bay—Cook's Monument—Review of Missionary Work—What has been accomplished—What should be aimed at—Institution at Honolulu—The Reform School—Departure from Sandwich Islands 110

CHAPTER X.
THE NEW HEBRIDES.

The *Southern Cross*—Settling down—Under weigh—The Loyalty Islands—Distress at Nengone—Mourning for Naiselene—A Ride across the Island—Havannah Harbour—An Island Trader—Shopping on an old French Frigate—The Volcano of Ambrym—"Yamming" at Aragh—Native Farming—An Inland Excursion at Maewo—Beautiful Scenery—The Club-house System—Curious Money—Barbarous Customs—Burial Places—Terrace Formation resembling Rotomahana—Visit to Opa—Caught in a Squall .. 119

CHAPTER XI.

THE BANKS' AND TORRES' ISLANDS.

The Banks' Islands—Mota—A White Trader—Banks' Island Customs—Santa Maria—Legend of the Greedy Bird-Catcher—The Torres' Islands—Lack of Water—Extraordinary Nose Ornament—Sandalwood English—Experiences at Port Mackay—Terrible effect of Disease—Character of Torres' Islanders—Their Industries—Value of Water 136

CHAPTER XII.

THE SANTA CRUZ ISLANDS.

Discovery of the Solomon Islands—Accidental discovery of the Santa Cruz Group—Murder of Bishop Patteson—Murder of Commodore Goodenough—The Island where La Pérouse was lost—Arrival at the Reef Islands—Boarded by Natives—Their Arrows—Their Canoes—Beauty of the Coral Reef—Sea-going Canoes—Formal Reception on shore—Presents—Mats and Money—An Eccentric Character—The Main Island—Enticing the Natives on Board—Appearance of the Natives—Ornaments—Arrows—Clubs—Landing at Nitendi—Entertained at the Club—Nature of the Country—Success of our Visit—A Santa Cruz boy—Nukapu—Nupani Natives—The Volcano of Tinakolo 145

CHAPTER XIII.

THE SOLOMON ISLANDS.

The Solomon Archipelago—Ulaua—The Natives—Their Canoes—A Disturbance—Deplorable state of things at Wango—Native bowls—Unfriendly Natives—An awkward Delay—Bartering—Solomon Island feasts—Thieving—Spears—Guadalcanar—The Florida Group—An Inland Excursion—A Native Congregation—The *Sandfly* tragedy—Centipedes—A Florida Chief—Headhunters—Tree-houses—Fortification—Canoes—Money and its value—Marriage customs—Tattooing—Hard times at Sea—A slight mishap 168

CHAPTER XIV.

NEW CALEDONIA AND THE LOYALTY ISLANDS.

Mr. Jones' Mission Station—A religious war—French Government—Crossing to Noumea—Difficult Navigation—New Caledonia—

Noumea—Resemblance to Port Said—Convicts—Libérés—The Neighbourhood of Noumea—Native Houses—The English in Noumea—The Australian Mail Steamer 192

CHAPTER XV.

LABOUR AND TRADE IN THE SOUTH PACIFIC.

The Labour Trade—Wages—What becomes of them—Traders—Naval Supervision—Murder of Lieutenant Bower—An Imperial Government Question—List of Massacres—Other Tragedies—Missionary Testimony—Ill-treatment of Natives—Conduct of White Men—Government Agents—Summing-up 203

PART III.

THE FAR EAST.

CHAPTER XVI.

THE CHINA PORTS.

Landing at Penang—The Malays—Singapore—Rough weather—Hong Kong Harbour—Chinese Children—Hong Kong—Swatow—A theatrical performance—Fan making—Pewter engraving—Amoy—A Chinese Review—Comical appearance of the Troops—Shanghai—The "Bund"—The China Town—The Native City—"Curio" shops—Tea-houses—A Nation of Merchants—The Famine—An illiberal Government 217

CHAPTER XVII.

FOOCHOW AND DISTRICT.

Foochow—The Min River—A Chinese Dockyard and Arsenal—Pagoda Anchorage—A Beautiful Panorama—The Bridge of a Thousand Ages—The European Settlement—The Paeling Tea Gardens—Preparing Tea—Carrying Tea to Market—Foochow City at night—The Ku-shan Monastery—Buddhist Relics—A Chinese Fanatic—An Ancient Bell—Chinese Houseboats—A Pleasant Dinner Party 228

CHAPTER XVIII.

THE JAPANESE PORTS AND KIOTO.

An old-fashioned Steamer—Nagasaki Harbour—First impressions—Tea-houses—The Inland Sea—Shimonoséki—Archery at a Temple—Kobe or Hiogo—Excursion to the Waterfall—A Native Entertainment—An untasteful Custom—Osaka—The Tycoon's Castle—The Mint—Kioto—The Temple of Chiomin—The Big Bell—Japanese Art—The Rapids near Kioto—Yokohama—Odawarra—Kango-riding — Myanoshita — Hakone — "Big Hell" — The Hakone Pass 240

CHAPTER XIX.

THE NAGASENDO ROAD.

Nagasendo and Tokaido—A Military Road—Otzu—A Japanese Steamer—Lake Biwa—Road-side scenes—The villages—Cottages—A happy valley—Tea-houses—Experiences at Tea-houses—The Mountains—Politeness of the People—Effects of the Revolution—The Japanese Race—Scenery—An active Volcano—Morality—Agricultural labours—A contrast—Takasaki—The new Régime—A native's testimony 259

CHAPTER XX.

NIKKO AND TOKIO.

A fresh start—Silk-worm raising—Soaking and unwinding—A mountain pass—An unfrequented valley—Nikko—The Temples—Their Surroundings—Yumota—The most beautiful walk of all—A mountain watering-place—Sulphur springs—The great Cryptomeria Avenue—Its neglect by the Government—The new régime again—Tokio—The shops—Asakusa—A Japanese Theatre—Good-bye to Japan—Statistics. 275

PART IV.
SPANISH AMERICA.

CHAPTER XXI.
CENTRAL AMERICA.

Exceptional interest in Spanish America—Mazatlan—A Mexican Hotel—Desolate aspect of the City—Manzanillo—Acapulco—Anecdote of Maximilian—Condition of Mexico—Tezcucan philosophy—San José de Guatemala—Costa Rica—Punta Arenas—Condition of the Republic—Panama—The Panama Railroad—Aspinwall—Buenaventura—Tumaco—The United States of Columbia—Guayaquil—The Cathedral—The people—The Republic of Ecuador 289

CHAPTER XXII.
PERU.

Incaland—Callao—Lima—The Chincha Islands—Lima Cathedral—The Amphitheatre—The Cemetery—Public Gardens—The Oroya Railroad—Construction—Scenery—Ancient Inca Irrigation works—Good steamers—Aspect of Coast—Mollendo—The Titicaca railroad—Arica—Iquiqui—Antafogasta—Retribution .. 303

CHAPTER XXIII.
CHILE.

Caldera—Cocquimbo and Yacan—Valparaiso—Aspect of City—English population—Santiago—The Hotel—Situation of the City—Santa Lucia—View from summit—The Cathedral—Monument on site of Jesuit church—Country to south of Santiago—Talca—Rural districts—Concepcion—View from the hills—Crossing the river—Southern Chile—Coronel—Copper works—Coal mines—Lota Bay—Straits of Magellan—Scenery—Punta Arenas—Enterprising settlers—The Atlantic side of the Straits 318

CHAPTER XXIV.
LA PLATA.

Great rivers—Monte Video—Appearance from the water—French aspect of the City—The suburbs—The Quintas—A monument of

Folly—River Plate steamers—Landing at Buenos Ayres—Dock schemes—The Plaza Victoria—Town mansions—a "Borraca"—The Foundling Hospital—The Paraná—Rosario—Aspect of the "Camp"—Cordova—Disgusting habits—The Opera at Buenos Ayres—The Cazuela—Cockfighting—A "Saladero"—Leaving Monte Video. 333

CHAPTER XXV.

BRAZIL.

The Bay of Rio de Janeiro—Comparisons—The city of Rio—Street scenes—Portugese traits—Tijuca—The Chinese View—The Botanical Gardens—The Organ mountains—Petropolis—Coffee—Scenery—The Pedro Segundo Railway—Bahia—The Churches—Natives—Export of Tobacco—Bad Times—Pernambuco—Fourteen thousand miles of coasting—General remarks—Conclusion 348

LIST OF ILLUSTRATIONS.

	PAGE
KANGAROO-HUNTING, FOUR-IN-HAND .. .. .. *Frontispiece*	
AUSTRALIAN BOTTLE-TREE	8
TREE FERNS, VICTORIA	25
LAKE WAKATIPU, NEW ZEALAND	33
A MAORI WARRIOR	43
"THE TOWN," NORFOLK ISLAND	54
FIJI HOUSES	79
LANDING AT SANTA CRUZ, SOUTH PACIFIC .. .. *To face Page*	89
PLAN OF CRATER, KILAUEA	102
THEORETICAL SECTION OF MAUNA LOA	108
MONUMENT ON THE SPOT WHERE CAPTAIN COOK WAS KILLED ..	113
A NEW HEBRIDES VILLAGE	128
INTERIOR OF HUT WHERE THE MATS ARE SMOKED	131
TORRES ISLAND NOSE ORNAMENT	141
SANTA CRUZ ARMLETS	150
SANTA CRUZ CANOES	153
SANTA CRUZ NOSE ORNAMENT	159
SANTA CRUZ ORNAMENTED CLUB	160
CLUB-HOUSE, SANTA CRUZ	162
"HE WORE THIRTY EARRINGS"	166
A LADY'S COSTUME, SOLOMON ISLANDS	169
SOLOMON ISLAND CANOES	170
ORNAMENTED BOWL, WANGO	174
SOLOMON ISLAND SASH	176
ORNAMENT WORN ON FOREHEAD	178
PLATFORM HOUSES, SOLOMON ISLANDS	180
TREE-HOUSE, YSABEL	185
SOLOMON ISLAND STATE CANOE	187
EAR PENDANT	190
NATIVE HOUSE, NEW CALEDONIA	200
A WINDY DAY IN JAPAN .. .. .. *To face page*	217
TEA COOLIE, CHINA	227
SCENE AT JAPANESE TEA-HOUSE	242

LIST OF ILLUSTRATIONS.

	PAGE
A Japanese Peasant	247
Kango Riding, Japan	253
Returning Thanks	257
Too Late for the Ferry	266
Irrigating	271
Soaking and Unravelling	276
Winnowing Rice	282
Scene on the Oroya Railroad, Peru *To face page*	289
The Cathedral at Guayaquil	301
View of Santiago	322
Monument, Santiago	325
Native Girl, Chile	332
Cordova Cathedral	341
View near Rio de Janeiro	353

MAPS.

Track Chart of the World, showing Author's Routes	*To face page* 1
Track Chart showing Cruise taken by the Author in Western Polynesia	*To face page* 119

PART I.

THE AUSTRALASIAN COLONIES.

. . . "Not the Irish, nor the Coolies are his servants, but Geology and Chemistry, the quarry of the air, the water of the brook, the lightning of the cloud, the castings of the worm, the plough of the frost. Long before he was born, the sun of ages decomposed the rocks, mellowed his land, soaked it with light and heat, covered it with vegetable film, then with forests, and accumulated the sphagnum whose decays made the peat of his meadow."—*Emerson.*

ABC# WANDERINGS,

SOUTH AND EAST.

PART I.

THE AUSTRALASIAN COLONIES.

CHAPTER I.

QUEENSLAND.

"Fresh woods and pastures new."—Lycidas.

I SAILED from Singapore in the month of July, and, crossing the Equator at about 104 E. Long., entered the Southern Hemisphere. Our vessel was one of the Eastern and Australian Line, bound for the Queensland ports and Sydney in New South Wales. Every one was glad to be at sea again, after the heat they had experienced on shore, for, although in the lowest latitudes, we ran into some beautiful cool weather while steaming along the north coast of Java.

The great volcano of Tambora, over nine thousand feet high, stood out clearly against the sky one lovely morning, and almost seemed to overhang our masts, we were so near the shore. There is a somewhat widely-spread belief that this volcano is the largest in the world, but its crater is not in reality more than twenty-one miles in circumference, and therefore ranks second to the great Haleakala of the Sandwich group. The eruption that occurred here in 1815, however, does I think exceed any similar event in magnitude; in Findlay's Directory it is stated that the ashes fell over an area extending fifteen hundred miles West and East, and nine hundred miles North and South.

So we steamed pleasantly enough in smooth water, past group after group of volcanic islands, through the Java Sea, the Flores Sea, and the Arapura Sea,—so on towards the great Southern Land.

The first Australian soil we came to was Booby Island, a little off-lying patch of land at the entrance to the Torres Straits. Here is a cave, where ships in earlier days left letters and small quantities of stores. It is still marked "Post Office" on the charts, and was visited by all sailing ships that came sufficiently near to make it worth their while. On the evening of the day on which we sighted Booby Island we anchored in the well-sheltered bay of Thursday Island.

This is the northernmost point of Australia, being situated at the extreme end of Cape York. It is marked largely on the charts, and is so often mentioned as a port of call, that perhaps one may be excused for being rather surprised to find that it consists of at most five small wooden "shanties." The white population of Thursday Island numbered at the time of my visit nine souls.

The chief, and perhaps only real value of this little settlement consists in its being the centre of the Torres Straits pearl fisheries. There were about six smart cutters lying at anchor in the harbour; they had come in to give to our steamer the results of their fishing, and we took on board, in consequence, some sixty tons of pearl shell, the value of which would be from £180 to £200 a ton. The men employed in the fisheries are all Kanakas, picked up in the Western Pacific Islands, and are in a dreadfully demoralised condition. They make far more money than they know how to spend and receive it all in a lump sum once or twice a year. When this occurs they take passage to Sydney, are kept perpetually drunk the whole way there by the bar-keeper of the steamer, and are immediately on their arrival in Sydney taken charge of by a class of people of whom perhaps the less said the better. A few weeks later they are put on board the steamer again, utterly unconscious and penniless, to be taken back to their former employers. I am not speaking of any exceptional case; this is practically the universal system.

We took half-a-dozen pearl divers down with us, whose fortunes during their holidays I took some pains to follow. They were such as I have described, and I saw the poor fellows brought down to the steamer some weeks later when she started on her return journey. One of the largest employers of this kind of labour travelled with us from Thursday Island, and he informed me that he paid away as much as a thousand pounds a month in wages.

Steaming through the Albany pass, we called for an hour or so at Somerset, a settlement of even less significance than Thursday Island—only three houses here. Opposite to it is Albany, shown in large letters upon the chart, but in reality even a smaller place than the others. The rateable property here consists of nothing more than a single one-roomed house and a small log hut.

The navigation of these Torres Straits is certainly an undertaking of no light character. The whole place seems one maze of shoals and banks and reefs. At night we anchored on a coral patch, or burnt blue lights as we groped along at half speed. The Queensland government are making great efforts to mark out the best passage, however, and lights and buoys will soon be plentiful throughout the more dangerous places.

It is not my intention to enter into any detailed account of my visit to Queensland; one can, I think, convey a better impression of such a country by describing generally the most noteworthy features of one's visit, rather than by setting down an itinerary which is apt to be wearisome from its monotony.

I visited, briefly only, many Queensland ports, and found them all very much alike. Cooktown was perhaps the roughest, as a gold "rush" had just been started on the Palmer river, a hundred miles or so inland. The town was full of hard-drinking adventurers, and sober dirty-looking Chinamen. The streets are broad and straight, lined with wooden shanties, every third one of which is a liquor store. The sun poured down mercilessly upon the corrugated iron roofs of these little weatherboard houses, and the whole place seemed to me burnt up, dreary, and comfortless. So also for the most part, were such other ports as I visited—always so barren, and shadeless, and scorched. There are no harbours along the coast for other than small craft, so that although from the shelter of the Great Barrier Reef the coast, perhaps, may be said to require no harbours, still it is a great inconvenience in every way for ships to be obliged to lie two, three, or four miles from the town.

The most pleasant thing I saw on this Queensland coast, was undoubtedly the Whitsunday Passage, which is formed by a little archipelago of green islets, lying a few miles from the mainland. We steamed through several groups of these islands, which were quite close together, and green as emeralds.

Native fires were visible every day as we passed along the coast; sometimes we counted as many as a dozen in a day, which I suppose would represent a similar number of different tribes. I am almost tempted to say something here about these luckless Queensland blacks, but the subject is of such infinite disgrace to all of us who have English blood in our veins, that I could never quite express my horror at our conduct towards them. Suffice it, then, for me to add my small testimony, with that of every other Queensland visitor, to the fact that nothing that has been brought before the English public regarding this matter comes near the real enormous truth. That if we have heard at home of white settlers shooting down natives ("potting blacks" is their grimly facetious word for it), in mere wanton sport by scores, they have really shot them down in such manner by hundreds; that if tales have reached us of the cruelty of the bush police, and the wholesale wiping-out of tribes for trivial causes, or no cause at all, such tales are within the mark, and may be capped with true stories of such massacres as are only paralleled in the history of the Spaniards in Peru. This thing has come before our British Parliament, and been the subject of enquiry as well in England as in Brisbane, but the truth of it has been hidden by those who were interested, and no approximately adequate measures have been taken for its punishment even yet. We are too just and right-minded a nation in these latter days to allow our colonists to make slaves of the natives of these new countries, but we have replaced that once popular system of slavery with a policy which, if not openly admitted, is at least not hindered, namely that of actively "wiping out" the native races during the progress of our white conquest.*

* Since writing the above I have come across an item of news in a Melbourne daily paper which I cannot refrain from printing. I copy it as it stands, but I hope my readers will not fail to notice and consider the deep significance of the last sentence.

"The following paragraph, extracted from the recent issue of the *Hodgkinson Independent,* of Queensland, affords an indication of the

Brisbane is the capital of Queensland, and lies some twenty miles up the Brisbane river. It is a sunburnt, dried-up, dusty place with fine bank-buildings, and poor wooden shanties—a very typical Australian city. Its hotels are of the meanest order, being mere public-houses with rows of small bed-rooms attached. We arrived, I remember, at midnight, but when shown our rooms felt immediately that some mistake had been made; the idea of sleeping in such little bathing-machine apartments seemed too absurd, so, saying good night to the landlord, we drove to the next hotel. We were not a little disconcerted, however, to find that hostelry even worse, and at last, in utter humiliation and contrition, were compelled to return to our original quarters!

sentiments with which the aborigines of this continent are regarded by some of the white settlers:—

'On Sunday morning last a person named Martin Doyle, while out on a kangaroo-hunting excursion, and when getting as far as Wooster's paddock, distant about three miles from Thornborough, came upon a mob of blacks camped, who, on perceiving Doyle, immediately made tracks in "double quick time." The dogs accompanying Doyle gave chase, and overtook one of the gins, and tore her to such an extent that she died almost as soon as they were drawn off their victim. Doyle, on returning to the camp suddenly vacated by the blacks, discovered that they had killed a cow, and were about to appease their appetites when they were disturbed. It is anything but creditable to the Government to allow such a state of things as this to exist. Blacks in the present day to be roaming about within a short three miles of a popular town like Thornborough, established now nearly five years, and slaying the cattle of its residents, is truly shameful.'"

Another cutting of a week later date (February, 1881) runs thus:—

"The Herbert correspondent of the *Townsville Standard* states that two whites and a Kanaka went to punish the blacks for trespassing on a potato garden, but failed to find them. They shot three gins, and burned the bodies, making the husband of one assist."

Again, I presume, it is anything but creditable to the Government to allow such a state of things to exist. Blacks in the present day to be roaming about within a few miles of a town like Herbert, and trespassing on a potato garden, is truly shameful!!

There is one fairly good street in Brisbane containing shops and banks and a Post Office and Town Hall, out of which branch a score or so of roads lined with wooden cottages, and beyond these again the suburbs may be found straggling far and wide. The river winds almost prettily along the foot of the slight hill on which the town is built, and steamers, small schooners and other vessels are plentiful.

It must be confessed that the attractions of such places as this are very small. There is no new life in the streets: there are no objects of interest whatever. The people themselves, although kind and hospitable, are busy and common-place, and so, in little more than a day after my arrival, I was anxious to be away again.

We started westward from Brisbane by rail. A small narrow-gauge railway runs over the coast range, and penetrates the downs and fertile plains beyond. It is a work of very considerable merit, for it crosses the formidable mountain chain which runs all down the Eastern coast of the Australian Continent. This range is only formidable in formation, not in height. It is split up into ravines and steep valleys to which there is probably no parallel except in the "barrancas" of Arizona, and Central America generally; for this reason the early settlers found great difficulty in pushing through in search of new lands. The ranges were first pierced much farther south, in New South Wales, where the chain is called the Blue Mountains. How wonderful a country was discovered beyond this barrier of hills, all the world now knows.

It took us six hours to reach the high lands known as the Darling Downs, the scenery being, as is all Australian scenery, ugly in the immediate foreground, but soft and pleasant to the eye in the distance. The green trees are so utterly dull and same in colour, and are so very shaggy and disreputable in individual appearance, that no pleasing scenic effects upon a small scale can be expected where they abound. These eucalyptus trees are to be found everywhere upon the Australian mainland, and such insignificant breaks in the monotony of form and colour as are produced by she-oaks, wattles, the curiously-shaped bottle-tree, and other species

AUSTRALIAN BOTTLE-TREE.

of Australian forest-growth have no perceptible effect upon the landscape.

We stayed some days at a little inland town upon the borders of the Downs. Its name was Toowoomba, a soft and pleasant word as are all those of the aboriginal languages; indeed, I think, the euphony of their speech is almost the only pleasing thing about these unhappy people.

Towns such as this of which I am speaking are all alike and I may as well describe them briefly once for all. The streets are very wide and quite straight, they are also cut up with deep ruts, and are muddy in wet weather and dusty in dry. The pavements, or more accurately "sidewalks," as the Americans would call them, are also very wide, also uneven, also dusty or muddy. In the leading street are several good bank-buildings, generally of stone or brick; all the other houses are of wood, and comprise one or two good saddlers and harness-makers' shops, and a few general stores. The rest of the street, roughly speaking, consists of public-houses, here known as hotels. From this one street branch out many other straggling thoroughfares, where the houses are sprinkled about more and more sparingly until the open country is reached, into which stretch broad roads in several directions, bounded by the invariable and universal post and rail fence which is made of gum-tree timber.

The air upon these Downs is beyond all praise, and I have known no single instance of its failing in its beneficial effects upon people with weak lungs. I should say, that of all places in the world for any one in a consumptive stage to resort to, a squatter's station on the Darling Downs is in every way the best. I have been recommended to try the Nile, the Cape, the Andes in Northern Peru, Tasmania, New Zealand, and even Guatemala, and of all these places I have had some experience, but I say, very unhesitatingly, that the Darling Downs is *facile princeps*.

The air is more bracing than that of Nubia or Upper Egypt, and life there is more enjoyable than in Natal or the Cape Colony. The people are hospitable even beyond most colonists, and there is good sport and good society. It is quite alarming to think of the hundreds of people who are sent out in sailing ships to Melbourne and Sydney by medical men of high standing in London, and who die miserably a few months after they land. These gentlemen are too little acquainted with the places to which they consign their patients, and I have come across cases in which men in far advanced stages of phthisis have been sent upon a long, cold, and trying voyage, only to land in Melbourne at the wrong time of the year, when the weather was as bad for them as it would have been at the same season in London. It is a fact, becoming daily more recognised, that the climate of the Australian capital towns, is not in any instance, except perhaps that of Hobart Town, a good climate. You must select your locality in Australia no less than in Europe. Sydney will not do, it is enervating and relaxing. Melbourne would be far more dangerous, its climate is changeable beyond that of any city in the world. Brisbane and Adelaide are both hot, glaring and dusty during the greater part of the year—indeed none of the towns of Australia are places for European invalids.

So great is the satisfaction of colonists with their climate, and so general is the feeling in England that all Australia is a paradise as far as weather is concerned, that I have placed below, in a note, some extracts from the papers of the summer months of 1880–1881 in confirmation of my statements.*

---

* "Amongst the items of Australian news, weather of unusual severity is reported, and especially in New South Wales. Heavy snow had fallen on the 20th of July in the Braidwood district, lying at least two feet

It may be urged that the Queensland plains are too hot in summer for any but the strongest to live there. If this is so a trip south for two or three months could be easily taken, but I have been repeatedly assured, and my own experience bears out the assertion, that although the heat is so intense it is not of an injurious kind, the air being so fine and bracing that one can stand very high temperatures. Even in Melbourne when the thermometer stands at 106° in the shade I do not find the actual heat very trying; it is the scorching and dust-laden wind that is so unbearable, made worse by the fact that one must dress warmly, as at any hour the wind may change and a fall of 30 to 50 degrees ensue in almost as many minutes. These rapid changes, however, are almost unknown upon the Darling Downs, which are as much as two thousand feet above the sea and possess a climate which is as healthful and even invigorating as that of any place in the world.

---

deep on the roads, and causing great destruction to flocks. In South Australia the cold is reported to be intense, and the fall of snow on the Flinders Range the heaviest experienced for the last twenty years.

"At Melbourne, in November, it was boisterous and squally on the 14th and 15th; fine and pleasant on the 16th; dull and sultry on the 17th and 18th inst.; thunder and lightning and a heavy shower of rain on the afternoon of the 18th, until towards evening, a strong and cold south-westerly wind set in, which lasted all through the 19th, with rain-showers at intervals, followed on the 20th by fine and pleasant weather. The highest temperature in the shade, 92·1°, was recorded on the afternoon of the 18th, the lowest, 42·1°, on the early morning of the 20th."

In December, the thermometer went down on the 26th from 104° in the shade at 2 P.M. to 62° at 2.45 P.M.

In February I notice from the meteorological report that the thermometer stood at 100° during the afternoon of the 22nd, and at 51° at 3 P.M. on the 23rd.

These are extracts cut from the papers as they happened to come under my notice. I have not attempted to search through the Observatory reports for startling examples of sudden changes.

From Toowoomba I drove sixty miles through an undulating and thinly-wooded country to a large sheep and cattle station upon the Downs. The sun was very powerful during the whole of our drive, but, thanks to the great altitude and bracing air, we did not suffer any inconvenience from either heat or fatigue.

The station at which I stayed is one of the finest in Queensland, but the details of station life and statistics have been so frequently given by travellers of wider experience, that I gladly refrain from entering upon them here, contenting myself merely with some of the less prosaic incidents of my very enjoyable visit in this district.

In Queensland the kangaroo hunting is magnificent, and there is also good duck shooting and emu hunting. I had only one experience of the last-mentioned sport, but of the two former we had many enjoyable days. The most general method of hunting kangaroos is by mustering as many guns as possible, and having a battue, but the more interesting way is running them down singly with dogs.

We started one glorious morning soon after daylight to make a raid upon these enemies of the owners of sheep. There were some twenty of us, I remember, with large cabbage leaf hats and no coats or waistcoats; with guns gleaming in the sunshine, and bright coloured sashes round our waists, and leather pouches and straps and swags. It was a most picturesque sight as we filed off from the homestead and away across the first paddock. Our horses were all good, but also impetuous and even opinionated, the first mile being in consequence a regular stampede. When about ten miles from the station, we told off six beaters to gallop round the piece of country where the herd of kangaroo were feeding, and we meanwhile all dismounted and posted ourselves in a long line at intervals of fifty yards or so, each selecting a suitable tree behind which to conceal himself. In a short time we could see the advanced guard of the herd, and a minute afterwards a body of perhaps fifteen hundred kangaroos were making towards us at full speed. At what a pace they come, bounding along fifteen or twenty feet at a stride and fairly flying past us! Bang, bang, went the first gun, and two great giants come bowling down upon their heads and shoulders. The firing then became general as the mob passed, and in five minutes we had thirty or forty big fellows lying around us. The country was a little too open to enable the beaters to turn them again and give us another volley, but we secured close upon a hundred, before the end of the day, which was considered a pretty fair bag.

Wallaby shooting was, I thought, better sport; these animals are much smaller than the ordinary kangaroo, and are usually shot over dogs in the scrub. They are very quick in their movements, and their peculiar hop makes them hard to hit at first; we had some very good shooting of this kind. I think it will be surprising to my readers to know that several of the kangaroos that we shot during my stay at this station were over eight feet from nose to tail, and that one whose skin was in the hall of the homestead measured nine feet over all.

The evenings after these long days on horseback were very delightful. We dined at seven, and although we had no ladies present, our host set us the example of wearing dress clothes, and I must say the dinners themselves deserved that much homage; and yet it seemed incongruous to be following May Fair customs in the Queensland bush. Such a visit as this of which I am writing, finally and for ever does away with the prevailing idea that all our cousins in the Australian bush lead hard and uncivilised lives. At this station there was every conceivable attribute of civilisation and comfort. There were even such out-of-the-way attractions as a photographic studio, and, upon the creek near the house, there was a steam launch. We could have a swim in the morning before breakfast, and during the day, if too tired to go out hunting or shooting, could play lawn tennis or sit out upon the wide balcony and watch the companion birds dancing on the lawn. Or again we could fill cartridges and clean our guns in the gun-room, or amuse ourselves with turning in the workshop or with photography in the studio. The pioneers in the back country, amongst treacherous native tribes and hardships almost innumerable, have rough times truly enough, but these old-established squatters of the Darling Downs lead lives that almost any one might envy.

One other experience had I of bush life which was no less enjoyable. This was in another part of Australia where I visited a bachelor upon a small station within fifteen hours' journey of Melbourne. The life here was more like what I had expected to find. We had, I remember, at that station no idea whatever of forms or even times. It seemed to me that as a rule we ate when we were hungry and slept when sleepy, and I had, I think, neither a coat nor waistcoat on my back during my fortnight's stay. Sometimes we went to bed almost at sundown, and at others, talking over old days in England, or playing at games of cards or moodily smoking countless pipes before the wood fire, we would sit up far into the small hours of the night. We had our share of sport here no less than in Queensland, but it was of a much more exciting character. Our host was famous throughout the whole country-side for his driving, and he even preferred hunting kangaroos in a buggy to riding after them on horseback. It was a most terrible ordeal at first to us who were novices, and it was several days before I could feel in any degree comfortable on such reckless expeditions.

We would start in the morning, driving four small well-bred horses in a buggy, and followed by several kangaroo dogs. Leaving the track as soon as we were some distance away from the station, we would start off at an easy trot through the well-wooded country, the dogs as well as ourselves keeping a good look-out. A few sharp yelps were the signal that game was in sight, and in a second dogs, horses and buggy might be seen flying through the forest at a terrific rate. Now was the time to see how horses could be managed; no one indeed who has not witnessed such an exhibition of skill could believe it possible. Our horses, fully alive to the sport, would lay themselves to their work "ventre à terre," and away we would go, over logs, across gullies, round tree-stumps and down hillsides in a manner that fairly made one's hair stand on end.* Of the several runs that we had, I think we were in at the death in every case but one, and when it is remembered that a kangaroo is nearly as fleet as a deer this will be seen to be no mean exploit. The trees, moreover, throughout this station were on an average certainly not more than fifteen feet apart, and were often too close for the buggy to pass without detours being made. It will easily be imagined, therefore, that there was no lack of excitement in these wild drives after kangaroo with four horses and a buggy.

* For an illustration of this incident, *vide* Frontispiece.

CHAPTER II.

NEW SOUTH WALES AND VICTORIA.

"The prosperity of a country depends, not on the abundance of its revenues, nor on the strength of its fortifications, nor on the beauty of its public buildings; but it consists in the number of its cultivated citizens, in its men of education, enlightenment, and character; here are to be found its true interest, its chief strength, its real power."—*Martin Luther.*

I WISH to write a short chapter about Sydney and Melbourne, the two rival capitals of the Australian continent. I do not intend to draw comparisons, or pit the merits of one against those of the other. That is already too much indulged in by the inhabitants themselves who, I fear, have the minimum of neighbourly good-feeling.

Let us take Sydney first, as it is the older city of the two. To steam into Port Jackson upon a sunny morning is an experience that the most blasé of travellers must enjoy. It is unnecessary for me to compare this land-locked bay with that of Rio de Janeiro or any other world-famed harbour; it can stand upon its own merits, and is as fair a sight as one may see upon this earth of ours. There are no high mountains, nor is there any magnificent coup d'œil; it is a simple and beautiful piece of water scenery, which, although it does not, as it were, take you by storm or astonish you with its magnificence, pleases and gratifies every visitor, whatsoever may be his tastes.

The distance from the narrow entrance to the city is five or six miles. It is a beautiful picture from whatever side you regard it. You are land-locked almost immediately after entering, and pass, in the short run up to the anchorage, perhaps a dozen little bays which run back from the main sheet of water.

Sydney itself is spread out upon the low hills at the upper end of the harbour. It is built with a delightful irregularity, very refreshing to meet with amongst the prosaic and painfully symmetrical cities of new countries. The streets are not parallel to each other, and are not, in many instances, even straight. The bays that form the upper end of the harbour cut the city up into dozens of capes, promontories, and peninsulas, and as one walks about the streets the slender masts of sailing vessels are seen in almost every direction. The largest ships can moor alongside the streets in Sydney, and there is an almost incredible amount of harbour frontage at the disposal of merchants and shipping firms. The streets and shops and buildings are like those of an English provincial town, such, let me say, as Nottingham.

There is nothing, therefore, of great interest in the city itself, but in the suburbs and in the many and beautiful drives, and in the splendid private residences scattered along the shores of the harbour, there is an infinite interest and delight. Perhaps nowhere are there such idyllic homes as upon the shores of Port Jackson; one cannot overdraw the beauties and comforts of these places, nor indeed the hospitality of their owners, who are very rightly proud of their newly-founded homes.

In the city are the usual public buildings and institutions, which I am weary of seeing, and of which I do not care to write. There is no architecture in these colonial towns, and but little art. The people here are not even as a rule satisfied with buildings essentially useful and avowedly untasteful; they too often make wild efforts at architectural

C

display, and at one and the same time mar the useful purposes of their buildings, and fall short of æsthetic excellence. I should mention, however, two buildings in Melbourne, namely the Public Library and the Town Hall, which are beside these remarks, being eminently sensible and suitable, and at the same time presenting a really pleasing external appearance.

Round Sydney are a score of pretty suburbs where one may go in search of rest and quiet; indeed I know of hardly any city more rich in " places to spend a happy day."

Pre-eminent among these outlying attractions is the Hawkesbury River, which Anthony Trollope has told us is superior to the Rhine, and has in the way of natural beauties "nothing equal to it, nothing second to it." I spent three days in a little steam launch upon that river, and I admired its beauties most thoroughly, but I will not hazard comparison with Rhine or Bosphorus; it would, I think, be foolish to enter any piece of river or strait scenery in the lists with those old established champions.

Another delightful trip from Sydney is afforded by the proximity of the coast range here known as the Blue Mountains. In the hot summer weather it is a great relief to retire for a week or two into those cool highlands, and there defy the fierce Australian sun, and night after night enjoy the comforts of a blanket.

The Blue Mountains are distinctly *blue*, and although from their eucalyptus forests, are in detail ragged and even ugly, form in distant sweeps and far-off backgrounds most lovely pictures. There are in these ranges several very curious ravines, or "gulches," which have the peculiarity of ending quite abruptly. They resemble in shape an ordinary dry dock with the pontoon end indefinitely extended. The most remarkable of these is called Govet's

Leap, and is, I think, the most entirely desolate and awful piece of scenery I have seen. It is not mountain scenery, the surrounding country being only what one would call hilly. You walk through the forest along an almost level path, and then, quite suddenly, come upon this great hole in the ground. It is two or three miles wide, and twenty or thirty long, the far end stretching away into a wilderness of shadows and beautiful blue and gray effects. You may stand upon the edges of this great valley and fling stones down two thousand feet into a forest upon the level floor of the ravine, the trees of which look like feathery blades of grass. It is an awful place, so still, so lonely, so gray and solemn; there is a cruel, God-forsaken aspect about it, too, which makes one shudder, and brings to mind those horrible plates of Doré's in the 'Wandering Jew.' The sunlight does not cheer, the rain cloud does not add to its sombreness; it is unique to me in its utter desolation. A cold damp wind blows up towards us from those uncanny depths, and we shudder again, and are glad to walk away.

There is no true story about the place. They call it Govet's Leap, but only because Govet, a surveyor, so wrote it on his plan of the district. Such a sight makes one realise a little what the pioneers who pushed their way through these ranges had to encounter, and what a number must have perished in their bold attempt, and been lost in these wild ranges. We were told by an innkeeper near here some stories of bushmen in this district, how wild they became through prolonged solitude, and how there were, even now, men and women who would run away and hide at the approach of a stranger, having lost every feeling of a gregarious nature, and become mere solitary animals with only their flocks for company. I could believe anything after seeing Govet's Leap. There is, moreover, truth in these tales. I have met men who, after long shepherding, are more shy than children, and can only with the greatest difficulty bring themselves to face a stranger; who even when returned to their families will slip away and mope alone sooner than endure the evident strain that the presence of companions puts upon them. There is something very unwholesome, I think, in that solitary bush life, and nothing seems to me more horrible than the history of those Australian pioneers who have perished in the interior. What an end is that deliberate lying down in the wide desert alone to die! What a revelation when it first bursts upon you that you are lost and "left alone and thirsting in a land of sand and thorns!" Perhaps these men go mad before the end comes, or do they calmly lie down and wait for death? It is singular that they almost always undress themselves, and fold neatly together their clothes, placing all they have in a small heap, and, if possible, securing them with stones. Then, utterly naked as when they entered the world, they go away into the wilderness and die.

Although I do not intend to mention or describe the "institutions" of Sydney—the university or museum or things of that kind—I cannot help expressing my surprise that in so pleasant a city, and one so much frequented by travellers, there is not a single house that has even the elements of a good hotel. There is, in broad fact, hardly a single place where one can without much unpleasantness take a lady. Through the courtesy of the members of the Sydney Clubs, most "unencumbered" travellers are spared the discomfort of these miserable inns. In the Union Club it is not too much to say that one can live as pleasantly and even luxuriously as anywhere in the world, and the kindness with which the members receive strangers is beyond all description. I have made no less than seven visits to Sydney, and in looking back have always the most pleasant remembrance of the many happy days I have spent there.

Melbourne has no external attractions, but it is from our nineteenth century point of view a very fine city, and in all such matters as width of streets and height of public buildings is foremost amongst the capitals of Australia. I am too incorrigibly insular and old-fashioned to like such cities as this, and whether in Sydney or Boston always feel attracted towards the low and crooked streets where the houses are old and out of all symmetry. In Melbourne, I believe, there are no old or crooked streets, nor indeed can I think of any modern city, except the two I have named, that possesses such attractions. Melbourne is to me quite painfully "spick and span," and the breadth of its streets makes one look upon the walk from one pavement to the other as something of a journey. The place is, in a word, immense; it stretches away far and wide, and there is no end to its glaring suburbs and straggling dependencies. Some one, I think, has discovered that, like Rome, it is built on seven hills, and no one I am sure will deny that its river—the Yarra Yarra—is quite as yellow and sluggish as the Tiber. Whether or not it has been found to be the exact centre of the civilised world I have not heard, but New York and many other cities have been shown to possess that highly-desirable attribute, so why not Melbourne?

There is one oasis in the wilderness of Melbourne streets and roads which I must not fail to notice. I refer to the public gardens. Here, as in Sydney and Adelaide, as also in most of the other important towns, are to be found lovely gardens most tastefully laid out and thoroughly well kept up. Those of Melbourne are the largest, the most beautiful those of Sydney; the most interesting, scientifically, those of Adelaide. It would be difficult to exaggerate the advantage it is to the inhabitants of these cities to have beautiful retreats where they can enjoy soft colours and cool shades, which are luxuries indeed to any one compelled to spend most of his day in the heat and glare of an Australian city.

Melbourne, just now, is passing through a very unpleasant period, a far more serious affair than the ordinary commercial depression, which, together with very exceptional weather, I have found to exist in every city or country that I have visited. It does not often fall to the lot of a country to descend so low in politics as Victoria has now done, and this political degradation affects every phase of both personal and national existence, from the water supply and street paving of Melbourne to the future of the colony. The very polar opposite of wise government seems to have been reached, and the prospect does not brighten. Manhood suffrage, with a system of taxation which does not reach the lower classes, has produced a state of things almost unparalleled in the history of independent government. Every form of extravagance is to the advantage of the lowest section of the community, and the result is the erection of public buildings suitable for the government of an European state, these works being almost avowedly undertaken in order to give employment to the working classes. Add to this the most narrow-minded protective system, and the ruthless expulsion from office of any man who makes honourable protest; add continual ill-feeling and hostility with the adjoining colonies; add, generally, the most ignorant and narrow legislation in almost every department, and you have an acme of misrule not easy to parallel. Quarrels between all parties are almost universal, and discontent and disgust prevail amongst every class but that which has nothing to lose and everything to gain.

The public service is no longer looked upon as an honourable employment, and all who can possibly do so avoid having anything to do with public life. I believe there are scores of men in Victoria who could direct wisely the affairs of their country, but they are either too fond of adding more and more wealth to their already great riches, or have too little public spirit, or pride in their country, to put themselves in political harness; and so we see the truth of the words of the philosopher—"the punishment that good men suffer, through abstaining from government, is to sit under the rule of worse men than themselves." Perhaps nowhere has this punishment proved more severe than in the colony of Victoria.

The pleasantest retreat from Melbourne—and with reference to all these modern cities I feel the vital question is, can one easily get away from them and are there any pleasant places to fly to near at hand?—the pleasantest of these places in the neighbourhood is Hobart Town. The little island of Tasmania is easily accessible, is cool, pretty, quiet, and has a lovely capital. One can go and rusticate at Hobart Town as pleasantly as anywhere in the world. There are pretty drives; there is a lovely river, a good harbour, in short, endless attractions of that quiet restful kind. The Tasmanians are a curiously satisfied and contented people. "We are a small community," they say; "and have no future; we do not wish for annexation, we are content to remain as we are." This is not satisfactory from our modern go-ahead point of view, but I think it very enviable. They are happy enough, they live to a great age, and although sleepy and dull, prosper fairly well. They can make no mark in the world, they do not aspire to that;

but are quite content to supply their neighbours with fruit and to hold the position of jam-makers for the Southern Hemisphere. Almost anything will grow and increase in Tasmania, and the climate is without doubt excellently good; it is, in a word, a thoroughly delightful and happy retreat.

Another very enjoyable excursion may be made from Melbourne, namely to the Black's Spur in the Plenty range, where are the highest trees in the world. I drove out there in a buggy on one most lovely day; it is fifty-one or two miles. The bush scenery in these ranges is the only beautiful forest scenery I saw in Australia. The tree ferns were gigantic, and all vegetable life seemed to thrive superlatively well. There are not merely a few detached groves of

TREE FERNS.

big trees as in California, but there are thousands of these giants, the whole hillsides being covered with them. When alluding to the Californian sequoias, the proprietor of the inn triumphantly said to me, " Why we can give 'em a hundred feet and lick their heads off." The greatest tree at present discovered was at Mount Baw Baw, and was measured by the government surveyor and found to be four hundred and seventy-one feet. It was an "eucalyptus amygdalina"; the highest tree, a sequoia gigantea, in California is only about three hundred and twenty-five feet.*

I received when visiting Melbourne as a traveller from England, the same courtesy that I had experienced in Sydney, and stayed at the very comfortable Melbourne Club in Collins Street. Here also, as in the rival city, there are no hotels that one can say a good word for.

Of colonial social life it is not my intention to say more than a few words. I think, however, there are two very notable facts in connection with the young people of our colonies. The one is the very universal musical talent which is noticeable throughout all classes, and the other the love of and skilful proficiency attained in out-door sports. We have heard of Australian cricketers ad nauseam, and I do not wish to do more than notice that every one in Australia plays cricket, and almost every one plays well. Horse-racing is carried on in the colonies to an extent, I suppose, quite unparalleled, the Melbourne spring meeting being, even upon the confession of the *Field*, the best-managed sporting event in the world. I have no hesitation in stating it as my belief that there is no racecourse any-

* In a report by Mr. Ferguson, the Inspector of State forests, a fallen tree is mentioned as having been found by actual measurement to be 435 feet from its roots to where it had been broken by its fall. The broken section was three feet in diameter, from which he estimated the entire length at over 500 feet.

where to compare with the Melbourne one, and besides this, at every little village where a few hundred people can be scraped together, you will find one or two race meetings in the year. The subject of musical talent is perhaps still more interesting, especially in connection with the question of climate.* I should almost think that the proportion, to the population, of people who can play a musical instrument in the Australian Colonies is greater than in any other country in the world.

I am tempted before passing on to New Zealand, which differs in so many ways from the colonies of the Australian Continent, to say something of a more general character concerning these new settlements of our countrymen.

Of the five colonies that I visited, I do not hesitate to place first in the scale of importance, New South Wales. It is the oldest and most stable; it is as a state the most steadily progressive; it is, I venture to think, in all respects the most substantial and dependable. In the quality of its land and in the nature of its climate it is at least as well off as its neighbours. It possesses, moreover, a great part of the Murray, the Darling and the Murrumbidgee rivers. It also possesses, and this of more importance than all, the only real harbour on the continent. The navies of the world might lie at anchor within the gates of its capital, and the largest ships of commerce can come up to the very streets of Sydney. The value to the country of such a possession as Port Jackson can hardly be exaggerated. If the colony shall owe its power to commerce it could have no more valuable acquisition; if to agriculture and home production, this harbour shall facilitate the sale

---

* I allude to the theory that the artistic, and especially the musical, pre-eminence of a nation is largely and perhaps mainly dependent upon climatic conditions.

of its creations and their export; if to war, in some dark future year, it shall be the nation's stronghold. One can estimate in no sufficiency the benefits that shall arise from the wisdom of Commodore Philip who chose to plant his standard of settlement in this little inland gulf.

There is one other thing on account of which New South Wales will rise above its fellow-colonies, and that is, the quantity and quality of its coal. "The power of England is in her coal," say Liebig and many more, with as much truth however as you please; if we are to think so, then shall New South Wales, too, have her share of power, and her modern Newcastle be the nation's mainstay. These are some of the reasons that make me place the oldest colony foremost in national importance. Minerals, such as coal and iron, are of greater value than gold and silver, and steady progress, than the feverish outburst of prosperity. Governments of moderation and temperate caution, even to slowness, have, I think without exception, always finally triumphed over the mushroom growth of more precipitous communities. It is not the lands of so great primary promise that have held stable positions among nations. Not Macedonia shooting up in a few decades, to such dazzling pre-eminence, not the great countries of Central and Southern America, which dazzled Spain and all Europe in the days of Cortez and Pizarro with their untold wealth of gold and resources inexhaustible. It is rather Egypt climbing up the steps of power through hundreds of generations, or Rome ever struggling sword in hand, or Germany through patient perseverance, or England through a thousand years of misrule and warful enterprise. These and of such are the nations that have become really famous. And perhaps here in New South Wales may be the nucleus of a great nation of vast natural wealth, of mighty Saxon race and grand old Christian religion.

It is almost impossible even to guess at the future of such countries as Queensland and Southern and Western Australia. It may be questioned whether the Saxon race can retain its present attributes under such climates as these lands possess. It seems to me that here we shall ever be more master than man; these are homes rather for the Chinaman and Malay than for us. We may grow sugar, and cotton, and maize, but the races of the East must work for us.

In South Australia, however, there seems great immediate prospect. In growing corn they produce what is more valuable to mankind than coal, iron, gold, or even wool. These founders of Adelaide, with their overland telegraph and projected continental railway, are men of great enterprise; their energy is indefatigable and their ambition endless. They own a strip of land from North to Southern shore; they are tropical and temperate—master of sugar, rice, and cotton, no less than of corn and wool.

What a land of promise this Southern world becomes when we view it as a whole, what a home for those already there, and for their descendants through coming ages! If not another shipload of emigrants were to arrive, there is yet in Australia every essential of national greatness; the country is now beyond the possibility of decline more than temporary; it is destined with certainty to attain its national majority, its manhood, its old age. It may not be that the present condition of the various colonies will remain, for there may be annexation and separation of many kinds before long, but as a whole this Southern land is now amongst the world's nations for a nation's natural lifetime, and that it may be a long one, and that its progress be arrested by no disgrace or misfortune, every Englishman will pray. All this is certain to come to pass if no newcomer landed upon its shores from to-day. What then shall happen, if year by year in ever-increasing numbers Europe shall send over supply after supply of intellect, and labour, from her own too well-stocked shores?

This opening up of Australia alone is a great blow to Malthusianism. We in England can even yet hardly believe that the flocks of Queensland squatters are grazing beyond the Barku, and that corn is growing hundreds of miles north of Adelaide, where but yesterday our geographers had written "inaccessible desert." Man is every day proving himself equal to his task; a tiller from the first of the soil from which he sprang, so shall he conquer the whole earth. How long since was Chat Moss a slough, and the Fen country of Norfolk and the Eastern counties an unwholesome swamp—and yet what do we see there to-day? And to-day, too, sheep on the interior deserts of Australia, and rain in Egypt, and anon, shall there be crops on the bed of the Zuyder Zee. The older a nation is, the more it can make of its lands: it is therefore difficult to estimate the productive capabilities of a country. So in China the very mountain-sides are gardens, and the steep valleys of Japan are mere terraced rice-fields. In ancient Peru, too, the Incas grew maize upon the western precipices of the Andes; there is indeed almost no limit to man's power as a producer of the necessities of life. This emigration question is one of quite boundless interest. What an exodus is now going on from the old world to the new, and as England becomes yearly more near that consummation so devoutly wished by the men of this iron age, as it approaches the condition of one great factory, filled from end to end with the smoke and pestilence of manufactures, men of peaceful, thoughtful minds will long the more for some land where they may live in quietude, and where the sun will still shine brightly, and the sky still be blue, and the trees green.

Active men, too, full of enterprise and energy, in ever-increasing numbers will seek out these new lands. Ere long, it will not be only men who are obliged to emigrate, that will go, but men who feel the present competition and struggle for supremacy in England too great a burden to be borne, will seek and choose for their homes these more natural, peaceful, and less-populated lands. Meanwhile, a more extended knowledge of Australia is absolutely necessary for young Englishmen, and should, I think, take precedence as a subject of education to the modern history of European states. Our ignorance of our colonies is truly disgraceful, and it is no wonder that we are objects of ridicule to our colonial cousins. Perhaps no wiser step in this direction could be taken than by admitting Australia into the Postal Union. It seems almost incredible that such places as Teheran, Pekin, Alaska, and Tahiti are within the twopence-halfpenny postal rate, whilst poor emigrants writing from Melbourne or Sydney to their friends at home have to pay sixpence. At first sight this may appear a small matter, but I hold it to be in reality a very serious one. Surely our children should be of first consideration to us, and that South American emigrants should have greater facilities for describing to their relations and friends the conditions of life in their new home, than emigrants to Victoria and New South Wales, speaks badly for our legislation, and the large-mindedness of our statesmen. Colonial geography, too, should be taught in our schools, for no one will deny that such subjects as the internal communication between Melbourne and Sydney, or the climatic conditions of Queensland, are of more importance than the names of Russian rivers, the number of departments in France, or any other piece of ordinary school geography book information.

CHAPTER III.

NEW ZEALAND.

"Give the Englishman a home and he is comparatively indifferent to society. For the sake of a holding which he can call his own, he will cross the seas, plant himself on the prairie or amidst the primeval forest, and make for himself a home. The solitude of the wilderness has no fears for him; the society of his wife and family is sufficient, and he cares for no other. Hence it is that people of Germanic origin, from which the English and Americans have alike sprung, make the best colonizers, and are now rapidly extending themselves as emigrants and settlers in all parts of the habitable globe."—*Smiles.*

AFTER a run of five days from Hobart Town in Tasmania, I arrived at the Bluff, a small port at the extreme south of New Zealand, and commenced my journey through the two islands. Over three months were spent in visiting the chief places of interest in New Zealand, and all my reminiscences of that beautiful colony are most pleasant ones.

The islands, generally known as the North and South Islands respectively, have each their individual sources of interest. The Southern one is pre-eminently the more picturesque; here are the high mountain ranges and beautiful groups of lakes. It is also probably the most valuable, as it possesses the Canterbury Plains, and the rich Otago lands. In the North Island, however, there are attractions of even higher interest to the traveller. There are the Hot Lakes, and the most curious pink and white sinter terraces of Rotomahana. There also is the remnant of that Maori race, in whose history and gradual destruction every Englishman must feel an interest.

I spent some days upon Wakatipu, the largest of the South Island lakes, a beautiful piece of water, some sixty miles long, and from five to ten in breadth. There is a small steamer upon the lake, which plies between the two little settlements of Queenstown and Kingstown.

At the upper end there is no township, but merely a woodman's cottage, where we passed a night and part of two days. It is a most romantic place, shut in by high mountains between whose peaks the pale blue glaciers may be seen. The highest elevation that has as yet been ascertained in this district is, I believe, a little under ten thousand feet; yet the shapes and arrangement of the peaks are such as to make one feel that they rival the Alps in altitude. The lake is a mere basin, hemmed in by gigantic walls of almost perpendicular mountains, the summits of which are all aiguilles and dents. The lake below, in strictest contrast, lies absolutely still and peaceful, as blue as Lake Geneva. Then come the bright green, yet steeply-sloping mountain-sides, and next the wild fearful precipices of black rock, and then again the aiguilles peaks, on one side glitteringly white, and on the other as black as ebony, cutting the sky like the pinnacled roof of the Venetian St. Mark's; and last of all, the deep blue silent sky as peaceful as the lake.

After a few days we started from Queenstown, the principal settlement upon the lake, to drive by coach to Dunedin. It was a very long and tedious journey of a hundred and eighty miles, almost entirely through mountainous country, cut up in all directions by fast-running streams which are being searched in every part, accessible or inaccessible, for gold. The whole country like that around Ballarat and Sandhurst in Victoria, is being quite literally turned upside down by the gold seekers, and we passed hundreds of small encampments of prospectors, and little colonies of patiently toiling Chinamen, on our journey.

VIEW OF LAKE WAKATIPU.

Dunedin is commercially the capital of New Zealand. It is the most populous city and I think the most prosperous. It is also one of the most beautiful. Perhaps nothing strikes the visitor to New Zealand more than the number of good harbours it possesses; indeed, while I am saying how beautifully situated is Dunedin, I find myself immediately, as it were, pulled up by the question " But what shall I say of Wellington? or what again of Auckland? or still more of Nelson?" The same jealousy —it really, amongst a great many people, amounts to ill-feeling—exists between the inhabitants of these cities as between those of the capitals of the Australian Colonies. One can hardly speak well of one city to the native of another, and to a perfect stranger whose habit it is to say merely what he thinks, this small-minded rivalry appears very absurd.

Dunedin is, as I have said, the leading commercial city and reflects great credit upon the keen Scotchmen, its founders. From here the already very complete system of railroads takes its origin; a line runs south as far as the Bluff—the southernmost port—and another railroad connects the city of Christchurch with the southern capital. At the time of my visit there was a through train every day between Christchurch and Dunedin, which traversed the 230 miles in eleven hours, and made three successive runs of two hours without stopping; this piece of enterprise has, however, of late been found to be too expensive, and only a slow train runs through now. After traversing some rather mountainous country for an hour or so, the line emerges upon the Canterbury Plains. The above name is given to the open and fertile tract of country lying between the mountain range of the west coast and the eastern shore. To the north of this valuable district is Christchurch, the capital of the province, and one of the most pleasant places in New Zealand.

Christchurch lies upon the open plain and is built almost entirely of wood. Through its very centre there runs a small winding stream, along the banks of which are willow-trees as fine as any at the backs of the colleges at Cambridge. There are large and very pretty public gardens along this river bank, and many delightful afternoons may be spent boating, under the pleasant shade of the weeping willows. In the museum at Christchurch is the finest collection of Dinornis skeletons extant, and these are truly of great interest. The Moa, as the Maoris call it, is a bird now very generally admitted to be extinct, although until within but a few years there were undoubtedly some specimens existing. The Maoris have songs of which the hunting of the Moa is the theme, and there are tolerably well-authenticated cases of pioneers away in the hills having seen them. Possibly like the Apterix they are night birds. The largest specimen in the Christchurch Museum is a little over twelve feet high, and its leg-bones are larger even than those of the African elephant.

The port of Christchurch is Lyttleton, a fine harbour separated from the capital by a small mountain range which, however, has been tunnelled.* This is a place of some interest as an example of the way in which people will now sacrifice everything to commerce. Christchurch, as I have said, lies upon the plains; it is a busy, hot, inland city: Lyttleton, its port, distant not more than ten minutes by rail, is situated on a lovely harbour sur-

---

* This tunnel was built many years ago at a cost of £200,000. It is a very considerable engineering work, being as much as a mile and three-quarters long. Its construction was necessary, as by no other means could the produce of this part of the Canterbury Plains be placed on board ship at a paying rate.

rounded by green hills. At this pleasant retreat so near at
hand, where the wind is always cool and the sea blue and
beautiful, one might expect to find some sign of rest and
comfort; one might at least look for a change from the hot
streets and busy life of the town. I went down therefore
on New Year's Day, when a grand regatta was to be held,
with every expectation of a pleasant afternoon. Special
trains ran at short intervals and by twelve or one o'clock
many thousands of holiday makers had left the city. On
arriving at my destination, I found what was to me a quite
unique and wonderful spectacle. These thousands of
visitors in their summer dresses of muslin and print,
escorted by cavaliers in all the elegance of lavender
trousers and bright blue ties, were, to my surprise, scattered
over a no less unromantic camping ground than the station
railroad sidings. The explanation of this state of things is
that Lyttleton, although built upon a very beautiful little
bay, as fair a spot as exists upon God's earth, has been
entirely monopolised by the railway people, and now in
consequence there are no sands for women and children to
sit on, no grassy slopes, not even a stone wall and lamppost
promenade—there is for sea frontage absolutely nothing but
this waste of railway sidings! Here, then, were booths and
penny shows (sixpence out here) and merry-go-rounds and
the whole paraphernalia of holiday-making erected and under
patronage upon a cinder-paved, scorching wilderness of
sidings. Nature could have formed no lovelier spot; the
little bay nestling under the steep green hills seems made
for the perfect enjoyment of tired and city-sick men of toil;
here they might have come to breathe the pure air and
forget the hurry and bustle of their everyday life. The
people to whom I talked on this subject, however, seemed
surprised at my train of thought, and very evidently con-

sidered the expeditious landing of coal and shipping of wool quite the only things needful.

I drove from Christchurch to the west coast. The coach road crosses the mountain range by the celebrated Otira gorge, and terminates at Hokitiki. The last part of the journey is a very wonderful experience, and consists of the worst piece of coaching I have known.

On the way up the pass one of our stages was twenty-six miles, which, having to be undertaken with one team of horses, took us six hours. For four hours we literally did nothing but crawl up the bed of a river, there being no road of any kind. In places the stream was so high that the bottom of the coach was in the water, and there was some danger of our being carried down by the current. Higher up still, the floods and frosts had completely washed away the road, and we could in places see the old track lying away down in the valley below, many hundreds of feet, the landslips having been so extensive that it was almost uninjured by its fall. The river that we followed on our way up is called the Waimakariri and is fully as terrible as its name. The scenery is certainly very magnificent, and may be compared to some of the finest Alpine passes. Mount Cook, which is 13,400 feet high and of very picturesque form, is clearly seen from the western side of the pass. The journey from Christchurch to Hokitiki took two days, on the first of which we travelled thirteen, and on the second sixteen hours; during the last nine hours of the second day we, moreover, had nothing whatever to eat.

Hokitiki is a played-out gold-field town—a wilderness of tumble-down, unoccupied wooden huts. We were glad to leave such a dreary spot as soon as possible, and so drove up to Kumara, a new and prosperous digger settlement. This place is in the middle of a dense forest: two years ago no human being had ever penetrated those woods, and to-day there were many thousands of inhabitants and all the usual surroundings of elementary civilisation. Opposite our hotel I counted six similar establishments, and our next door neighbours, both to right and left, were in the same line of business! This was the only place I have seen where a "rush" was actually going on at the time of my visit; every other gold-town that I have been to had seen better days or was immediately expecting a revival. These diggings at Kumara, however, were in full swing, and the township at the zenith of prosperity, presenting a far from edifying spectacle.

A tramway runs down to the coast, in flat forest country such a road being very easily constructed. A line is marked out through the forest, and a clearing some twenty feet wide made; the timber is then cut roughly into lengths and laid down as are railway sleepers. Upon these logs the lines, which consist of long pieces of timber about four inches square, are laid, let in about an inch and wedged up tight. The spaces between the sleepers are filled in with any sort of ballast, and the road is then complete.

We travelled upon this tramway to a small port called Greymouth on the coast. The journey was a beautiful one, through the best New Zealand forest scenery I have seen. The trees are very high and the road is so constructed that no damage has been done even to the immediately surrounding forest; there is absolutely untouched jungle on either side and infinity of creepers and fern varieties. The most distinctive feature in New Zealand forests is the growth of creepers which almost cover the trees, sending down long shoots to the ground, up which again climb convolvuluses or ferns. Even grasses at times may be seen in great bunches growing up above among the branches, so that in places the ordinary undergrowth of flowers, ferns and moss seems tossed aloft and sprinkled all amongst the higher branches as in some bright fairy scene.

Before we reached Greymouth we had to cross the Teramakau river, which runs through a deep gorge. Wires have been flung across the river from one high cliff to the other, and we were drawn along these in a small cage, the distance from bank to bank being over three hundred yards.

I went by sea from Greymouth to Wellington, calling in at Nelson and Picton on the way. These two little places are only notable for their extreme natural beauty, which in some respects can hardly be exaggerated. I have made three short visits to Nelson, and have found it on each occasion more charming than before. It is one of the most peaceful and beautiful places in all the world.

Wellington is the political capital of New Zealand. It is spread out along the shores of a beautiful harbour, with a back-ground of fine hills. The government buildings are enormous wooden structures, looking as though they were built of dressed stone. I think, however, all the buildings are of wood, but, as in San Francisco, it is impossible, without touching them, to know whether they are of wood or stone. In Wellington is to be seen the best collection of Maori curiosities now extant. There is also at the museum a native meeting-house taken from one of the villages and re-erected here; it is very complete and most interesting as showing of what these people are capable. The carving of the pillars is intensely elaborate, the designs resembling those of Chinese or Japanese temples. I have seen a modern building of this kind near Masterton, quite recently completed; in that case also the elaborate carving of the columns and frames of the house was most remarkable.

At the back of Wellington and over the mountain range lies a large and fertile piece of country known as the Wairarapa plain. This tract of land lies at a considerable elevation, and is shut in on all sides by mountains: the soil of a great part of it is poor and weak, capable of producing nothing much beyond rank grass and reeds. I stayed, however, for a month at a farm on the upper part of the plain where the land was of much better quality and yielded very fair returns. A tribe of natives whose "pah" was only a mile from the house gave the place a rather more than purely agricultural interest.

To the north-east of this plain lies a forest known as the Seventy-Mile Bush, beyond which is Napier, the capital of the Hawke's Bay province. From this town, which is of no great interest, I started with some friends to ride overland to Auckland.

The country between Napier and Lake Taupo, in the centre of the North Island, is very mountainous and romantic in character. When the ranges are crossed, however, the traveller enters an entirely new kind of country. Lake Taupo is a large sheet of water, twenty-five miles by twenty, situated at the south end of a wide plain; beyond it, still farther to the south, are two picturesque mountains; one, Ruapehu, snow-capped and imposing; the other, Tongariro, the volcano which is the Fuziyama of New Zealand. The Waikato river, a stream of quite historic interest since the Maori war of 1863, flows out of Lake Taupo, and, some miles from the little collection of native wharés and huts which constitutes the settlement of Taupo, forms a waterfall of very great beauty. These falls are in all respects similar to those of the Niagara river, only upon a very much smaller scale; the same kind of deep ravine with dark blue eddying water and black perpendicular cliffs is found below the falls.

The place is well worth a visit. Near Taupo are some very pleasant hot spring baths, at a point where a hot stream and a cold one converge. Over the confluence an awning has been spread, and upon the bank an enterprising individual has put up some native huts for dressing-rooms. It forms a most delightful bathing place, for one can swim from hot water into cold, and cold into hot as one pleases.

We did not follow the coach road from Taupo, but having been most kindly provided with constabulary horses and an orderly who knew every mile of the country, we struck out across the plain to another place of interest on the Waikato river known as Orakei Korako.

Here was a very considerable gathering of natives from the country around, who had met to settle some land disputes with the government. The village was crowded beyond its capabilities, but when we arrived with a constabulary escort we were immediately received with every kindness, and a wharé was cleaned out for our accommodation.

During the afternoon we visited some alum caves and curious volcanic formations in the neighbourhood, returning after an hour or so to hear a little of the debate then going on. The speaking was very impressive, and it is not too much to say, that although we could understand nothing we were much interested. There was one magnificently tattoed warrior whose commanding voice and manly action, I think I shall never forget; at times he would make long pauses, then again walk a few paces up and down, pouring forth a volley of words to which every one listened with riveted attention. Some hundreds of natives had assembled, and the deliberations were to last over a week. At sundown an old woman brought us some potatoes, which we ate with our fingers and relished exceedingly. The chiefs also sent us presents of fat pork and other delicacies.

Later on the natives were persuaded to perform a "hakka," or Maori dance, for our edification. The entertainment was given upon an open plain of a white formation, perhaps an acre in extent and almost flat. An enormous bonfire was lighted upon this place, during which performance an old ruffian with a short flat club went roaring about, hitting his thighs, and calling the people together. Fifty or sixty men and women soon assembled, and formed in a semicircular double row, the rest of the people squatting down behind us, forming a considerable audience. Both men and women took off nearly all their clothes, and settled down to work as though something very serious were going to take place. They began with regular gesticulations, slapping their thighs loudly and beating the ground with their left feet; between each beat they shook their hands in the air to one side. Their roaring was at first low and fierce, but terminated periodically in a frantic howl. After a time two leading men came out from the ranks and strode up and down in front of the line, uttering yell after yell, and contorting both their faces and limbs into a hundred frightful shapes. This seemed to work the whole party into a frenzy, and as the flames of the bonfire leapt up we could see every face contorted into fiendish aspect, eyes rolling, and tongues hanging out. I have seen nothing more absolutely horrible in my life. The excitement now became greater and greater. The women commenced beating their breasts and tearing their hair while the men gave way to every conceivable and inconceivable paroxysm of lunatic frenzy. There in the midst our orderly pointed out Ta-hau, the late outlaw, now pardoned for the sake of his tribe, who befriended us in the war. He it was who, on the East Coast, had committed atrocities too awful to mention, and who is still known as Te Kooti's butcher, for his awful deeds of cannibalism and murder.* Beside him were a dozen other ruffians as fierce and frenzied as he, and I confess we felt a little nervous as the madness seemed to increase with these people, and their shouts and actions grew more and more fiendish. There were but five of us among a hundred very hellhounds. As the fire burnt low, their faces seemed more weird and horrible than before, their eyes, mouths and distorted features being such as I have seen in nightmares. It was the most awful and terrorful experience. We saw a dozen or more dances, some of pleasure and some of war, but not differing materially from each other. About midnight we left them, and tried to curl up in our little hut and sleep, but the distant shouting of those who still kept up the dance, and the flickering light of the bonfire shining through the rough timber walls of our wharé kept us awake. The dogs, too, were like those of an Arab village in the persistency of their barking, and several times in the night we were visited by pigs and other intruders. There was nothing for it but to plunge into

A MAORI WARRIOR.

* The notorious cannibal Te Kooti who caused so much trouble during the war and who, it is said, has had 1500 men in the field in his pursuit, is still alive and at large in the King Country.

the cool river at daylight, and be off on to the hills again. We had to swim our horses across the Waikato at this place, as it is very deep. There were two slight canoes in which we crossed, leading our animals by their tethers. It was a long and dangerous process, and we very nearly lost one horse, which was carried many hundred yards down the stream, but found a landing ultimately.

After a ride of thirty-seven miles along a hardly discernable bridle track, we came upon the Wairoa lake, where is a small wooden inn and a Maori village. Here we put up, and after a night's rest, started across the water to visit the Pink and White Terraces of Rotomahana.

These terraces are situated about a mile from the larger sheet of water upon a lake which is almost circular, of a deep blue colour, warm throughout, and perhaps a mile in diameter. It is the centre of a little district of curious volcanic formations, the chiefest of which are the two geysers which have formed the Pink and White Terraces. These geysers are situated about a hundred and fifty feet above the lake on the hill-side. Their water is strongly impregnated with silica, which has been deposited as the stream runs down in the form of beautiful terraced slopes.*

We first visited the White Terraces, over which no water was running when we arrived. The sweep of the lowest platform is about two hundred yards and is almost flat. As we ascend, however, the steps become gradually more and more deeply hollowed out, forming a series of basins. The incrustations upon the outside of the terrace steps forms exquisitely minute tracery, resembling frost upon a

* For a very complete and wise treatise upon the nature of these terrace formations, see a paper by the Rev. R. Abbay in the Quarterly Journal of the Geological Society, May 1878.

window pane, the basins, themselves, in brilliant contrast to the snow-white silica, being filled with turquoise, or sapphire-coloured water. At the top we found a large cauldron, shaped like a crater, from which the geysers flow intermittently. In the morning when we arrived this was empty, but before we left it had commenced to fill, its condition appearing to depend upon the direction of the wind. We walked from the top of these terraces to a place where little mud craters were bubbling in all directions. It was almost a comical sight although somewhat uncanny, reminding one of the refinements of torture in the Inferno. Passing these we came upon a steam vent-hole; the noise was terrific, but there was no water, merely dry steam escaping at a high pressure. Beyond this again were more boiling mud craters and then a mud terrace at the head of which was a brilliantly emerald-green pool, still and clear. Close by were inactive basins of light drab-coloured mud which the natives eat, and we tried some, but did not find it very palatable. The next curiosity was an intermittent geyser, which was also very curious. For five or ten minutes the water would be quite calm and clear, then, rising slowly and becoming turbulent, a large jet of boiling water twenty to thirty feet high is thrown into the air.

After satisfying ourselves with these extraordinary sights we went down again to the lake, and were paddled across in little canoes to the Pink Terraces, which lie on the other side. These are of a light salmon colour, not so large as the White Terraces, but in many ways quite as beautiful. There are twenty terraces, the formation being identical with the others, excepting only the slight colouring matter. Water was running over them at the time of our visit, so we took off our shoes and socks and walked up barefooted. When we reached the deeper holes we took off our clothes also and had a glorious bathe. The pools are three or four feet deep and their sides as soft as velvet. There is any temperature one may wish for, according as he goes higher or lower, nearer the geyser where the water is boiling, or nearer the lake where it is only tepid; the water, moreover, is most deliciously soft, and I suppose the bath is the finest in the world.

The Maoris who own the lakes are of the Arawa tribe, and are very outrageous in their black mail and canoe charges, but the government is, I believe, trying to acquire the place as public property. There is no natural beauty near the terraces, the lake being, on the contrary, swampy, unclean and greasy in appearance. The surrounding country is scorched up and sulphurous, and covered only with stunted growth: the terraces are, however, curious beyond most of the world's sights, and in such points as the traceried carving of their steps and the exquisite sapphire-coloured water are very beautiful.

We rode from Wairoa to Ohinemutu, on the large lake of Rotorua which is the Lake Titicaca of New Zealand. To this lake are attached all the earliest Maori legends, and there is an island upon it in connection with which you are told of a Hero and Leander episode.

We visited this island and were shown certain battle fields, and a pah where some desperate struggles took place, and a hoary, rusty old villain with no teeth whose age was a hundred and two, but to whom sixpences still had a charm. At the village are warm baths, in which the natives splash about all day; there is, moreover, a civilised and public-house air about the place, which is not pleasant, and we only stayed one day.

From Ohinemutu we started to ride across to the Waikato through a country which is utterly barren at present, and where there are neither white men nor Maoris for between ninety and a hundred miles. We rode steadily on through one day, having started very early. The track was almost lost, and we took a Maori guide with us. Hour after hour we pushed on, availing ourselves of every bit of level ground for a spurt, but too often having for miles to climb up hills, or pick our way along ridges, where trotting was impossible. By eight o'clock in the evening, to our great surprise, we noticed the smoke of a fire, which turned out to be at the encampment of a surveying party. Here, after a ride of between seventy and eighty miles, we halted, leaving the remaining distance to the next day. We got into Hamilton by noon the following morning, and went on to Auckland by railroad, after a very delightful riding tour through the most interesting part of the North Island.

During the last fortnight we had, of course, seen a good deal of the Maoris, but what we saw was almost more distressing than interesting. The race is undoubtedly dying out very fast, and the causes are the old causes—everywhere the same—drink, tobacco, wearing European clothes, and adopting European customs. These people are dying, in a word, of civilisation. There will be no more serious Maori troubles now, for the colonists have adopted a method of dealing with these people which will very soon end in their destruction; I refer to what is known as the "sugar and flour policy" which is as disastrously effective as a deliberate scheme of destruction, the Maoris being given enough necessities to enable them to afford luxuries, such as tobacco, gin, and blankets, which are rapidly killing them from the face of the land.

Their King country is still not broken into, and perhaps nothing astonishes a visitor more than finding this great tract of land, in the centre of New Zealand, still alienated from the Crown, and in absolute possession of the natives. No white man may go in there, or if he does he very surely does not come out. The constabulary force recognise the difficulty and merely leave the district alone; it is, however, a place of refuge for defaulters, who are often willing to take their chance with the natives.*

When Captain Cook discovered New Zealand, there were probably as many people as in the Sandwich Islands, whence the natives originally came. There are now hardly one-tenth of that number. From 1861 to 1879, they fell in numbers from 55,336 to 43,595, or about 20 per cent. in seventeen years. They were in many respects a notable race, and have been spoken of as the noblest of savages. They were great warriors, great military strategists, great upholders of the creeds of honour; they were brave to a marvel, had many redeeming points even in their social lives, and were certainly powerful orators. In the early days the missionaries doubtless did much good amongst them, but their work seems to have borne but little fruit of late, and the condition of the people is far from satisfactory. They have seen too much of the white man to have any great belief in his religion. "You point to heaven," they say; "and whilst our eyes are looking there, you take away the land from under our feet."

A half-caste race is springing up in considerable numbers, which, indeed, is said to be physically finer than either the European or Maori, from which it has sprung. Ere long, however, this strain of native blood in the New Zealand

---

* I cut the following from a paper of Nov. 23, 1880:—"The King natives at Upper Wanganui have killed a pakeha Maori named Moffat, who formerly lived amongst them making gunpowder, for which he received a sentence of two years. He returned to the district to look after some property left there. The natives held a meeting, and ordered him to be shot, as no white man was allowed there."

colonists will be the only remaining trace of the once famous Maori race.

I steamed out of the very beautiful harbour of Auckland for Honolulu in the Sandwich Islands, feeling quite sorry to leave what I always remember as the most delightful, most attractive, and most English of the Australasian colonies.

CHAPTER IV.

NORFOLK ISLAND.

> " It was a wild and breaker-beaten coast,
> With cliffs above, and a broad sandy shore,
> Guarded by shoals and rocks, as by a host,
> With here and there a creek, whose aspect wore
> A better welcome to the tempest-tossed ;
> And rarely ceased the haughty billows' roar,
> Save on the dead long summer days, which make
> The outstretch'd ocean glitter like a lake."—*Byron*.

NORFOLK Island, lying in the Southern Pacific in S. Lat. 29° 2′ and Long. 167° 58′ E, of Greenwich, was discovered by Captain Cook in 1774. It is six hundred miles from Auckland in New Zealand, and about nine hundred and fifty miles from Sydney, N.S.W. It appears to have been formed by the eruption of volcanic matter from the bed of the sea, and is estimated to contain about ten thousand acres. Until 1788 the island had remained uninhabited, but in that year a small number of convicts, with a party of marines, was sent from Australia. The convict establishment was finally withdrawn in 1855, and in the following year the inhabitants of Pitcairn's Island (a mere dot in the Pacific, only four and a half miles in circumference), descendants of the Bounty mutineers, who had outgrown their diminutive home, were, at their own request, removed to Norfolk Island. The Melanesian Mission under Bishop Patteson, established its head-quarters on the island in the year 1866.

So much of Norfolk Island from the books of reference. It is not quite an Australasian colony, and yet its position is one of almost as great independence. The descendants of the Bounty mutineers are now to be found upon two islands in the Pacific. The larger part are on Norfolk Island, but a few still remain upon Pitcairn's Island in the far east, where Christian, the originator of the mutiny, first settled. Pitcairn's Island is rarely visited by any ships, but Norfolk Island is more accessible, for the steamer that runs from Sydney to the Fijis passes within a few miles of it, and upon a certain payment, and under certain conditions, will call in to land an adventurous passenger.

Hearing, whilst I was staying at Sydney during the summer of 1879-80, that this was the case, and being very anxious to escape, if only for a short time, from the hot winds and dried-up desolation of an Australian summer, I started with a friend in the Fiji steamer, having made arrangements to be put down on Norfolk Island on the outward voyage, and picked up again on the way back. We steamed away from the Australian coast in a north-easterly direction, and in two days sighted a little oasis in the waste of sea known as Lord Howe's Island. We ran in quite close to the land, passing between the main island and an outlying sugar-loaf rock called Ball's Pyramid. Both the Pyramid and the island itself are very high and well-wooded. Here, although there are only a few acres of land, about twenty solitary spirits have made their home, and earn a scant living by exchanging their fruits and vegetables with such few whalers as may give them a call.

On the morning of the fifth day, after a very rough and comfortless run of about a thousand miles, we made high land and steamed up to our destination.

Norfolk Island is of most forbidding aspect. There is no

shelter round its iron-bound shores; there is no permanent anchorage, and landing is almost always a matter of difficulty. We knew we were in for a rough experience that morning, for it was blowing fully half a gale, and even on the lee side of the island, where we ran in somewhat near and fired our gun, the sea was running very awkwardly. After an hour or so a whale boat came off and battled out towards us through the boisterous sea. She was manned by four splendid fellows, and had at the steer-oar a weather-beaten old mariner whose very hat inspired confidence. Getting into this boat was a matter of great difficulty, for the steamer herself was pitching and rolling in the wildest way, and a dozen times I thought the whale boat would have been dashed to pieces under the vessel's quarter. We watched our chances, however, one at a time, and then jumped; a few small bags were thrown after us, and in two or three seconds we were clear of the vessel and comparatively safe.

But what waves there were, and how utterly fragile and puny our little craft seemed in that great sea! It was for all the world like the pictures on the Life Boat Association's money boxes! I could not have believed it possible, however, to manage a boat so splendidly; excepting the driving spray from the waves' crests, we shipped no water whatever, but rode over mountain after mountain of sea in glorious defiance.

We had been dropped from the steamer fully two miles from the shore, and had a very long and fatiguing pull towards the land. Our troubles, however, we learned after an hour or so were still all to come; we had the actual *landing* to do yet; this boating in the open sea was mere child's play to the work before us. I think our brave "Norfolker" crew took some delight in indicating the dangers ahead. They were too hard at work and too much out of breath to do more than hint brokenly at what we had to go through, but this they did with dramatic power. As we approached the breakers we could see, dimly, a low stone pier which runs out twenty yards or so, and upon the end of which were many figures watching. Our helmsman now stood up and the crew lay upon their oars for a moment's breath; then we pulled slowly on, and then rested again. A man on the pier-head was watching the rollers as they came breaking in; for a moment or two we lay rising and falling with the waves, then there was a shout and a signal from the pier and a "lay to lads" from the helmsman; the right moment had come and those great weather-beaten sailors *did* lay to in real earnest. For one moment we half stopped, surrounded by a great seething cauldron of foam, and the next, shot round the pier head and into smooth water.

There was a small crowd on the shore to welcome us, a quaint crowd of weather-beaten men, and yellow-skinned black-haired women, and bright girls without stays or stockings, and curious peering boys and children. Through these we made our way to a small stone cottage, and there were refreshed with hot tea and relieved of our drenched clothing. Then away across the island to the Mission Station, where we were most kindly received, and given a cheerful bungalow for our residence.

Upon Norfolk Island there are two communities. Firstly that amongst which we landed, secondly that of the Melanesian Mission. The "Norfolkers," as the proprietors of the island are called, were brought from Pitcairn's Island at the Imperial Government's expense, and were landed at their new home in 1856. They drew lots amongst themselves for the chief buildings and most valuable pieces of land, and straightway settled down as proprietors of the island, and all the old convict buildings thereon. Each married couple received fifty acres at first, but of late years the marriage settlement has been reduced to twenty-five acres.

The majority live in the old convict "town," as it is called, on the south side of the island. There are vast buildings

"THE TOWN," NORFOLK ISLAND.

here which served as prisons and barracks, and more desolate piles of masonry one could hardly conceive. The larger ones it was found hopeless to try to maintain, so these are in ruins and look hundreds of years old. The officers' houses, also of fine hewn stone, and the smaller buildings are still kept up and serve as the homes of the more well-to-do inhabitants. On several occasions we wandered through the labyrinths of prisons and barracks and were told stories of those dark melancholy days of old. They were the most desperate of criminals that were sent here, and I am afraid the history of their lives would form no ornament to our country's annals. We saw the old gallows where so many hundreds have been led out to their doom, and where fifteen and eighteen have been hanged in a morning. We saw the chapel, too, now in ruins, where the prisoners all assembled for prayer and service. There is a raised dais at one end upon which a company of soldiers was drawn up with loaded arms. As we stood in the ruined chapel our thoughts could not but wander back to one fatal day, when some sign of rebellion being shown, during God's service and before His very altar, the word " Fire" was given and twenty or thirty were killed or wounded. What a ghastly scene! the service stopped, the chaplain hurrying to the vestry, the officers' wives and children fainting and crying, and the stern soldiers shooting down the prisoners in the very house of God! Of such was the life in those old convict days. I believe no one could draw too dark a picture. Witness this solemn report from the House of Commons proceedings.

" As I mentioned the names of those men who were to die, they, one after another, as their names were pronounced, dropped on their knees and thanked God that they were to be delivered from that horrible place, whilst the others remained standing mute, weeping. It was the most horrible sight I ever witnessed."—*Evidence of Very Rev. Wm. Ullathorne, D.D.*, 1838. *Q.* 267, *Report of Select Committee on Transportation.*

And again.

. . . "Two or three men murdered their fellow-prisoners, with the certainty of being detected and executed, apparently without malice, and with very little excitement, stating that they knew that they should be hanged, but it was better than being where they were."—*Evidence of Sir Francis Forbes. Q.* 1335, 1343, *in same report.*

The same sad memories are awakened down by the water's edge a mile or so from the little town where is a walled-in plot of land. I have never seen so sad a sight, I think, as this God's acre neglected and forgotten. Its old stone monuments sloping this way and that, and the rank grass growing above the graves. Here a captain's little son, and here a colonel's wife; here a mother's new-born child, all lying beneath the green grass in this far-off Pacific island. Here, too, many private soldiers and many officers who had escaped a hundred dangers, only to be laid low at last by a felon's hand. Brief records are on most graves of the nature of the tenant's death, "barbarously murdered whilst in the execution of his duty" occurs many times, but most frequently of all items, "drowned while endeavouring to cross the bar." Graveyards are never cheerful places to visit, truly, but there is a desolation about this forsaken spot, out of the way even there on Norfolk Island, that is beyond all telling.

Norfolk Island is always spoken of as one of the most beautiful places in all the world, and, indeed, although the list of most beautiful places is so long, it is not said without reason in this case. Its beauty is not the beauty of the tropics, although it is in a latitude that admits of tree ferns and others of nature's richest decorations. The beauty of the tropics is one thing, but there are sights in our temperate zones that no tropical glories can approach. As I think of nature's grandest spectacles, Brazilian forests, and South Sea islands, and mountains in Malay, and jungle-skirted Andes, I feel that they do not possess the poetic beauty of the English lakes or the valleys of Japan. I remember Kingsley somewhere says, that one day there will be West Indian poets and tropical artists, as far above ours of the Lakes and Highlands, as the scenery of those sunny lands is above our own; but this is, I think, a grave error, as all who have known more than the first wild delight of those intoxicating spectacles must feel. The scenery of the tropics is like its fruits and flowers, too rich, too gorgeous; we are for a time dazzled by its splendour, but the joy passes and we long for our Highland Lochs and English Fells. I was walking this year along the shores of Derwentwater, and I felt that no Andes Peaks, Himalayan slopes or tropical forests could delight in the way that those soft cloud shadows delighted me, as they chased each other up the green hillsides, or down along the water's edge, blending the soft hues of green and blue into sweet picture poems.

The scenery of Norfolk Island is like that, nor can the fringes of tree ferns, and groups of giant pines destroy the peaceful, quiet English beauty of its valleys and hillsides.

What rides are there among the glades and uplands of that little island! Great reaches here of meadow, cleared of every stone or stump in the old convict days. What lovely paths, too, cut through the dense forest; what gallops one can have along the high cliffs, and in and out amongst the partially cleared woodlands! The whole island is but fifteen square miles, and yet so undulating is it, and so even mountainous in its small way, that there seems no limit to the number of rides one can take. In the old days, before the great works had fallen into decay, it must have been a demi-Paradise; fine English-looking roads ran round and about the island, gardens were laid out in almost every gully, the grass was mown upon the hills, in short, the whole place was one large park. Even now, its character is more of a park than of anything else, and I shall never forget our rambles on horseback through the beautiful woods and down the valleys and along the high cliffs, the bright fresh air, the yellow sunlight through the trees, the grand effects of light and shade across the great far-stretching ocean.

It is a queer, simple little community that owns this lovely island; the venerable Mr. Nobbs, whose history has been too often told to need repeating here, is at its head. The men are strong, hardy-looking fellows, but in the women one sees a little of the old Tahitian blood; they fade very soon and are only of two kinds, children and old women. The patois of these islanders is somewhat curious; it is that of a race of sailors with the slightest touch of foreign accent.

Life is surely easy enough for these good people; all kinds of fruits and vegetables grow with the maximum results for the minimum amount of labour, and there are pigs, cows, sheep, fowls, and horses upon the island in abundance.

Whaling is almost their sole source of revenue, however, for they are incorrigibly lazy, and seem to care nothing whatever for more than meat and raiment. The young men are grand boatmen, being brought up to face all manner of danger from their earliest years. Perhaps the most interesting feature about these people is their attachment to the island; many of them would not leave it even for a few weeks; their whole ideas seem bounded by the narrow margin of their island shores, and they are most singularly free from all curiosity with respect to the outer world. So much then for the rightful owners (by special Crown grant) of the island.*

Another community exists on the island, as I have already said; this is the college of the Melanesian Mission, whose head-quarters are now permanently fixed here. A thousand acres were given over to the Mission upon payment to the islanders of two pounds an acre. Upon this land a very complete missionary station is placed. The Mission college is upon the model of an English public school, there being

---

* The islanders are governed by a chief magistrate, who is selected by ballot, and who performs his magisterial functions for a limited period. The only punishment for any offence is the infliction of a fine. Capital offences must be tried in the Supreme Court at Sydney. The £2000, obtained by the sale of land to the Melanesian Mission, is invested in Sydney for the support of a doctor upon the island, and for other expenses.

seven "Houses" with school-rooms attached, in each of which live a clergyman and twenty or thirty natives of the Western Pacific Islands. In the centre is a large hall where all meals are taken and which is also used as a school-room. In connection is a printing-shop, also carpenter's, and blacksmith's shops, farm-bailiff's house, farmyard, &c. &c. Last of all, but most important of all, there is the chapel, built in memory of John Patteson, the martyr bishop.

The system that the Mission has adopted is briefly this. Their vessel, the "Southern Cross," sails to the islands two or three times a year, and brings back native boys and girls, who are placed in the various houses. Here they remain three or more years, and are taught to read and write, plough and plant, make clothes for themselves, and live decent civilised lives. They are then returned to their islands, either permanently or merely for a visit, after which they are brought back again, and, if promising pupils, are further taught and finally turned out as teachers or deacons. The hours of their labours are, I think, very sensibly short. They have three spells of three quarters of an hour each day, also an hour or two for working in the fields, and lastly two services in the chapel at which there is not, as with us, any "call over," but at which practically all attend.

The principle of the Mission is distinctly wise—first that which is natural, and afterwards that which is spiritual. They do not attempt to alter more native customs than are absolutely needful to be altered. They do their utmost to cultivate friendly relations everywhere, entering into all the pursuits, pleasures, and troubles of their pupils, with results which are, I think, very satisfactory.

I cannot refrain from describing the native service in the chapel, which is the most impressive sight of its kind that I have seen. The building is of dressed stone and will last for ages; as far as the interior is concerned it is very beautiful; the pavement is a fine marble mosaic presented to the Mission in memory of a Mr. Freemantle. The stained windows are, however, its greatest adornment; they are six in number, and were designed by Burne Jones and executed by Morris. Nothing can exceed the exquisite colouring of these windows, which certainly are the finest specimens of glass painting in Australasia. The interior of the chapel, then, without entering into more particulars, is very impressive and beautiful. As the bell tolls, the barefooted islanders walk silently in, each one kneeling at his or her place for a few seconds before sitting down. As the hour strikes, the doors are closed and service is commenced in the Mota (an island in the Banks' group) language. The responses are uttered by everyone, and I have seen nothing to equal the quiet, earnest devotion of these pupils. The singing is really very good, and in all details the service is identical with the ordinary English Church service, but the attention and devotion of the congregation are beyond all praise. At the end there is a long pause; not a sound is made; there kneel these two hundred natives, after the blessing has been pronounced, and one might literally hear a pin drop upon the marble floor. Then they all rise and steal noiselessly out.

The usual half-holidays are given to the pupils, and cricket and other games are played with some enthusiasm. They also make up large fishing and picnic parties on Saturdays, and wander all over the island in twos and threes, enjoying the luxury of needing no weapons, and being free to wander where they will.

It would be unjust if I did not say a word about the social condition of this little community of two hundred souls. There are no servants amongst them, a purely communist system of life being aimed at. The work of cooking, washing, farming, gardening, and the like, is divided, as equally as may be, amongst the pupils and teachers from the bishop downwards, and none are too proud to lend a hand anywhere and at any time. The position of the clergymen to their pupils is absolutely paternal; no long-faced, stern disciplinarianism or hollow-cheeked, unapproachable Christianity, but genial good-fellowship and unrestrained enjoyment in both work and play. They seem, these missionaries, almost to have eradicated the old-established feud between youth and lessons, the boys running off to school with almost as much good will and merriment as to their games. Not the least remarkable feature of the whole school, perhaps, is, that although they live so freely together, men and women, and boys and girls, there is practically no immorality amongst them and but little quarrelling, and I doubt if as much could be said of any community of white people that have ever been brought together in present or historic times.

We spent a fortnight on the island, riding, and playing cricket, and even shooting now and again; the sport, I confess, is not of the very best, although there is a fair number of imported pheasants could one only get more easily at them.

It was during my visit here that I was invited, and finally persuaded, by Bishop Selwyn to accompany him in his voyage down to the islands that year (1880). His intention was not only to visit the New Hebrides and Solomon Islands as usual, but, further, to make an attempt to land upon the main island of the Santa Cruz group, and, if possible, to establish friendly relations with those dreaded natives, who have been entirely neglected by the outer world since the disastrous visit of Commodore Goodenough in 1875.

The voyage would not commence until early in July, after the "Southern Cross" had returned to Norfolk Island from her first trip of that year in the South Seas. I returned, therefore, to Sydney, and spent a few more months in Australia and New Zealand, determining to visit the Fiji group in June, and arrange to be put down once more on Norfolk Island, on my way back from Levuka, in the beginning of July.

CHAPTER V.

FIJI.

> " The mat for rest; * * *
> * * for board the plantain spread
> With its broad leaf, or turtle-shell which bore
> A banquet in the flesh it cover'd o'er;
> The gourd with water recent from the rill,
> The ripe banana from the mellow hill;
> * * * * *
> The cava feast, the yam, the coco's root,
> Which bears at once the cup, and milk, and fruit."—*Byron.*

I LEFT Sydney in the winter month of June, delighted at the prospect of entering more warm and genial latitudes (for if people in England imagine that the weather in Australia is all sunshine and dry crisp warmth, they are mistaken) and sailed in the same steamer that had six months before taken me to Norfolk Island, for Levuka in Fiji. The vessel in question is under contract with the Government of Fiji to carry Her Majesty's mails monthly from Sydney to that group of islands, and belongs to the most execrable fleet of steamers known in the southern world briefly as the A. S. N., in consequence of the well-sounding name of its owners, the Australian Steam Navigation Company.

We were about seven days battling with the winds and waves of the most misnamed Pacific—the distance being nineteen hundred miles—before we sighted the land. For a few hours we skirted the coast and outlying reefs of

Kandavu and Viti Levu, finally running through the entrance to the reef at Levuka on a beautiful sunny morning, and dropping our anchor in front of the little town.

The Fiji group is one of the largest and most valuable in the Pacific. It has been known to the western world for more than two hundred years, but, like so many of these Pacific islands, was left unvisited, after its first discovery, for many generations. It was not until the beginning of this century that any real knowledge of the group was acquired.

The archipelago consists of about three hundred islands with a total area equal to that of Wales. Not more than seventy of the islands, however, are inhabited, and of these the largest and most important, is Viti Levu or Great Fiji. From this word Viti the name for the whole group has been taken, Viti, Fidji, Fiji, Fidgee, Feejee, &c., all being forms of the same word.

Between Viti Levu and the island of next importance (Vanna Levu or Big Land) lies the little mountainous island of Ovalau upon which Levuka, the present capital of the group, is situated. In the harbour we found quite a little fleet of ships; German barques and San Francisco schooners, small craft from New Zealand and Australia, island traders, and finally H.M.S. "Cormorant," looking very large and important.

A coral reef runs round the entire island, without which is the ocean broken and rough under the influence of the strong trade wind. Within the reef is a calm blue lagoon with tiny waves rippling upon a sandy beach. One cannot well, I think, exaggerate the beauty of a coral reef, and I, at least, have no words with which to convey the effect of that glorious fringe of snow-white breakers which ceaselessly thunder upon the coral breakwater.

Levuka is a mean, straggling little village of the usual new-world order. The houses are of wood, with iron roofs and flimsy balconies. Immediately behind the one long street rise the fanciful mountain peaks that we admired so much on entering the harbour; there is not, I suppose, in all Levuka a quarter of a mile of even reasonably flat ground, and I am afraid no town of any size can ever spring up in so unfavourable a situation. The land is even more "steep to" than at Hong Kong, and it would be, one may almost say centuries, before the amount of labour expended upon our little China colony could be equalled here. This is only one of the many reasons why it has been resolved to move the seat of government to another spot of which I shall speak later on.

In the streets of Levuka, or rather in its street, for there is but one, the stream of humanity flows up and down all the day long. The merchants and planters pass and repass, transacting their daily business. They are a broad-hatted, coatless, red-sashed and leather-belted community, glad, I think, to see strangers in their little island home. Their club is a pleasant house with balconies hanging over the water, and cool, open rooms for reading, writing, billiards, &c. They are not a contented community by any means, having more grievances than even an English farmer is entitled to. I have never anywhere been so beset by men with troubles. I was buttonholed, and cornered, and "stood drinks," and wedged into chairs, and surrounded at all times by such importunity of denunciation against the powers that were, that I felt as if I were engaged in a Fijian Rye House plot, and was almost ashamed to accept Sir Arthur Gordon's hospitality at Government House. It would be out of place for me here to enter at all into the subjects of dispute so disastrously prevalent in Fiji. It quite goes without saying that the late Governor's policy is the outcome of a most conscientious regard for the best interests of the Colony, and if any one wishes to learn the particulars of the controversy between the planters and the government, they must refer to the various pamphlets upon the subject that have appeared from time to time.

The second, but most important feature, numerically, of Levuka street life is the crowd of natives who pass and repass ceaselessly. These do not hurry to or from their work, but glide noiselessly by with that leisurely dignity so characteristic of native races. The men are dressed merely in the " sarang" of Java and the Strait Settlements, called here a " sulu" ; the women also wear a sulu, and occasionally a short chemise. Their frizzly heads need no covering, the hair standing up in a substantial aureole-like mass, the more careful natives, however, wearing a sort of turban made of native cloth to keep it from wet or dust. This crown of frizzly hair varies in colour from white to darkest brown according to the time that has elapsed since last it was coated with lime. The most general condition is a rich yellowish-brown, which is not unbecoming.

Of pure Fijian life one sees nothing whatever in Levuka. Even the natives in the streets are mostly from other islands, brought here under the well-known "labour" system.

There is, however, about two miles from Levuka, a charming little native village to which I went more than once, and where one could lose sight of ships and houses and for an hour or so, at least, hide oneself in a little world quite primitive and natural. Here lives in native fashion, **a young Englishman** whose business is in Levuka, but who prefers this pleasant native village to the poor wooden English cottages of the settlement. Here we sat on one or two evenings upon the cool, clean mats, in his well-built Fiji house. Natives were lying all around upon the mats, and a low fire burnt quietly in a corner. The roof was dimly visible by the light of the small oil-lamp upon the floor, and as one looked up, dark smoke-stained rafters loomed forth, and spears across the rafters. On one side was the small square doorway, not four feet high, and the large moon cast its rays a little way within and shone upon the bronze chest and arms of a sleeping servant. Without, the waving palm-shadows and the calm lagoon, and beyond the breakers thundering on the reef. I have known nothing more peaceful or beautiful. Now and then some dark, noiseless figures would pass along and disappear among the palm-trees, and then perhaps above the distant never-ceasing roaring of the reef, would rise some wild fragment of a native song— a weird, yet peaceful home this of the Englishman in far Fiji.

A day or two after my arrival I made arrangements with a native chief, who was crossing in an open boat to Mbau, the little island home of the late king Thakombau, to take me to the large island known as Viti Levu.

We walked away from Levuka, past the very pretty and native-looking Government House, to the village I have spoken of above, and here waited for the boat to pick us up. Whilst lying on the clean mats of a pretty hut near the shore, to my surprise, a negro entered, and we soon struck up a conversation. He was born in Virginia an indefinite number of decades ago, and had been in Fiji for many many years. He told me that his name was Black Bill, adding with some pride that he was generally mentioned in "the books." He seemed to have visited most parts of the world, and was, —as what negro is not?—full of narrative and humour. In his time he had been a kind of factotum of King Thakombau's, and informed me with much pathos that had he served his God as he had served the Fijian king, he would not be mending sails in that village that day. We talked for an hour or so of the Southern States and the war, and Baltimore, where he had lived, and San Francisco, where he had begged in the streets, and London, where he had been in a hospital, and half a hundred other places and subjects. Time is hardly a recognised institution in Fiji, and, although we had arranged to start at nine, it was past noon when we finally waded out to our boat.

Sailing down the coast was very pleasant—the sea smooth and blue, high land richly covered with vegetation to the right of us, and the thundering, snow-white surf to our left. The enjoyment of this, however, was but of short duration, for our course lay beyond the sheltering reef, and across half a dozen miles of very choppy and unpleasant channel. Our boat, moreover, proved to be a newly-imported one, having arrived from New Zealand but a day or two before. It soon showed its quality; before we left the lagoon the gaff was carried away, and just as we were running for the passage several minor "fixings" came to grief, and we had to anchor. Having patched up the rigging as well as we could, we made a rush for the opening in the reef. To one who has never crossed a reef before this is a *mauvais quart d'heure* indeed. The men stood up in the bows to look for "patches:" the breakers seemed furious, both to right and left; on we scudded, however, through the partially broken water, and finally out into the rough open sea. For a moment it was really dangerous, for had our most indifferently-repaired gaff given way again, we must have drifted upon the lee breakers, and one has only to see them when the trade winds are fresh, smashing themselves upon the reef, to know what that means.

For an hour or so we scudded along over the high waves, sometimes almost lost in their yawning troughs. It is never pleasant work sailing in a small open boat when the sea is running high, but somehow it was less pleasant than ever that day, for our chief had gone to sleep after crossing the reef, and I had no confidence in the other men and did not know in what direction to steer myself. However, we soon began to feel the shelter of a long outlying reef that runs away from the eastern corner of the big island, and in an hour more were again in smooth water, whereupon I indulged in a few minutes sleep, but was soon roughly roused by a crash, and starting up found the sail and rigging utterly demoralised, and the mast very nearly over the side. We had brought up short on a patch and there lay half out of the water. After the usual hauling and shoving, all of us waist-deep in the water, which reminded me of the Nile, we floated once more, and about sundown dropped our little anchor close in shore at Mbau, the royal island of Fiji.

This historical little island is almost part of Viti Levu, being only separated by a narrow, barely-covered channel. It is about half a mile long and a quarter wide, but is as pretty as green slopes and numberless native houses and palm-trees can make it. All the families on the island are of more or less exalted rank, and here, most important of all, lives the venerable Thakombau, whilom King of all the Fijis, greatest of known cannibals, most dread of savage potentates. His glory is in these days departed and his title of King cannot be said to be more than complimentary; he has, however, a very large pension from the government, and after his fashion maintains some state.

We were taken on landing to a very clean and comfortable house where the greatest hospitality was shown us. Our chief was not in his own territory here, being lord of Suva, but he was treated, and I also for his sake, with great consideration and kindness.

There was soon prepared for us a most luxurious evening meal in entirely native fashion, and amongst other dishes were some turtles sent by Thakombau, and a banana leaf full of a delicious compound of plantain, coco-nut, maize, &c. Everything we had was served to us cleanly upon the matted floor, wide banana leaves being used as plates and plaited palm leaves as dishes. The house was, as usual, an oblong building with thickly-thatched roof and sides; the rafters and roof were crusted over with soot from the wood fire which in Fijian houses burns unceasingly in one corner; the floor was very soft and springy, being made of layers upon layers of mats, commencing with coarse palm-leaf ones at the bottom and having for final covering the beautifully-made white ones for which the South Sea Islands are celebrated. At one end of the room is a sort of dais, raised about a foot from the rest of the floor, and upon this the principal members of the establishment sleep. There are two small holes or windows at this end of the room through which the pleasant cool trade wind blows refreshingly.

The houses of the well-to-do natives are almost always well-kept, clean, and comfortable; at the doorway there is frequently a hollowed log with water in which to wash the feet before entering, a rough mat being placed beside the log to wipe them upon. Both the doors and windows, as one must call them, have sliding palm-leaf shutters, so that on cool nights they can close all up and be comfortable. I have visited numberless native houses in all parts of the Pacific, but unless it be the platform and treehouses of the Solomon group, I have seen nothing that can be compared with these Fijian ones for comfort.

After our evening meal the inevitable ceremony of "Kava" drinking had to be gone through. Some very clean and fairly pretty girls were brought in having as little clothes on as well could be, and seated themselves in a row on one side of the hut. Sundry friends of the family also assembled, and in a few minutes we were quite a large, and a very merry party. An enormous bowl was taken from its peg upon the wall, and placed between us and the pretty girls. It was a splendid piece of furniture, and had been in the family for many generations; its diameter was over four feet, and a cream-coloured enamel covered the greater part of its shallow surface. It had four short legs, and was carved from one solid piece of hard black wood.

The Kava, or as it is generally called in the Fiji group, the "Yangona" root, is in appearance not unlike a large horse-radish; this is scraped of its soiled outer skin and cut into little lumps which are handed over to the girls, who put them into their mouths and commence solemnly and methodically to—chew. I know Lord Pembroke has insisted that ruminate is the only right word to use, but try as I would to surround the process with romance and hide the stern realities, I could not persuade myself that they were doing anything less repulsive or more refined than plain *chewing*. It seemed to me from the first to be a very unbecoming occupation for these dusky maidens, but when they stuffed into their mouths lump after lump of the crisp root and chewed solemnly on with swollen cheeks and distended eyeballs, I began to think the operation positively frightful. When any one of the girls deems her individual mouthful of the needful consistency, she puts her hand to her mouth, grasps the whole mass and places it into the great Kava bowl. Then she rinses her mouth with water and begins again. A considerable number of masses of chewed Kava ("blobs" or "dollops" as of mortar they really are) at length accumulated in the bowl and on to these water was poured until they were well covered. Then a stringy, coco-nut fibre thing, which I felt Thackeray would have compared to old Miss Mac Whirter's flaxen wig, "that she is so proud of and that we have all laughed at," was brought, and the contents of the bowl were filtered by being wrung, in a washer-womanly way, through the fibre wig, the more solid parts adhering to the fibre and being afterwards shaken out upon a mat: the liquid in the bowl was then fairly clear and ready for use. The drinking of the Kava is no mere convivial pastime; it is almost a ceremony. A beautifully polished coco-nut bowl was given to me, and into it one of the maidens poured from another bowl the soapy-looking beverage. I winced as I realised that my bowl held a pint and a half, for I knew it was etiquette to swallow every drop. I drained it off however, at one fell gulp, and, as previously instructed, flung the empty coco-nut shell upon the mat with a spinning motion amidst clapping of hands and deep-toned cries of "ah mata." It is a most unpleasant beverage to a stranger, tasting as I imagine diluted earth and Gregory's powder would taste.

Being compelled to drink it frequently during the ensuing few days, I found the palate quickly became used to the peculiar flavour, and before I left Fiji I almost liked Kava; great numbers of Europeans drink it and not seldom to excess. I have known nothing but a rather soothing effect from it, resembling that of tobacco, somewhat, but the natives undoubtedly become intoxicated with it frequently, although I believe not boisterously so; it usually "goes to their legs" as the phrase is, and they fall down and go to sleep before they become riotous.

Later on in the evening I noticed my first finger had

begun to show signs of inflammation, and before an hour had elapsed was rather seriously swollen. I knew it must be from the bite of a venomous insect, and asked as well as I could what was best in such a case. My host, who spoke a word or two of English, said, "Oh! native doctor," and away some one ran. In a few moments the doctor arrived, no hoary old fakir of ninety years as I had expected, but a very shy and well-looking young girl of sixteen or seventeen. She sat down beside me with great solemnity, and for half an hour, without speaking or smiling, just stroked, with lightest touch my finger with her own swarthy one. I confess to being quite cured in the morning, but that the cure was due to the treatment of my pretty physician, I neither affirm nor deny. In the morning they gave me a delicious bath of clear water in a large black wooden bowl; I then started to ramble over the island.

One white man lives upon Mbau which is, as I have said, the historic island of the group; this is Mr. Langham, the Wesleyan missionary, who has been there since the very early days; he was away at the time of my visit. I walked out alone, therefore, in the cool morning and saw the place where the great feasts were formerly held. The old tree whereon were marked the numbers killed at various carousals was blown down in the last hurricane, but the ruins of the native oven were there, and the great gong or "lali" as it is called, which was sounded before the feasts. These gongs give out a weird but not unpleasant sound, and can be heard at almost incredible distances. The one in question was about five feet long and a foot or so wide; it had a deep rich tone. What scenes have been witnessed within sound of that gong! Not twenty years ago this little open space was the place of rendezvous whenever any great occasion demanded a ceremony or a feast. Not twenty years ago this very same King Thakombau, whom I am to see in a few hours, was the habitual author of the foulest butcheries; this was the scene of their enactment and awful consummation. I tried to call up those dreadful times and picture to myself the human sacrifice and greedy faces, round the low stone oven; but there were children playing on the grass, and the bright morning sun glistened on the water, and my mind could not realise those brutal days of old.

After breakfast I went to see the native school; this is held in a large, low building in the middle of the island; it is built exactly like the other houses, but is much larger. There were about a hundred scholars ranging from four or five years to grown men and women even with babies. They seemed very happy and bright, girls and boys, men and women all mingling amicably together. The noise they made would, I think, have somewhat astonished an English schoolmaster, but their evident enjoyment of their work, and the entire absence of that feeling of *school* which is inseparable from the mind of English youth, fully made up for seeming lack of discipline. There were native teachers only, of course, and these took charge of the scholars in what I suppose were classes. Some were dividing and multiplying by 3, 5, 7, 9, and the like; others were slowly spelling out little Fiji words, but all were happy and cheerful, and very evidently thought it capital fun.

Presently they all gathered round one teacher, and squatting down upon the mats, without a moment's warning burst out into a wild and curious chant. There was no laughing now; their faces were all as earnest and solemn as though it were a religious ceremony. I think, indeed, the words they used were from the Psalms, but the chant itself was purely native. One big, handsome girl sang a kind of refrain of a weird and curious nature, and the others joined in methodically. Their time was quite perfect, and I shall never forget the effect produced by their now and then stopping instantaneously; it is done at the most unexpected moments, the sound ceasing absolutely, as if cut off with a knife; then the leader would break out again and the rest join in with their monotonous refrain. I left them singing, but the sound filled the whole island, and they kept it up for some hours, and wherever I happened to be, the quaint notes of that wild song would break upon my ear.

Later on in the day we were summoned to an interview with King Thakombau. He lives in a house which is in all respects like those of the common people; his garden is, however, more extensive, a sort of avenue of banana trees leading up to his door.

As we entered, escorted by various chiefs of the island, we saw him lying on a mat at one end of the house; he affected not to notice our entrance, so we sat down by the door and waited for a few minutes.

Presently he aroused himself, and, asking an attendant who we were, called me, and I was led forward, and as it were presented; I said, "Saiandra," the native salutation, and shook—not without a shiver—his cannibal hand. I then sat for what seemed an interminable time going through a sort of conversation, of which I understood but little beyond my own part. I did, however, make out that he asked me about my travels, and how big Russia was, and what I thought of India. It was an absurd farce altogether, this interview, for I half-believe the old villain knows a good deal of English. I could not, with my head full of the olden times, get over a feeling of disgust and anger as I saw him sitting there. I began to picture him passing along the rows of condemned wretches, and marking out those for his own use. Here, in this very room, had he eaten of many a score of human beings, and but a few years ago the roof was hung with the sculls of his victims. There he sat, a hard old man with a worried, peevish face, white whiskers, and small, bloodshot eyes. His house is plain enough and just like another, there being no signs of royalty beyond a Hong Kong chair given by the governor, and an old French print of a fair-haired lady, leaning against the wall!

After leaving the royal presence we returned to the house of our host, and before saying good-bye, I received a very good club with the marks of two victims and the small Kava drinking-bowl I had used the night before, which I was given to understand was very valuable as it had been used for many years by Thakombau.

CHAPTER VI.

FIJI CONTINUED—THE REWA DISTRICT.

> " The palm, the loftiest dryad of the woods,
>   Within whose bosom infant Bacchus broods;
>   While eagles scarce build higher than the crest
>   Which shadows o'er the vineyard in her breast;
> * * * * *
> The bread-tree, which, without the plough-share, yields
> The unreap'd harvest of unfurrow'd fields,
> And bakes its unadulterated loaves
> Without a furnace in unpurchased groves."—*Byron.*

FROM Mbau we sailed across to the large island of Viti Levu. After running some distance along the coast, but inside the reef, we entered one of the mouths of the Rewa river, up which we rowed for ten or twelve miles. The Rewa is the great river of Viti Levu; it is a very large stream for so small an island, and empties itself into the sea by means of a great number of mouths, like a miniature Nile. It is certainly a fine river, and navigable for little steamers for about fifty miles; upon its banks are the leading sugar plantations of Fiji.

The delta of this river is in appearance the most unhealthy place I have seen anywhere. It is a mass of rank vegetation and muddy swamps, and mangroves amongst the water, and water amongst the mangroves. It is like pictures of central Africa; it is like the river valleys of Ecuador and Columbia; it is like everything that is feverish, and one would naturally say at once that it would be fatal for a white man to live there. Yet, strange to say, there is in all the Rewa district no fever or ague at all, and indeed the whole of the Fiji group is practically without that great tropical curse. How to account for this is surely a worthy subject of inquiry, but one concerning which the medical world has at present left us in utter ignorance. I have seen Englishmen living in Fiji on the borders of almost stagnant estuaries, with the densest and most rank vegetation around them on all sides, with mosquitoes and a hundred such insects infesting the district like a plague; in dry seasons their houses will stand in the very centre of great plains of reeking ooze; in times of flood the muddy river will rise to their very verandahs, and yet these people are robust and healthy. I have gone from there and a few weeks later have visited islands in the Solomon group or New Hebrides, where I have found a dry coral soil and high land upon which the pure trade wind blows freshly month after month; steep land too from which the rain water is quickly borne downward to the sea, and all this but a few hundred miles from the Fiji group and in the same latitude and blown upon by the same trade wind; and yet in these places it is almost death for a white man to spend more than a few months in the year on shore, and practically no one who lives ashore at all can hope to escape frequent and severe attacks of fever. Now surely, in these days of scientific enlightenment, some reason should be offered to account for this. It is to my thinking an infinitely more vital question than the extent or existence of fields of Bactyræ in the South Pacific.

I was landed at some such " Eden " looking spot as has been depicted above in the evening of the day I left Mbau, and, having engaged a native to carry my bag, started to walk to a place known as Harry Smith's, where I had been told I could put up for a night.

Our walk lay across a part of the Rewa delta, and I was pleased to find it entirely native land, owned and farmed by the villagers themselves. It seemed to be very rich soil, and was certainly made the most of by the natives.

We passed little patches of maize, tobacco, yams, kumaras, taro, sugar, then again more open pieces where would be growing breadfruit trees and coco-nuts and lemons and bananas. All these things seemed to be in a flourishing condition, and at every hundred yards or so was a small cottage or group of cottages.

FIJI HOUSES.

Our path was a mere foot-track winding in and out among the little plots of land, in many ways as like the paths in the agricultural districts of China as could be. I liked the look of this quiet, peaceful, homely district; the people seemed contented and prosperous, and it was indeed hard to realise that so few years ago this was one of the most dreaded cannibal islands of the South Seas. I reached Harry Smith's after a walk of seven or eight miles in the cool evening, having seen very much that delighted me, and entertaining quite new ideas about Fiji. Not the least pleasant sight was that of a little native canoe scudding down the river as I walked along the bank. It came so silently and moved with such ease upon the mirror-like water, that I did not for a moment notice something strange about the two figures in it; as it came nearer however, I saw that the paddler was a little fair-haired Saxon boy, the other figure was his elder sister, also with long fair hair glistening in the slanting sunlight. Nothing could form a prettier picture; they were as much at their ease in their little craft as any native, and their laughter and happy English voices sounded like music across the water.

I passed the night at Harry Smith's in company with two or three planters and a hundred million mosquitoes.

The following day I hired a boat and a good crew of natives, and pulled up the Rewa to the sugar mills. The distance was some twenty miles each way, so we had no light day's work before us. We went up merrily enough with the tide, my men pulling splendidly; the heat was, however, intense.

There are two or three sugar mills on the upper part of the Rewa, but they are of a most primitive order and will be very shortly entirely eclipsed by the grand new mills of the Colonial Sugar Company, who are spending £100,000 on the Rewa; they are prepared to give ten shillings a ton for all cane landed at their river frontage, and expect to crush about a hundred and fifty thousand tons of cane from an area of three thousand five hundred acres. The labour employed upon these sugar estates is almost entirely imported. The natives are brought from the New Hebrides and Solomon groups and hired by the planters for a three years' term. I was told that they worked on the whole fairly well, and as I saw them during my few days upon the Rewa they seemed cheerful and well content. Of the labour system I shall have more to say, however, when I come to the islands whence these natives are collected.

It would be difficult to overrate the beauty of this Rewa valley; it is flanked towards the river's source by a lovely range of mountains so weird in shape, so exquisitely blue that I found myself comparing them to the Organ Mountains of Rio de Janeiro. Their brilliant colour was made the more remarkable from the intense richness and fertility of the river basin. For miles on either side are plains of well-cultivated land, laid out in farms bearing crops of sugar, bananas, and oranges. There is a path along each bank and upon this I walked for miles, enjoying the lovely scenery, and being every hour more astonished at the wealth and prosperity of the Rewa plantations. I could hardly believe I was really in Fiji; it seemed like a land that had been enjoying civilisation and prosperity for years. There were bungalows now and then upon the hillsides, and flower gardens and orange groves and small settlers' houses by the river bank, and healthful, bearded colonists smoking pipes at the doors of their thatched houses, and once I even saw a prim English housewife sitting at her door-way sewing at some Liliputian garment, just as one might have seen her in England fifteen thousand miles away. I was sorry to leave the Rewa, it all seemed so peaceful and beautiful, but my stay in Fiji was to be short, and I had therefore to hasten back to Levuka. I went down the Rewa and across to Overlau in a small iron steamer which was as exquisitely uncomfortable as soot and oil could make it; the absurdities that little six-ton vessel indulged in while crossing the chopping channel between the islands defy all description.

I must say a word about the very beautiful Government House at Levuka. It is built in a little valley, or "chine," as people in the south of England would call it, about a mile from the town, and is most delightfully suitable to the country and climate. The building is as it were an aggregate of one-storied houses strung together with balconies. The walls are mostly constructed of thin canes placed close together perpendicularly, through which the air can freely pass; in this respect it resembles the houses of Ecuador and Central America. The public rooms are decorated with native curiosities of all kinds, and in places are hung with "tappa," or native cloth. At one end of the drawing-room is a fine collection of Fijian pottery, which in so many respects resembles the ancient Inca pottery of Peru, that theories as to the origin of the Fijians have been based upon their similarity. It is of a rich brown colour, coarse in workmanship, but good in design, and often exceedingly quaint and grotesque. The floors are covered with Fijian mats, upon which the bare feet of the splendidly-formed and handsome native servants fall noiselessly.

On one evening a dinner-party was given, and I cannot refrain from remarking upon the admirable way in which all the details of that entertainment were carried out, yet there was not an European servant in the room. Behind our chairs stood a row of fine-looking fellows, in white tunics cut low to show their broad bronze chests, who waved great oval palm-leaf fans the whole evening, and amongst these stately figures, moved the waiters, gliding in and out, and doing their work as faultlessly as Indian or China servants might have done.

Nothing can exceed the quiet beauty of Levuka upon a

fine evening; the air so fresh and balmy, the high weird hill-tops standing out darkly against the bright starlight sky, the long white fringe of breakers glistening in the moonlight.

The governor had occasion to visit Suva, the new capital, about this time, and accordingly the mail steamer was ordered to take him there on its way from Levuka to Sydney. This gave me an opportunity of seeing what in future will be the most important place in Fiji. In little more than six hours from the time we left Levuka, we were running through the reef and into the fine harbour of the future capital. I was several hours on shore, and could not but admit the wisdom of the choice of site. This removal of the seat of Government has met with much opposition, but I am convinced it is a wise measure. The site of the new city is very beautiful, indeed I think it would have been hard to prepare a more healthful or pretty spot than this which is provided by Nature. The mountains of Viti Levu stand out gloriously in the west, and as the sun went down behind them no effects of colouring could have been finer. Of course the greatest advantage in this new capital is its proximity to the sugar district of the Rewa. There will be a good road before long from the capital to the centre of the large island, and the great expense of re-shipping and carrying produce across to the island of Overlau will be avoided.

After a pleasant day on shore, we steamed away through the passage in the reef, and the island of Viti Levu soon began to sink beneath the horizon with the setting sun.

It would be presumption on my part to attempt to write of the resources and possible future of Fiji. Nothing as a rule can be more valueless than the opinions of travellers who visit foreign countries, and after a few weeks' kindly treatment from hospitable friends, go home and write as though they had lived in those places all their lives. I have had a pleasant visit to Fiji. I have spent long evenings talking to its best friends, and listened not a little to the grumblings of its worst enemies; I have spied out the land with such powers of observation as I possess, and have found it truly a land of fair promise.

A very rich country indeed has been added to the British Empire, and it does not require a long residence in Fiji for one to learn that the future must contrast almost as favourably with the present, as these present days do with those of the early pioneers twenty and thirty years ago. The cotton of Fiji has long been known, and will be still more known. The sugar, although as yet only just appearing in the market, will, even in a year from now, be no mean rival to that of Queensland. Coffee is grown with most satisfactory results, and but for the question of labour, would very soon be a great industry. Even tea has been tried with some success. Labour however is the great stumbling-block to the colony's progress, but of that I hesitate to speak in this place lest there should be no end.

When walking among those plantations in the great Rewa valley, I could not but feel astonished at what had already been done to make a civilised country of a few savage islands, the most striking evidence of all perhaps being the fact that two Saxon children were paddling their canoe along the river for mere exercise and pleasure, with not a white man even near them, but native villages upon the banks, and naked savages walking along the paths, or paddling home with canoe-loads of yams or other food. This very generation have been cannibals, and those same men who call perhaps "Saiandra" or some such salutation to the English children had but a year or two ago been praying to their heathen gods such prayers as this: "Let us live, and let those who speak evil of us perish. Let the enemy be clubbed, swept away, utterly destroyed, piled in heaps. Let their teeth be broken. May they fall headlong into a pit. Let us live, let our enemies perish."*

To the Wesleyan missionaries one must in great measure give the credit of this great change, and it would not be just to close this chapter on Fiji without a word in praise of their great work. No one can deny them the highest admiration. Their work was amongst a very fierce and cruel race, but has been carried on with the greatest courage and perseverance, and to show what terrible things have happened upon the little island of Mbau, and to illustrate one aspect at least of missionary life in the old days, I may perhaps be permitted to introduce the following lines from William's "Fiji and the Fijians":

"The report soon crossed over to Viwa and reached the mission house. Fourteen women are to be brought to Mbau tomorrow to be killed and cooked for the Mbutoni people. Mrs. Calvert and Mrs. Lyth were alone with the children. Their husbands were many miles away on another island. The thought of the horrid fate that awaited the poor captives aroused the pity of those two lone women. But what could be done? Amidst such fiendish excitement it would be a desperate thing for any one to venture into Mbau for the purpose of thwarting the bloodthirsty people. Those two noble women determined to go. A canoe was procured, and as they went poling over the flat they heard with trembling the wild din of the cannibals grow louder as they approached. The death-drum sounded terrible, and muskets were fired in triumph. Then, as they came nearer, shriek after shriek

---

* In Fiji a salutation is shouted to the sneezer by the bystanders, "May you live." It is proper to utter a good wish in return—"Thanks! May you kill" (i.e. an enemy).

pierced through every other noise, and told that murder was begun. . . . Surrounded by an unseen guard that none might break through, the women of God passed among the blood-maddened cannibals unhurt. They pressed forward to the house of the old king Tanoa, the entrance to which was strictly forbidden to all women. It was no time for ceremony now. With a whale's tooth in each hand, and still accompanied by a Christian chief, they thrust themselves into the grim presence of the king, and prayed the prayer of mercy. The old man was startled at the audacity of the intruders. His hearing was dull, and they raised their voices higher to plead for their dark sisters' lives. The king said, "Those who are dead are dead, but those who are still alive shall live only." At that word a man ran to stop the butchery, and returned to say that five still lived; the rest of the fourteen had been killed."

Of such—and there are dozens of similar true stories—was the life of the pioneers in Fiji twenty years ago. In our comfortable English homes we think perhaps too little of what the opening up and settlement of new countries really means. In Fiji to-day one might walk alone without great danger in almost any part of the group, and it is not too much to predict that in another five years these islands will be as safe a place of residence as New South Wales. So much then of civilisation has been accomplished in the Pacific during the last quarter of a century.

PART II.

THE PACIFIC ISLANDS.

"They sat them down upon the yellow sand,
 Between the sun and moon upon the shore;
 And sweet it was to dream of Fatherland—
 Of child, and wife, and slave; but evermore
 Most weary seem'd the sea, weary the oar,
 Weary the wandering fields of barren foam.
 Then some one said, 'We will return no more';
 And all at once they sang, 'Our island home
 Is far beyond the wave; we will no longer roam.'"—*Tennyson.*

LANDING AT SANTA CRUZ, SOUTH PACIFIC.

CHAPTER VII.

OAHU AND MAUI.

> "To stand upon a windy pinnacle,
> Beneath the infinite blue of the blue noon,
> And underfoot a valley terrible
> As that dim gulf, where sense and being swoon
> When the soul parts; a giant chasm strewn
> With giant rocks—asleep, and vast, and still."

I AM afraid the island of Oahu will not present itself to the mind of the majority of my readers even as it appears on the map with its neat little fringe of queerly-spelt names, standing out like spiders' legs, and its broad clean margin of blue sea. Nor, I fear, will the word Maui be familiar to many either in or out of the geography class room: and yet Oahu can boast of the royal city of Honolulu for its capital, and upon Maui is situated the largest volcano in the world!

We steamed into the harbour of Honolulu after a pleasant run of fourteen days from New Zealand. It was much like what I had been lately expecting. It is like Penang, like all the small tropical ports I have visited. There are trees amongst the houses, and houses amongst the trees. There is the broiling sun overhead and the bright green foliage that such a sun produces. There are the hills behind, blue and beautiful. Unlike most tropical ports, however, there is a capital hotel to which we hasten forthwith. It is an American hotel "run" by a Swede, whom I promptly ask for "Smergesbrod" and "Branvin" and am in return given the best of rooms and taken everlastingly to his heart!

In the streets are strange stores where you may buy needles or anchors or what you will; there are wooden verandahs over the pavements, and Kanakas in all costumes everywhere, albeit not in *native* costumes, but in Manchester ones always. Nothing native do we see save the sable skins of these islanders; all here, in Honolulu, is European and American. More American than European, moreover, for the United States have made this place almost a colony, and are first favourites against all comers with the king and government.

In wandering through the streets of Honolulu, and in shopping and paying visits to the Chinese stores, and being photographed, and eating ices at the ice-cream palaces, we pass our first few days on shore.

Then the inevitable sightseeing begins, and we fain must go and see the public buildings, gardens and the like. The Government building is *the* lion of the place, and under the guidance of His Excellency Governor Kapena, who, if these lines should meet his eye, will accept the writer's warmest thanks, we solemnly visit that architectural pile. It is of stone, well-built, clean and suitable, the rooms being large and pleasant; this is the Educational Department; this the Lands Office; this the Inland Revenue, and this the home of Common Pleas. The whole machinery of government is housed in this one building, and an admirably-devised piece of machinery it is. Our host, who is foreign minister and gold-stick-in-waiting for all I know, shows us all over with pardonable pride, and, notwithstanding his exalted position, is the best of fellows. There is a museum in the building, not, it seems, open to the public, which is of considerable interest. Here are relics of the olden days and natural curiosities collected on or near the islands. Here is the old feather helmet that Kamehameha's grandfather wore; it is the fellow to the one with which Agamemnon struck terror into the hearts of the Trojans, and although made of feathers, is, I understand, quite as valuable. Here is the cloak of some great chief, its value more than a thousand pounds they say, though also made of feathers, not of gold. Here, too, are spears and swords and clubs and bows and such other toys in which savages delight. We also were shown treasures of modern times, such as the stars and orders which adorn the manly breasts of the swells surrounding the throne. Treaties also and letters from our Gracious Queen and records numberless of greater or less interest. There is a large room under the museum which serves as House of Parliament and Royal Reception Chamber. It is hung with the most droll portraits in vast gilt frames, representative of divers Kamehamehas, their wives and sisters. There is a so-called mint also in the building, which consists, however, of merely an office where a few notes are printed. This department, indeed, is upon a very small scale, as the coinage of the country is foreign.

We visited the king during our stay in Honolulu, and surely a few words are due to this enlightened potentate. His palace is at present not imposing, but a new one is to be built and the bricks are already piled in a formidable heap within the gardens. The amount of royal pomp and state is very small. A seedy sentinel there is at either gate who flings open wide the portal with melodramatic air, and presents arms as though his snider were a warclub; within the walls, however, there are merely a dozen wooden shanties which do not deserve even the name of bungalows. In the garden are some tamarind trees and clumps of bamboo and an old fountain and some flowers. The king receives us in one of the wooden shanties and his room is pleasant; there are bookshelves, photographs and a table covered with papers. He sits at his table in a gilt, Frenchified chair with a large crown on the back, and we are given similar chairs, only without crowns. An ancient native of ninety years sits in a corner, and the Foreign Minister and private Secretary are in attendance. We discuss various topics, the islands, the volcanoes, his new palace, his late visit to America. When are we in Europe to receive a visit? In 1880 or 1881, he hopes; it is the ambition of his life; England he holds to be the land of foremost interest. In such small talk we pass a pleasant twenty minutes. His voice is soft and even musical, his English of the best. We were most glad to have had this pleasant interview.

There are two or three drives round Honolulu which are of some interest, the one of chief importance being to the so-called "Pali." The question in Honolulu always is, "Have you been to the Pali?" Just as in Sydney it is "Do you admire our harbour?" We hasten, then, to see the Pali, and almost think of printing the fact on the corner of our cards when we have done so. It is a fine pass in the range of mountains at the back of Honolulu, the distance being about six miles to the top, and a most villainous road after the first mile. The pass lies between some splendidly-shaped needle Peaks, and from the summit the views both to north and south are very fine. On the northern side is an open and fertile plain producing sugar; Chinamen are passing along the road and are, could one see them, working on the plain below. There is a great precipice at one side, over which a large number of natives were driven during one of the fierce battles that were so frequent in the good old times; the word "Pali," I believe, means precipice.

Another drive is to Waikiki, a charming watering-place,

where is grand sea-bathing, and a palm-tree grove and other such delights.

I must not waste more words on Honolulu, which, indeed, except in a very small measure, is not at all Hawaiian, but, as I have said, American and European and civilised. We took steamer, after spending a week in the capital, to Maui, which is the next island to this and contains the great extinct volcano of Haleakala.

The queerest little steamer plies between the islands, and I confess I can say nothing in its favour. There are no cabins but only berths arranged round the saloon, and in these men, women and children, Chinamen, Englishmen, Hawaiians, are promiscuously distributed. The effect can be better imagined than described, the spectacle the saloon presents being something terrible, as the passage is nearly always a rough one.

We reached the island of Maui the following morning and landed at a queer little place called Maulaia Bay. The great volcano lay to our right. It is over ten thousand feet high, and does not look six thousand. The scenery of the island requires little description. It is a dusty, treeless wilderness; there are no palm-trees, there is no timber of any kind, there is no grass; the two sole products of the island are sugar and red dust. We drove about twenty-five miles, passing by the sugar and through the red dust until we reached the station of an American gentleman, at the foot of the mountain. Here we were received most kindly, the more so as we were unprovided with letters of any kind, and had simply to throw ourselves upon his hospitality. We stayed several days, seeing all there was to be seen, and making the ascent of the mountain. There are, in the neighbourhood of this "ranch," some very extensive irrigation works being carried on by an American company, which, when completed, will convert into sugar-growing land some thousands of acres of the dusty plain that we crossed on our way from the landing-place.*

The ascent of the mountain is long and tedious, but I think repays one for the fatigue. It is a hard, glaring, windy ride of twelve to fifteen miles, the path, for the last few miles, being intensely steep, and covered with loose lava boulders. We were nearly five hours in reaching the top, and were right at it all the time. The wind was bitterly cold at last, and there was snow in the crevices near the summit; we were glad enough, therefore, to dismount and walk to the crater's edge, from where we could look down into the great chasm below.

There is no beauty in this great God-forsaken hole, yawning like the jaws of death or gates of hell, under one's feet. It is terrible and very wonderful and fascinatingly awful, but quite beautiless, even hideous. The surveyors say it is seven miles across and four miles wide; it does not look seven miles across, but it looks every yard of its depth, which is over two thousand feet. The floor of the crater is fairly flat, but from it arise something like sixteen small craters, each larger than that of Vesuvius, one indeed being as much as ten times as large! These little cones (they appear little), are from five to eight hundred feet high, and look like mere pimples upon the floor of the crater. The whole chasm is of a reddish brown colour, and

---

* I may notice here that all the pipes used in this undertaking are of light *wrought* iron $\frac{3}{32}$ and $\frac{1}{8}$ inch in thickness. They are covered with an asphaltum composition, and are used up to as large a size as four feet in diameter. The joints are "butt-ended," and covered by a tight ring, round which a coating of lead is run. Four sizes are imported which admits of their being telescoped, and by their use a saving of 80 per cent. over cast-iron pipes is effected. The Spring Valley water-works in California have had pipes of this description under ground as long as sixteen years.

one sees no green whatever, although I am told there are a few acres of grass somewhere down below. There are none of those brilliant sulphurous and metallic colours such as one sees at Vesuvius, but then this great volcano of Haleakala, Temple of the Sun, has been quiescent since Hawaiian history began.

We flung great boulders of the hard red scoriated lava down the crater's side, and saw them break into a thousand dusty fragments far below. It was a cold, cheerless, uncanny place—can you conceive what a hole twenty-eight square miles in area, and two thousand feet in depth, looks like? It is not earthly, but an utterly fearful and awful sight. Of the view looking outwards from this ten thousand feet island-mountain I can say but little, for it was shut away from us nearly all the time by an endless, interminable, infinite field of snow-white clouds, which lay before us like a sea of cotton wool. At times, beyond these fields, we saw a deep blue distance, and, once, standing out grandly, the two great peaks of Hawaii appeared slightly snow-clad, but with these exceptions we were unfortunate, and had to return to the ranch after our day in the clouds without being rewarded with a good view. It was a tiring excursion, we were in the saddle nine hours, and most tedious hours they had been.

Having accomplished the object of our visit, we drove once more across the dusty plain, and past the sugar plantations to the port. The sugar growers on this island have been very successful hitherto, the climate being eminently suited to this industry, and the land rich and productive. A great incentive has been given to sugar-growing by the late American treaty, by which Hawaiian sugar is imported into that country free of duty. This arrangement sadly handicaps the West Indian market, and as a result Hawaiian sugar is used almost universally to the west of the Rocky

Mountains. I should mention here that telephones are in very general use amongst the planters on this island. From ranches to mills, and mills to "townships," we found them everywhere, and very useful and successful they appeared to be. Civilisation is surely a capricious mistress; here was the island of Maui in the Sandwich group at the date I speak of (1879) further advanced in telegraphy than London!

We boarded our little steamer once more, with no great reluctance, for the island is a cheerless spot, and not attractive to visitors. We called for an hour or two at Molokai, the leper settlement, which island has been set apart for the exclusive use of persons affected with this distressing malady. A medical man lives in the little village, and the steamer calls now and then to take stores, and embark or disembark patients.

In a few hours, but after a somewhat stormy passage across the channel between Oahu and Maui, we reached Honolulu once more.

CHAPTER VIII.

HAWAII AND ITS VOLCANO.

> "And one a foreground black with stones and slags,
> Beyond, a line of heights, and higher,
> All barr'd with long white cloud, the scornful crags,
> And highest, snow and fire."—*Tennyson.*

AFTER a day or two in Honolulu, we started again, on the coasting steamer, bound, this time, for the furthermost island, the one that gives its name to all the group, the one most interesting both to traveller and merchant, the richest as well as the largest—the home of the great volcano.

After calling at various ports on the lesser islands as before, we ran along the windward or north-eastern shore of Hawaii in a rough and unpleasant sea. The coast is magnificently bold, the cliffs of black and lowering rocks are hung beautifully with creepers and ferns, and now and then relieved by a silver thread of waterfall many hundred feet in height. This rocky coast is cut up at intervals of a few miles or so by great ravines, "gulches" as the Americans call them, which make travelling by land a matter of extreme difficulty. We were fifty hours out from Honolulu when we steamed into the little port of Hilo, our present destination.

At Hilo we stayed with an American gentleman whose bungalow, standing in a beautiful tropical garden, is one of the most delightful retreats I can imagine. He has two of the sweetest little children, with large round eyes and long fair wavy hair, such as those with which Kate Greenaway delights us. The place seems quite home-like therefore to us in our long pilgrimage. There is a simplicity and sweetness about children, which stimulates all feelings that are highest, for they are the most natural of creatures, and everywhere and always the most natural thing is the most beautiful and admirable. How often I seem to see this in my wanderings—artifice and affectation ever despicable as compared with Nature. It is of course the most so in new lands, where Art, the link that binds the two and makes their union bearable, is hardly perceptible. Happiness too often flies from the artificial conditions which accompany modern civilisation and is distributed most generally amongst the simple peoples of the earth. Those childlike peasants in the uplands of Japan, those Saxons, free as air, upon the downs of Queensland, those Swiss in the unfrequented valleys, if there still are unfrequented valleys of central Europe, can we show any from our cities as happy and contented as they?

Hilo is a pretty village; this is a kind of spot to which we looked forward. Telephones and American "notion" stores seem out of place in the Sandwich Islands; palm-trees and bananas, and thatched cottages, and almost naked natives are more what we have been expecting.

We went down one afternoon to a valley near at hand, through which the Hilo river flows in a deep ravine. Here we witnessed feats of swimming and diving, and also saw the great leap of which travellers speak. The man jumps ungracefully from a height of ninety to a hundred feet, clearing five yards or so of projecting rock in his descent. It is an awful exploit, and I dare say he will kill himself some day. At present he makes a fair profit from this daring exhibition, and falls feet foremost into the stream with apparently no sort of injury.

There are falls at the upper end of the ravine and over these the natives in scores are sliding and re-sliding. Girls and women, and men and boys, all plunging about in the water, climbing up the rocky walls and hurling themselves in again for quarter dollars, and enjoying it amazingly. We left them when our stock of silver was exhausted, but they splashed and paddled and dived about in infinite enjoyment for hours afterwards.

Having viewed the lions of Hilo to our satisfaction, we started early one morning, upon a long ride up to the crater of Kilauea which lies on the side of the great volcano of Mauna Loa. The mountain itself is 13,600 feet high, and its summit is sixty miles from the sea; the main vent, however, of its inward fires is at the crater of Kilauea thirty miles from Hilo on the mountain slope.

The crater at the summit is smaller than this vent-hole in the side, and is only active on grand occasions, such as during the eruption of 1868, when, as always on the occurence of an eruption, *it* discharged the volumes of lava, there being no greater disturbance at Kilauea than the sinking of the floor of that crater some eight hundred to a thousand feet.

There is a bridle trail across the thirty miles that separated us from the object of our visit, and along this we made the best of our way in the early morning. Our track lay for some miles through a sort of scant jungle, then into a piece of dense and lonely forest, then out upon an almost barren wilderness of lava. The wealth of vegetation in the forest is simply wonderful. We rode under great ferns, not tree ferns, thirty feet high, and every turn of the trail disclosed fresh glories, lovely creepers, and great glowing flowers, and broad green leaves. We rested at a small native house at about the fifteenth mile, where we had a luncheon fairly cooked by two old Hawaiian women, and then proceeded on our journey.

I may here notice that nowhere in the Sandwich group may a drop of spirituous drink of any kind be sold or given to a native. We had been considerably impressed by this and by the apparently effective working of the law: what then was our surprise on finding shortly after starting again that our guide was hopelessly and incapably drunk! He must have obtained the spirit from some native cottage, for he had not touched our flasks. The most disagreeable feature of the case was that here we were in an entirely unknown country, with but the merest trail for our guidance. It was a trying and provoking circumstance; he would keep with us for a time, then fall helplessly on the ground, and remain behind for half an hour or so. Darkness settled down upon us, and we still plodded wearily on, hardly ever, from the nature of the ground, able to travel at more than a walking pace. At last we noticed a red glow in the sky, and knew we were near our destination. Then came an open piece of country, then the low, wooden inn looming through a sulphurous mist.

It was the most homely little place this "Volcano House"; and we found a cheerful room with a huge log fire, a clean wooden floor, an old-fashioned clock, loud-ticking—the very acmé of comfort and warmth.

From the windows we could see the great fiery abyss, and later in the evening we walked to the crater's edge, and looked across the plain of lava, where were a thousand streaks of fire. The great chasm, between four or five miles across, lay eight hundred feet below us, infernal, Stygian, desolate.

After a day's rest, in which we wandered round the crater's edge, and visited great sulphur beds, and steamed ourselves, Russian bath-wise, over little vent-holes, and gazed across the terrible abyss, we prepared for a descent.

After descending the pathway down the crater's side, which is steep and dangerous, we commenced the weary trudge across the lava plain. This plain resembles more nearly than anything else I can think of, a short chop sea solidified; the lava is exactly like hard pitch, but the surface is not as level as a sea, bearing traces of fearful squeezes, and being in one place bent up into a great ridge.

As we advanced the lava became slightly warm, and hot sulphurous air arose from the crevices. Here and there were places where molten streams had forced their way through from beneath, and were rolling slowly across the surface; and now and then we would pass a cone or vent-hole covered with a brilliant yellow crust of sulphur. At last, after some two to three miles of hard walking, we commenced a slight ascent of a hundred feet, and found ourselves upon the edge of the lake of fire.

I hope my description conveys clearly the nature of this crater. First the great hole or "crater" proper, say twelve or thirteen square miles in area, and eight hundred feet in depth. The floor of this, a cracked and broken lava sea, covering as a crust, the liquid fire below. Then in the centre of this, an open cauldron upon the edge of which we now were standing.

The lake of fire was at the time of our visit divided by a lava ridge, and only one of the divisions was accessible, but upon the very edge of this, and within say fifty feet of its seething surface we could stand.

I cannot describe to any satisfaction this spectacle. It is, I think, the most impressive of the world's sights. There lay the lake below us, Hale-mau-mau it is called, "the House of Everlasting Fire"—a burning lake more than five hundred by two hundred feet. Beyond, a ridge, and then

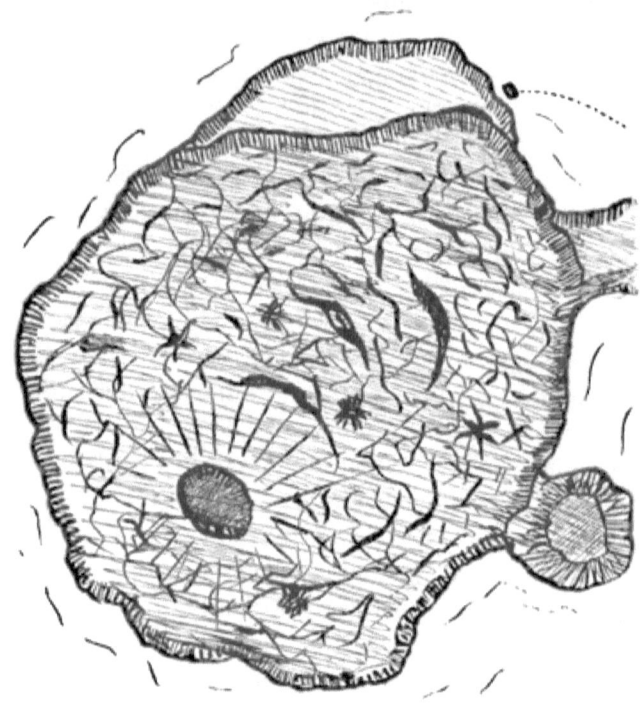

THE CRATER OF KILAUEA.

another lake somewhat larger, but hidden in fiery spray and smoke.

The surface as we first found it was covered with an ash-coloured scum, and the whole cauldron was heaving intermittently as though threatening an outburst.

In a short time an active panting begins and the scum parts and the pure liquid fire is hurled high into the air, and falls a golden shower. To this succeeds a beautiful geyser, and to that again six or eight others, until the whole lake is spouting and roaring fearfully. From these fountains waves extend and meeting other waves they rage and toss across the lake, now flinging themselves against the rock-like lava sides, now hurling their whole force into the caverns opposite, and tearing themselves ruthlessly into a thousand jets and sprays, with a weird lashing sound, staining the lake's wall blood-red, and lighting the whole sky with crimson spray. Then for a time succeeds a lull, the ash-like scum begins to form again, and we advance nearer, and wait for what shall come next. The whole soft heaving scum begins in a few minutes to move slowly from east to west. Then great seams form across the surface, which breaking in, give place to molten waves, and the western end towards which these waves are moving, seeming to resent the onslaught, lashes itself fiercely against the lava rocks. And now to right and left, and here and everywhere the golden geysers play again, and we, quite awestricken, shrink back a yard or two.

We stood for many hours on the thin crust-like edge and watched, unable to take our eyes away lest we should miss some grander spectacle. The sun fell down behind the high crater walls, and a dull, threatening darkness enveloped the whole place. If the sight had been weird and wonderful in the broad daylight, what of it in the black night some hours later? Let us try and picture that scene unequalled, I maintain, amongst the world's wonders.

From the high storm-tossed lava crags above the lake streamed a sulphurous cloud of steam and smoke. Let us picture this as it holds the changing shades of orange, red and gold reflected from the cauldron at our feet. Let us remember it as with a thousandfold iridescence of reflected light it curls and wreaths itself across the sky. On every glittering spangle of the sulphurous stream there shines the soft and ever-varying light, now brilliant as the sunshine as some more than ever high-reaching geyser flings its fires aloft, now softly luminous as the great source of light grows slowly more dim; that smoke curling across the sky contains, alone, beauties worth all the labours of our journey. What then of the fire itself? what of the gently-breathing crust, the slowly-moving blood-red waves? what, still more, of the angry caverns by the lake's edge, and the mighty storm-tossed waves—waves of fire from whose jagged crests were blown far-reaching streams of fiery spray? What of the strange noises that issued from that subterranean sea? How weird in the still night! How wild and unutterably fearful when no other light was there, but of that very sea itself!

The lake beyond the ridge added to all these terrors. It seemed, I think, even more fearful to us than the one we saw. The strangest of noises came from there, boomings as of cannon, and shrill loud cracks, and now, as from some distant gala scene, a jet of spray like rockets was hurled high into the air with unspeakable magnificence, against the coal-black sky.

After many hours we turned our backs upon the furious and infernal lake. The return journey across the lava was intensely tedious and nervous work. From all those cracks that we had crossed, there now shone a dull light, and any false step almost would have been attended with severe burning. Our guide led us cautiously along with utmost skill, we stumbling and struggling in his footsteps.

Soon we passed by a lava stream, and watched it creeping slowly across the cooler crust. It felt soft and spongy as we thrust in our sticks. At times we would pass some wider crevice, and peering down would see the molten stream below running harmlessly. On again over the broken lava-crust with its blood-red cracks, and strange, unearthly fires shooting from curiously-shaped holes. The distance seemed endless, and we were almost exhausted when our guide pointed upwards to a small speck of light, looking like a single star in the dark sky. It was a lantern on the rim of the crater above, showing us where the path lay. So with infinite fatigue we reached the lava's edge, and clambered up the steep ascent to the comfortable inn, most thankful for our safety.

On our way back across the lava we had noticed a light far away in the sky, which we found, on reaching the inn, to be the cause of some excitement. It was indeed the summit of the mountain shewing signs of activity.

There had been no eruption there since the great one of 1868, when a vast stream of fire flowed from the top for sixteen months, running right into the sea, and forming a promontory two miles long. It was the general opinion that an eruption would take place. The reflection in the sky was visible at Honolulu, where we also found the same impression. There has, however, been no noteworthy sequel to this threatening aspect of the mountain, beyond the following, which I take from a letter from Dr. Coan to Professor Dana printed in the *Times* of September 18th, 1879.

"One feature of the last eruption of this remarkable volcano in the Sandwich Islands is the fact that the great molten lake of lava, occupying a huge cauldron nearly a mile in width, and known as the 'South Lake' was drawn off subterraneously, giving no warning of its movements, and leaving no visible indication of its pathway or the place of its final deposit. Other eruptions have blazed their way on the surface to the sea, or while on their subterraneous way have rent the superincumbent beds, throwing out jets of steam or sulphurous gases, with here and there small patches or broad areas of lava. But as yet no surface-marks of this kind reveal the silent, solemn course of this burning river. Our theory is that it flowed deep in subterranean fissures, and finally disembogued far out to sea. Our ocean was much disturbed during those days, and we had what might be called a tidal wave of moderate magnitude."

I have since heard that the lava sea has commenced to rise again as it has steadily done with the above exception, since 1868. The appearance of the "Lake" after the lava had left it—a vast black, infernal hole—has been described to me as unspeakably awful.*

---

* The eruption which these events so significantly portended has at last commenced. The following extract from a London paper of January 14th, 1881, may interest some of my readers.

"A recent despatch from Honolulu says :—'For some days past the people of the island of Hawaii have been greatly excited by an eruption of the volcanic Mauna Loa, which far exceeds any former outbreak of that celebrated mountain of fire. The eruption began early on the evening of November 5, a few miles north of the summit crater, and the lava flowed rapidly down to the plateau lying between Kea and the Mauna Loa. It formed two branches, one running towards the old crater of Kilauea, and the other towards the east. On being first observed, it was seen that the great stream of liquid fire was making its way towards Kea, but some twelve hours after the outbreak it was noticed that a second flow appeared, and was rapidly running towards the beautiful town of Hilo. The greatest alarm was felt, and for a time there was every fear that the place was destined to be overwhelmed. But before the stream had reached half the distance to a deep wood which stands in the way, it suddenly and, without any apparent reason, turned abruptly to the northward. So the flows continued for some days, when the two streams ran beside each other for a considerable distance, presenting one of the grandest sights which could possibly be witnessed. From both rivers of red-hot matter there ascended dense columns of steam and smoke, and these, as they went upward and united for a time, formed an arch-like avenue, through which there could for miles be seen the dull glare of the boiling and bubbling mass which steadily moved on its way. Suddenly, here and there, great cones would be thrown up, and again streams of lava, as if unable to find a vent in any other direction, were forced upward in columns to the height of scores of

I may here be permitted to give a short description of some experiments made by Professor F. L. Clerk, which have resulted in a very plausible theory as to why the crater of Mauna Loa at the mountain summit is the one from which all eruptions take place, whilst that of Kilauea, the more extensive and more continuously active, one has never been known to overflow in any destructive manner.

An arrangement of tubes representing the supposed subterranean passages was fixed above a preparation of fat which in its cooling properties resembled lava as nearly as might be.

Upon heat being applied from below, the Mauna Loa passage, although longer and more narrow, was the first to break out; there was, however, but little difference between the two. The apparatus was then allowed to cool slowly until the smaller passage was closed, the larger one remained molten in virtue of the greater volume contained therein. Here was the existing state of things, Mauna Loa quiet, Kilauea active. Heat was then again applied from below. The direct and smaller passage was this time very decidedly the first to break out, and a temperature was obtained at which the narrower passage would discharge, whilst the wider one remained in statu quo. The reason for this rather curious result lies probably in the fact that the more narrow channel

---

feet. For more than thirty miles from the outlet the liquid fire rolled on, the width of the streams being from 100 to 200 yards, and their depth varying from 6 ft. and 8 ft. to 20 ft. and 30 ft., according to the nature of the ground over which they made their way. If the lava continues to flow in the direction which it has now taken, there will be hardly any danger of its doing any damage to Hilo, as it would have to fill up the great valley below Pemblo and Walluka swamps before reaching the neighbourhood of the town. Still there is danger that a stream may strike and follow the course of the "flow" of 1855-6, which lasted thirteen months, and sent the burning lava over an area estimated at 300 square miles.'"

is a direct one, also, perhaps, that the wider channel, containing so vast a store of lava, would produce a resistive pressure from sheer weight.

From the above experiments I think we may conclude that at least some approximate arrangement to that in the diagram exists under the great Hawaiian volcano.

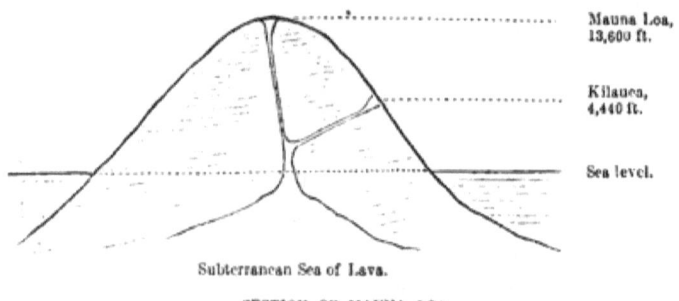

SECTION OF MAUNA LOA.

We did not visit the crater at the summit of the mountain; the journey is one of great fatigue, and would not be worth undertaking unless considerable time was at one's disposal. Mauna Loa is the most obtuse-angled mountain I have seen, the ascent being so gradual that from no point of view does it look anything like thirteen thousand feet high. Both this and the extinct volcano of Haleakala on the island of Maui which I described in my last chapter, are essentially what the Americans would call " mean " mountains as far as appearance is concerned. The visitors' book at the Volcano House is one of the very few compilations of its kind that I have found interesting. It abounds in careful surveys and descriptions, several of which have been made by scientific expeditions. Amongst the remarks of the expedition sent up from H.M.S. *Challenger*, I take the two following which are of interest:

" Magnetic observations were made with a large dip-needle

in front of the hotel. Then again on the lower platform (300 ft. below), and a difference of two degrees was found, indicating the powerful influence of the iron in the crater."

"Spectroscopic observations were made of the furnaces with a small direct-vision spectroscope which gave a continuous spectrum, the red showing brightest. An occasional flare of green."

There are whole pages written by the indefatigable Miss Bird, who not only visited Kilauea, but also the summit crater of Mauna Loa. There is one little entry, which, as it always runs in my head when I take myself back in memory to our days at the volcano, I am tempted to give entire:

> " Nine-and-twenty miles we rode
>   Kilauea's fires to see;
> An hour o'er crushed lava trod,
>   And on the brink stood we.
>
> Forty feet our eye beneath
>   Lay a raging burning sea;
> Hearts with awe and wonder filled,
>   Full slowly turnéd we.
>
> Our pipes well filled, the lava stream
>   A ready light supplied;
> The crawling liquid's steady flow
>   We, musing, sat and eyed.
>
> With tired feet, the weary steep
>   Up to Kane's house took we,
> With food and rest ourselves refreshed,
>   Then back to Hilo's sea."

CHAPTER IX.

HAWAII CONTINUED.

"Perhaps no science ever received greater additions from the labours of a single man than geography has done from those of Captain Cook. . . . Those who are conversant in naval history need not be told at how dear a rate the advantages which have been sought through the medium of long voyages at sea have always been purchased."—*Cook's Third Voyage to the Pacific Ocean*, 1776-80.

A FEW days after our experiences at the crater, we were sailing once more in the little coast steamer. From Hilo she makes the circuit of the large island of Hawaii, every other week, taking her passengers round the south-west coast of that island. The natives of the Sandwich Islands are, in their way, great travellers, and the ship is always full of them. Natives eating "poi" in twos, in threes, in fours; natives sprawling on mats, or asleep in the sun; natives loquacious, too, and even argumentative but never angry; always good-humoured and gay, and always, as it were, holiday-making. Flowers in the richest profusion are to be seen everywhere, round their necks and hats in most pretty garlands called "leis," or in large flower and fern wreaths worn as sashes. One cannot speak too highly of their love of flowers: it is a national trait. In the streets of Honolulu, or in the smallest village of Hawaii, you see neither girls nor men without their wreaths of flowers, more attention being, indeed, paid to that portion of their apparel than to any other. We do not see any of the feather "leis" in these days of civilisation, they are of too great value. The very beautiful yellow feathers of which these are made are very scarce now, being worth a shilling apiece, when purchasable, and very many hundreds are required to make a "leis."

It is amusing to see the natives eating their "poi." The varieties are "one finger poi," "two finger poi," &c. These names denote its consistency. It is eaten with a curious twist of the hand, which prevents any of it dropping before the fingers are thrust into the mouth. "Poi" is the universal food, and is prepared from the root of the "taru," a sort of sweet potato. After the vegetable is baked it is pounded by a heavy stone pestle, then mixed with water until a thick paste is made, after which it is left to ferment a little, thereby acquiring a bitter taste. The most curious sight connected with "poi" is that of the mothers feeding their children. It is really not disgusting, although it may sound so. The mother takes a finger full of poi, and perhaps a bite of fish, screwing them round together in her mouth. The little urchin holds up its face as though for a kiss, the mother stoops down, both their mouths wide open and close together, the mother's tongue is thrust quickly out, and the urchin, smilingly satisfied, swallows the dose—all done with a neatness and cleanliness quite marvellous.

There is nothing of interest in the appearance of this south-west coast of Hawaii. Everywhere is scoriated lava, and I do not know how the people make a living, for the land is barren and blasted with fire and ashes. We call, however, at many little ports where there is always a large number of natives. The women wear long, yellow and red dressing gowns, the most sensible of costumes, and have black, frizzly hair, strong, muscular frames and protruding figures. The men are slim and active, and are usually dressed in blue trousers and coloured shirts.

Belonging to these men and women there is the inevitable

bowl of poi, and a little fish sometimes, and mats and blankets always, and children with quaint, old-fashioned faces. At times we pass a tract of country, which the devastating lava-flows have left unharmed some fifty or a hundred years, and here are fine forests and rich vegetation as near Hilo, but for the most part the country is a dreary lava wilderness.

There are no minerals on the island whatever, no precious stones—fruit, indeed, constitutes the only natural wealth. Of this there is no lack either of quantity or variety. Bananas, yams, sweet potatoes, bread-fruit, coco-nut, arrow-root, sugar-cane, strawberries, raspberries, ohelo, ohia—all these are indigenous; all the common tropical products have also been acclimatised. Of animal and insect life there is singularly little, a few of the common field insects, and a small lizard, but no reptiles, frogs or the like. I have seen guavas lying on the ground by hundreds in all stages of decay, yet not a single fly or insect near them. Of birds there are but few varieties, the useful ones comprising geese, snipe, plover and wild duck. There is also a small owl, which I noticed to be very common.

We saw near the villages numbers of caves in the lava cliffs, which were used in the old pre-missionary times as burial places. Ordinary chiefs and priests were buried in a lying position, and the common people were placed in the caves with their chins upon their knees, like the mummied Incas of Peru. The chiefs of highest rank, it appears, were not buried in these caves, but were converted into skeletons and kept in the temples.

The natives all along the coast use canoes with a single outrigger, which are very deep and carry heavy loads; I need hardly add they handle them skilfully—all natives do.

We put in to the historical Kealakeakua Bay, where

Captain Cook was killed, and we went on shore and saw the monument that has been erected on the spot. It is a plain concrete obelisk, with an inscription on one side, and is certainly a great improvement upon the copper

MONUMENT ON THE SPOT WHERE CAPTAIN COOK FELL.

plate fastened to a palm-tree stump, which to within a few years ago was all that marked the spot.

The place was of great interest to us, with the details of the fatal day fresh in our memories from lately reading a dozen accounts. The American writers, mostly missionaries, are very bitter about the great navigator, and one of the latter, a Mr. Bingham, has the narrow-mindedness to speak of the providential way in which Cook was led back to the Bay, in order that heaven might be avenged for his wicked

I

conduct, and so mete to him his deserved punishment. One can hardly imagine a man seriously advancing so irrational a theory.

The Bay is not a prosperous place, the fifteen thousand natives and three thousand canoes, spoken of as assembled there in Captain Cook's time, have given place to a population of perhaps a hundred, and the canoes at present do not exceed six in number. Clearing from Kealakeakua Bay in the evening, we proceeded on our way, and after the usual most wearisome delays, rounded the misnamed Diamond Head and steamed into Honolulu once more.

Our visit, limited to a month, had by now almost drawn to a close. The few remaining days we spent pleasantly enough in Honolulu, where are many delightful people, all anxious to do everything in their power to give pleasure to their visitors. Hawaiia, as the group is sometimes called, is indeed a most delightful place to visit, there is such a variety of interest and even of objects of study. The great volcanoes are of themselves much, but the added interest attached to a race but so recently rescued from barbarism must not be omitted. The Sandwich group is, I suppose, the most thoroughly cultivated missionary field, not excepting Madagascar, that exists. The work, as purely missionary work, is completed, and the result is, I think, of the highest interest, but I cannot say that to me the consummation of all this praiseworthy labour is quite satisfactory.

The whole mode of life has truly been changed, but the new order of things has not been made a success. A race of Christian natives has been produced; but it is not a race that can sustain itself, but one that is surely and certainly vanishing away. Such a result I hold to be only partially successful, and I feel that until our missionaries can point to some more satisfactory results, they must not complain because so many outsiders are in the habit of finding fault with their system.

A century ago Captain Cook discovered this group, and made his customary explorations at various points. He found a nation of savages of the usual Polynesian type, some four hundred thousand in number, ruled over by chiefs and weighed down by the most fearful superstitions. They were not a hostile people, but eager to trade and still more to steal. Amongst themselves they were warlike to an extremity, waging everlasting internecine warfare, and fighting pitched battles of extermination whenever the smallest pretext arose. Cook they thought a god, and they treated him well until, by a mere chance and in a heated moment, they killed him.

Vancouver and others followed Cook, and then in a decade or so came the invading army of missionaries. What they found we may read in a score of their books, published in America and elsewhere.

The usual "taboo" abounded, and human sacrifices, and perhaps a little cannibalism, and tyranny of chiefs and addiction to war dances. The usual nakedness and uncleanliness of habits, the usual superstition and weakness of moral character, all this the missionaries found in about their normal abundance. There was a shade less missionary appetite and desire for white scalps and foreign blood; indeed, on the whole, the most peculiar characteristic of these islanders seems to have been their pacific tendency and willingness to tolerate the missionary inroad. Upon this soil the seed was sown with such ten, fifty and hundredfold result as we have for the past month been observing.

I am always at a loss how to gauge this missionary work. I know it is not measurable in numerical computation of converts, any more than in the circulated or verbally delivered exhortations of the enthusiastic missionaries who deliver lectures during their holidays in England or elsewhere for subscriptions. I feel it cannot any the more be computed from such evidence as the numerous churches and schools gleaming on the green hill-sides in the bright evening sunlight, nor from the more pretentious square conventicles that tower above the roofs of every half dozen huts that may be collected on the sea-shore. I cannot but accept with reservation, also, those earnest, but all too biassed, accounts, which the missionaries will pleasantly entertain you with in social intercouse. All this tells us a great deal, but it is not satisfying, it does not tell us the right thing. Can these natives now live honest and prosperous lives? Can they bring up their children to maturity, and start their sons in life, and so increase both the wealth and numbers of their community? Can they, in short, advance, not only as individuals, but as a nation? Nothing less than this, I think, should be the aim of mission work, and this we do not find in the Sandwich Islands.

The results in these islands of missionary labour are broadly, that we hear no more of idols and barbaric sacrifices or infernal carousals; we find the natives no longer in the primitive condition of the noble savage, which every thoughtful man since Buffon has known to be the very essence of ignobility; we hear no more of their burning their grandmothers as an absolvence, and killing their friends for eating "poi" with a wife, or letting their shadows fall upon the person of a chief; we do not find them indulging in the amusement of cutting deep gashes in their arms and breasts on high days and holidays. These things have passed away, and with them every vestige of the life of those olden, wicked, idle times. One cannot but wish, however, that there were more signs of national health and prosperity amongst the natives themselves, and although I think most highly of the zeal and courage that has been shown by the pioneers of Christianity in these islands, I do not hesitate to examine very closely the *results* from which alone experience and wisdom may be learnt. Those who have the welfare of native races at heart should look to the Sandwich Islands as the most instructive example of completed missionary labour; the successes attained there may undoubtedly be taken as grounds for encouragement, but the points of failure should none the less serve as warnings to those engaged in similar work in other countries.

It seems to me that we must look for greater things than the mere wiping out of barbarism. That would have come ere long, had we sent out Californian gold diggers instead of Christian missionaries. More hopeful sights are the institutions in Honolulu. The Queen Emma Hospital, a model of cleanliness and usefulness; the Insane Asylums, the State Prison, the Reform School. This last is of more interest than any. Here are fifty boys from five years old and upwards, who for small offences are entered and retained at this establishment until they reach their majority, when they are turned out, useful members of society. They are taught a trade, they raise their own food —poi, rice, sugar and a little meat. They are in every way well looked after, and the scheme is an entire success. If only this kind of work could be done by missionaries, if only we could save the people before it was too late, then, I think we should have something to be proud of. Is it not too late in the Sandwich Islands? But a century ago there were four hundred thousand souls to reclaim; now there are barely forty thousand, and in another half-century there will be in such great proportion the fewer. It is the old, old tale; the savage race not being reclaimed to civilisation, but being surely and rapidly civilised off the face of the earth. The natives will lessen in numbers every year, the Americans and Europeans will increase. It must inevitably be so, and our children will probably see the Hawaiian group a mere outlying state or territory of the Union, peopled by a sugar-growing and store-keeping community. Where then will be the results to which these good missionaries will point?

We sailed away from Honolulu, with no too cheerful thoughts concerning the future of these poor people. As in New Zealand, as in South Africa, so here, strive as our good men will to Christianise the natives, there is a stronger power at work, which gradually and surely takes possession of their ground, and when the harvest time comes and they look around them for the realisation of their hopes, lo! the land is barren, and there is a new and different class of labourers in the field.

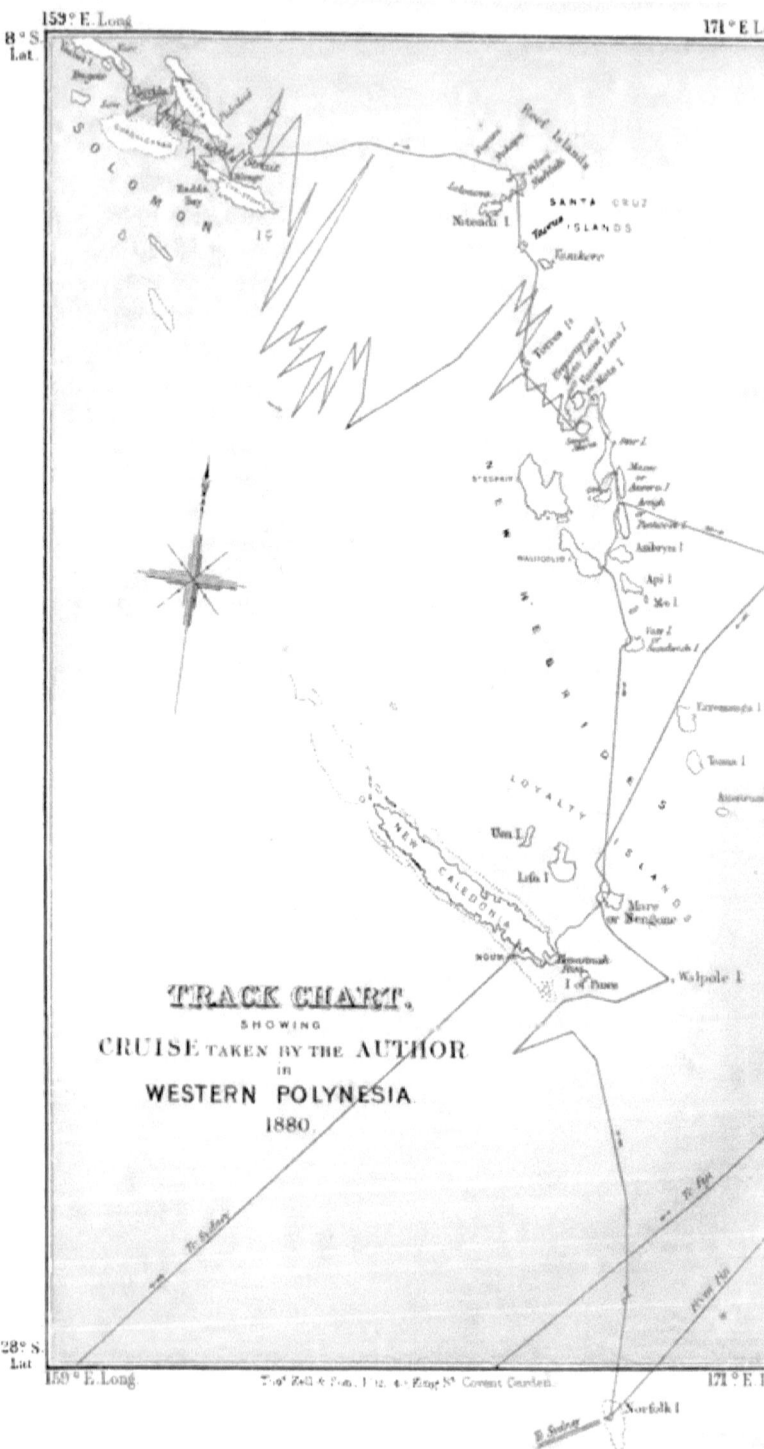

CHAPTER X.

THE NEW HEBRIDES.

"And we came to the Isle of Flowers; their breath met us out on the
    seas,
For the Spring and the Middle Summer sat each on the lap of the
    breeze;
And the red passion-flower to the cliffs, and the dark blue clematis,
    clung,
And, starr'd with a myriad blossom, the long convolvulus hung."—
                                                  Tennyson.

ON the first of July, 1880, I found myself for the second time upon Norfolk Island. A mile or so from the shore lay the little mission bark *Southern Cross,* flying the Royal Thames Yacht Squadron's burgee and the blue ensign. She is only 125 tons register, but carries a little auxiliary engine, generally known on board as the "coffee mill," which is sometimes useful in a lagoon or during dead calms. This vessel was to be my home for the next three months, and I looked at her from the high cliffs near the Mission Station with considerable interest. There were several boats plying between her and the shore, taking on board stores, yams, pigs, cats, boxes, baggage and boys. About forty natives were to be taken down this time to their homes, and I must say forty Cook's tourists could not have made more commotion. Some had pigs, many had cats, all had boxes and bundles, some even had babies! Amongst the number were seven or eight women who had a little room to themselves abaft our cabin, the boys were all to live together in a large room forward, and ahead of that again was a small forecastle for the eight seamen.

We were a merry and very noisy crowd that evening, and did not indeed settle down for some time. I almost doubt if we ever should have done so, had not a fresh breeze sprung up, and the ship being "put by the wind," soon commenced a kind of hurdle race movement, which did more to shake every one into his or her respective place than anything else could have done.

We were five or six days making our way to Nengone (Maré) in the Loyalty group, which was our first place of call. It was my first experience in a sailing ship, and although I am willing to admit that in many respects "sailers" are far ahead of steamers in point of comfort, still a hundred-and-twenty-ton barque can do more in the way of demoralising one's sea-going capabilities than any steamer in which I have travelled. I was ill all the time—ill first of all with a fair breeze; ill next scudding along "full and by" six points from the wind; ill "wearing"; ill "tacking"; ill running with a good stiff slant; ill finally "hove to" off our destination! Whenever I began to recover the wind would alter a point or so, and an entirely new motion commence; I was very glad therefore of a run ashore after six days, and looked ruefully forward to twelve weeks of this kind of thing.

The Loyalty Islands are low and flat, the outline running in terraces which show most markedly where at different times the sea level has been. They are very evidently rising rapidly. The pines that cover the leeward side of the island are of the same species as those from which the Isle of Pines takes its name. They are thin, quaint-looking trees, in shape like worn-out pipe cleaners. I believe they are closely related to the Norfolk Island pines but do not resemble them except when very young. They rejoice in the distinctive name "Cookii" after the great Navigator.

The Loyalty Islands belong to France, and are technically

part and parcel of New Caledonia. The French interest in them does not, however, go farther than keeping a 'Resident' on the island, who periodically endeavours to establish a reputation by bullying the natives.

After running along the coast for ten miles or more in the early morning we came to a little bay where were some houses, off which we hove to and lowered a boat.

When we had made our way in the gig through an intricate passage in the reef, we were met by a number of natives, who towed our boat in and out among the patches in the small lagoon, and finally landed us on a little sandy beach.

We found the people in great distress. Naiselene their old chief was dead, and, after the manner of loyal subjects, they were truly inconsolable. The more distinguished islanders had their faces covered with soot, down which the tears ran freely as they related the events of the last few weeks. I never saw a more entirely hideous object than the dowager queen, who must have been nearly a hundred years old. Her hair was perfectly white and very shaggy, her face was covered with soot, down which the grimy tears rolled plenteously, falling upon her old bare shrunken breast. There she stood bowed down with years and sorrow, the picture of savage woe. Her son had been a fine man truly, and his loss to the island is quite irreparable.

After a few hours, during which we were surrounded by a hundred or more savages of every size and age, squatting upon the ground, or lolling about under the coco-nut trees gazing and listening, we were, to our surprise, given horses. Upon these four of us started to ride across the island, nine or ten miles, to where Mr. Jones of the London Missionary Society lives. This group, I should perhaps say, does not belong to the Melanesian Mission, but was given up to the London Missionary Society by the elder Bishop Selwyn some twenty years ago. Our ride was not a beautiful one, the path stretching for the most part across a rather barren coral plain upon which nothing of consequence grows but coco-nut palms. The island seems to be so young that there has not as yet been time enough for more than a very thin coating of soil to cover the coral rock. After a long ride, for riding over either a coral or a lava path is very slow work, we found ourselves at the top of a steep cliff below which lay a small strip of land and then the sea. Upon this narrow strip was the Mission Station, to which we scrambled down on foot.

On my return from the islands some three months later, I was set down here by the "Southern Cross," and spent five pleasant days with Mr. Jones, the missionary. I will not, therefore, run the risk of repeating myself by entering upon a description of this place here, but will merely say that, after a pleasant hour or so at the Mission Station, we rode back in the cool evening, and, shortly after dark, joined the ship, which had stood off and on for us all day.

From Nengone we ran northward for about two hundred miles, and in forty hours found ourselves off the entrance of Havannah harbour in the island of Sandwich, one of the New Hebrides.

This place is marked conspicuously on the charts, and is a favourite place of call for men-of-war and traders. It is indeed a splendid natural harbour, formed by a deep bight in the land, across the entrance to which lies an island. At the upper end is a good anchorage, where we found three vessels and an old hulk lying. One of these was an American three-masted schooner, which had put in to repair her rigging, after a lengthened cruise in the northern islands. She had just returned from the Admiralty group, where she had been collecting bêche de mer. The condition of this ship's company was very lamentable. The captain had died of all manner of complications on the coast of New Guinea; the mate was unpopular, and the crew discontented and mutinous. I had a long talk with an Americanised Italian who was in some mysterious way connected with the expedition. He told me that they had been for three months in the Admiralty Islands, and had even lived on shore there for some time, narrowly escaping a carefully prearranged massacre. Evidently their negotiations with the natives had been unfortunate, but who could wonder with such a captain and so lawless a crew? It is such vessels as this that sow the seeds of South Sea tragedies, and the all-prevailing hostilities between the natives and white men.

We went on board the hulk, which turned out to be what was left of a French frigate called the "Cheviot." She had been filled with "trade" for the islands, but had been dismasted and reduced to her present condition by the late hurricane. We found such a splendid stock of trade on board, that we bought up beads, knives, tobacco, turkey-red, looking-glasses, axes, &c., &c., to the extent of £35!

We landed later on, and found a couple of traders living near where the ships lay at anchor. Their stores, one flying the American, the other the English flag, were tumbledown shanties, the contents of which consisted chiefly of cheap liquors and rusty old rifles.

From this place, which I suppose is the town of Havannah harbour, we walked three miles along the shore to the Mission Station. The island belongs, spiritually, to the Presbyterian Missionary Society. At the Mission we found Mr. and Mrs. Macdonald, and three little fair children; they all looked delicate, and I thought low-spirited. Their work here is indeed not very encouraging; there are but thirty or forty natives around them, and, although they had been here eight years, Mr. Macdonald told me that he had never penetrated more than three or four miles into the interior of the island. The little native village looked clean and pretty however, and in front of the missionary's house was a pleasant garden sloping down to the white coral-sand beech, where the tiny waves were tumbling musically.

There have been several attempts to settle this island of Sandwich, or Vaté as the natives call it. Australians and Germans have been here, and have cleared acres of bush, and landed sheep, but as far as I can learn the experiment has been abandoned of late, and is now regarded as almost hopeless. The hills that surround the harbour are very beautiful, and one could hardly wish for a more peaceful picture than this land-locked bay afforded, as we glided slowly out with a light breeze in the evening sunlight.

From Vaté we steered northward again, passed Mae and Api, and through the passage between Mallicollo, and the great volcano of Ambrym, and so on to the island of Aragh or Pentecost. I should very much have liked to land at Ambrym, and find out something definite about the volcano there. From the appearance of the sky above the mountain, it has been thought that possibly this crater may exceed in size even the great Kilauea of Hawaii. No white man has, however, made the ascent, and the natives are utterly unconquerable in their dread of the place. They have the same superstitious awe as the Maoris have of Tongariro, and indeed as the Hawaiians had of Kilauea before the missionaries overcame their fears. The ascent is, moreover, from all that I have heard, of great difficulty, and even if one had the time and native co-operation, it would probably require a Whymper to reach the summit.

The island of Aragh is long and narrow, running due north and south. The hills are as much as two thousand feet high, and clothed from base to summit with the most luxuriant vegetation. A few villages are scattered along the shore, and at the extreme north of the island is a little open bay into which we ran, and let go our anchor.

When a vessel has a number of native passengers on board, one operation is periodically necessary, to wit, "yaming;" that is taking in stores of yams, the staff of life of the South Sea Islands. At this little village on the island of Aragh we resolved to go through this operation. Two boats were lowered, and a plentiful supply of knives, tobacco, axes, &c., were stowed in the lockers. Then we pulled in to the edge of the reef, which is here merely a "fringing reef," and only a few yards from the shore. Hundreds of naked ruffians, knee-deep in the water, surrounded us in a few minutes, and then such a babel arose as I had not thought possible out of Egypt. It was not that they all spoke at once, but that they all shouted, yelled, shrieked at once!

Each man or woman had a small "kit" of yams, and for these we paid according to their size. There were some ill-looking fellows amongst them truly, and the people here have not a good name, for two boats' crews were cut out a few miles down the coast last year, and several lives taken. Care had accordingly to be exercised to prevent any disputes or over-excitement. Of any excitement beyond what prevailed already I was, however, unable to conceive.

When we had purchased several boat-loads of yams, the people calmed down a little, and we struggled over the jagged and cruelly sharp boulders of the reef and so on shore. The village is not upon the beach as one would expect—indeed we seldom found houses down by the shore upon any of the islands—but is perched up on the top of the cliffs, and is reached only by a rugged and very steep path. These island paths, by the way, in wet weather—and it is always wet weather—are simply agonising. The continual passage of bare feet up and down reduces them to the condition of a glissade, in consequence of which the booted European comes continually to ignominious grief. There were maize and yam plantations on the hill-side, upon which a very considerable amount of labour must have been expended. I shall not say anything here about the houses or villages upon this island as they are in every way similar to those upon the one we next visited, and having had more time there, I shall do my best to describe what of New Hebrides home life I had the opportunity of seeing, when I come to a short excursion I took upon the island of Maewo.

The view from the hill-top was magnificent, and we spent some hours at the little village overlooking the sea. The men and boys for the most part carried bows and arrows, and I made some boys try their skill with their toy bows. The arrows used in this case were tipped with a blunt lump of coral, and with these they can very skilfully knock over small birds without killing them. I did not see any men shoot, their shooting constitutes a rather more serious affair as a rule, but they should be good shots, as they carry a bow from very infancy.

Our next stopping-place was on the northern end of Maewo, which is an island very similar in shape to Aragh, its chart name is Aurora. Here is a double water-fall formed by a most lovely stream. We lay nearly three days at anchor off the little river's mouth, and bathed and washed to our heart's content, and filled up the ship's tanks with clear, beautiful water.

There are no villages or houses near the watering-place; we accordingly started as soon as the work of watering the ship was over, for a short excursion to the villages on the high table-land in the centre of the island. Our walk as

The Island of Maewo.

usual commenced with a very steep and difficult ascent; numbers of natives had come down to see the vessel, and these formed an escort for us on our way up to the village.

There is no island amongst those that I have seen in the Pacific to surpass this island of Maewo in natural beauty. It is, indeed, an earthly Paradise, and I despair of giving any right account of the glories of our walk that day. The steep hill-side up which we climbed was covered with a beautiful convolvulus-like creeper, between which and the black, fern and moss-sprinkled rocks we made our way. Now and then at a turn in the zigzag path there would be an opening in the wall of creepers, through which, while resting a moment or two, we could gaze out upon a beautiful scene of blue sea and distant isles. I shall never forget the delight of leaning back against the moss-covered rocks in the deep, cool shade, and looking across the path at these lovely pictures with their flower frames.

At the top of the path the view was of course more extensive but it was far less enjoyable; the strong sun could shine through the forest trees as it could not through the wall of creepers. The sea lay spread out before us like a great sapphire carpet, but it did not look so perfect as in those little creeper-framed pictures that were hung for us along the gallery of our ascent. The path we had come up by was literally a gallery cut in the rock face as are the passages in the rock of Gibraltar, but the defence afforded was not that of live rock against an enemy's cannon balls, but of thick walls of bright green foliage against a burning sun.

Proceeding on our way we found the path level and pleasant for the next few miles. It wound in and out through the forest, now under a great banyan tree, which we roughly calculated must cover nearly two acres; now along the river bank; now through the river, and so away towards the centre of the island.

After about four miles' walk, we came, quite suddenly, upon a good-sized village. It was the most pleasant and unexpected sight. Instead of the usual little cluster of

A NEW HEBRIDES VILLAGE.

squalid huts among the trees, we found a wide clearing quite level and free from either grass or weed. Perfectly clean, moreover, so that one could not so much as see even a coco-nut shell lying out of place. Sprinkled about upon this level clearing were about a dozen little houses. Some of them were fenced around with white cane fences, but all had, planted beside the doors, one or more handsome flowering shrubs or trees. It was—to be horribly common-place— like a fairy-scene in a theatre! The ground was so clean, the colours so bright, the little houses so smart and toy-like! Some of the flowering shrubs, planted purely for their beauty's sake, were really magnificent, great scarlet flowers on one; cream-coloured honeysuckle blossoms upon another; bright-yellow bell-shaped flowers upon a third. Alas! not one of us was botanist enough to know the names or families of these flowers, and although some of us had been in many countries, we could not compare more than a few of them to any we had seen before.* The leaves of many of the trees were no less beautiful than the flowers, and I have seldom seen a more gorgeous display of crimson, gold and brown foliage.

The houses are small, and have, strictly speaking, no walls. They consist of a deeply-gabled roof set upon the ground, and are, in fact, like very large and long hencoops. The workmanship is, however, as I have said, very neat and good. A small square doorway, perhaps two feet high, leads into the single room, and the floor is covered with rough mats. There were very few natives about the village, the greater number being away at work upon their little plantations. I did not think them a good-looking people by any means. They are very naked, the men wearing merely a small banana leaf stuck into a string round their waist. The women wear nothing whatever in the ordinary way, but many, in consequence of what the missionaries had taught them, when we appeared donned a leaf or strip of calico if they had it. Naturally, however, the women of all ages on this island are

* By "we" in these chapters I always mean Bishop Selwyn, one or, at times, two, of the Melanesian clergymen, and myself. Both Bishop Selwyn and Mr. Bice have spent one or two weeks on this island. With this exception, no white man has probably been beyond the sea-board. Neither the traders, nor, indeed, the officers, from such few men-of-war as visit this part of the Pacific, care to go inland or out of sight of their ships. The inland tribes are generally hostile and almost always distinct from the coast tribes: hence complications are liable to occur. Although I cannot claim to have been the first white man at any of these islands, I earned the title, laughingly bestowed upon me by the members of the mission, of "the only unarmed layman."

K

entirely nude, and even express great unwillingness to wear any covering, pleading bashfulness and that they are ashamed at being made so conspicuous! Upon the island of Opa, only a few miles off, on the other hand, one never sees either a man or woman without a little finely-woven mat for covering.

Passing through this hamlet we followed the path for a few hundred yards, winding as usual through the forest, and then came upon another level clearing sprinkled with houses, and after that another, and another. This is the way the people live; their villages are aggregates of little villages, the inhabitants of each hamlet being as a rule connected by birth or marriage.

To each village is attached a club-house or "gamal" as it is called. A club-system prevails throughout almost all the Western Pacific Islands, varying merely in detail. When the boys of the village have grown out of actual childhood, they are sent from their homes to sleep and eat in the village gamal, which is generally in a central position. Upon entering the club they pay a small fee, and sleep and eat at what is called the lower end. From this position—which may be compared to the lowest rank in a Masonic lodge—they work their way gradually upwards, at each advancement paying the chiefs of the club-house certain fees. The gamal is generally thirty or forty feet long, and divided up into small divisions, there being, however, no actual partitions, but merely palm logs laid on the ground. In each division is one or more bed-places; bows and arrows hang above the bed, and a wooden bowl or two upon the wall. The gamals that we visited were as a rule empty, with the exception, perhaps, of an old chief at the upper end, who was too old or too dignified to go out to work.

In connection with the fees paid for advancement in these

curious lodges, I must not forget to mention a curious custom on this island. Of course the money is different in every group of islands, just as in every country of Europe, but here it is so singular that it deserves special mention. Near the centre of the village at which we stopped, was a small and rather exceptional-looking house. It was fenced around, and had a more elaborately-constructed front than the common dwelling-places. This we learned was the money house. We were taken to see what was inside, and crawled through the very small doorway for that purpose. From the roof of the hut were suspended eight or ten mats, their sizes as they

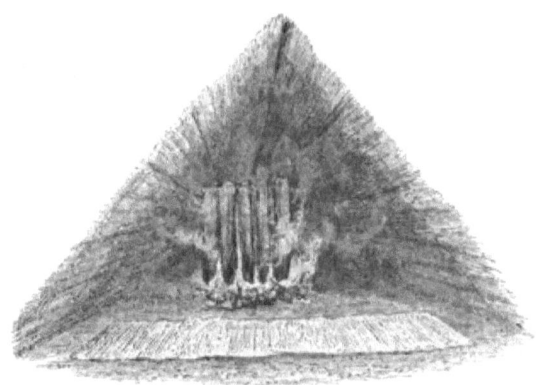

INTERIOR OF HUT WHERE THE MATS ARE SMOKED.

hung down from the beam being about two feet by fifteen inches. They reached to within a foot of the ground, and under them a small wood fire was kept ever burning. In course of time the mats become coated with a shining black incrustation, which gradually accumulates in such a quantity that it hangs down in stalactite forms, called by the natives "breasts." The fire, it will be seen, requires very constant looking after, for if it became at all large the mats would be set alight, and if it went out, the process of coating them would be arrested. A man has, therefore, always to be kept watching these curious moneys, and it is the time thus spent upon them that makes them of value. This kind of money is, as far as we could learn, only current in the matter of club advancement. A fairly old mat is worth as much as a large boar with finely-curved tusks. Of all the forms of money that I have seen this is certainly the most curious, for it cannot even be carried about, and is, if possible, never moved even when it passes from one owner to another.

The people here had built a very clean and pretty little house for the use of Mr. Bice, the missionary, during his visits, and we had the most favourable account of their advancement in decency and civilisation. Only a year ago, when the bishop was at this place, they buried a woman alive, and it is still a very common occurence to hear of an old creature being killed off when any one is afflicted by the loss of a child or a parent, but they are gradually giving up these customs, and never allude to them without shame. The burial-places of these people are most beautiful as well as singular. They build a little wall, say a foot high, of stones round the grave, and plant the enclosure with the most beautiful flowering trees and shrubs they can find; thus the graves are like little flowery plantations scattered about on the cleared plain of the village, and are peculiarly picturesque. All the small hamlets we passed—and these were very many—were alike prim, clean, picturesque. They are really model villages, and the care bestowed upon the trees and shrubs is beyond all praise.

The path that we followed back to the coast was even more beautiful than the one by which we came. We crossed the river—which below forms the waterfalls—many times; crossed it at lovely little pools and tiny cataracts enclosed on every side with steep and creeper-hung rocks.

These pools and little waterfalls were gems of scenery. In two places we discovered terraces, the steps and basins of which are identical in form with those of Rotomahana in New Zealand. The formation here, however, is not silica as at Rotomahana, but a very similar substance of a gray colour. The interest attached to the existence of these terraces lies in the shape of the basins and the overhanging character of the steps, from which, if the theory of the deposition of the New Zealand terraces, as described by Mr. Abbay * before the Royal Geographical Society in 1878, be correct, it is proved that the water at the period of their formation must have been hot. This idea is confirmed by the fact that lower down the stream, where the water would have been cooler, although the deposit still fills the river basin, the terraces give place to a mere inclined plane. In one or two places, notably in one known as *the* waterfall, this plane becomes exceedingly steep, yet so tenacious is the deposit left by the water, that, although not without much difficulty and even danger, we were led by our native guides right down the fall on foot, the rushing water, ankle deep, adding to the difficulty of the descent. The sensation was most curious, for had the ground consisted of any other material, our feet must have slipped. When we reached more level ground, we passed through numerous yam plantations, and also taru fields. Taru is grown, like rice, under a few inches of water, and the irrigation works in connection with these little patches were very elaborate, resembling those of the paddy fields in China.

I visited only one other island of the New Hebrides group, namely Opa or Leper's Island. It is magnificently moun-

---

* Vide a paper in the Quarterly Journal of the Royal Geographical Society, May 1878, upon the building-up of the white sinter terraces of Rotomahana, by the Rev. R. Abbay.

tainous, and stands out of the water to the height of 4000 feet, its outline resembling in shape a whale's back. We visited Opa on three occasions, and lay at anchor on the N.W. or leeward side of the island. The people are better-looking than those of Maewo and Aragh. The women are very elaborately tattooed, the designs covering the whole of their bodies like those of the coolies of Japan. Some of the men wear their hair in numberless, oil-soaked ringlets, like those of the ancient Egyptians and the Nubian women of to-day. The females in almost every case had their hair cut short after the manner of our convicts. None of the people on this island are naked, the women wearing a short skirt, and the men a narrow native mat passed between the legs and tucked into a waist-string before and behind.

The condition of Opa just now is peculiarly deplorable, as several "cutting out" cases have recently occurred, and the action taken by the Commodore and the High Commissioner has not as yet produced any satisfactory results.* We visited the small village, where Johnson, a white trader, was shot a few weeks previously in cold blood; the people, however, seemed friendly enough, and many assured Mr. Bice that if any attempt at hostility were shown they would stand by him. We found one poor boy lying under a banana tree in great pain, and almost breathless, suffering from acute inflammation of the lungs. We put a hot yam poultice on his chest, and covered it over with banana leaves. He was very quickly relieved, and when we called again, eight weeks afterwards, appeared quite well as far as his chest was concerned, but had

---

* Since the above was written, accounts have reached the English papers of a visit paid by H.M.S. *Miranda*, from which, even after allowing for the usual inaccuracy of such news, it appears that some very definite punishment has been inflicted upon the perpetrators of the *May Queen* and other massacres.

severed his large toe with a tomahawk, and this had been neglected so sadly that mortification had set in, so I suppose the poor fellow will have died after all. In the club-house at this village were many bows and poisoned arrows, also a few loaded rifles. The place was dirty, smoky and out-of-repair, but picturesque.

We had a long sail back to the ship, and were caught by a squall from the hills, and as nearly swamped as I suppose any of us will be again in our lives. These squalls are peculiarly violent and sudden amongst all the more mountainous islands of the New Hebrides, but perhaps are nowhere more dangerous than at Opa. On this occasion we had taken a boat-load of yams as a present to the poverty-stricken people of the village. It was quite fine early in the day, and on our way there we had pulled against a light breeze with no great difficulty. The return journey, however, was a different matter, for we had not sailed more than a mile from the shore, on our way across a bight in the coast, when a terrific squall caught us, and our boat, being flying light, was almost literally blown out of the water. It was at the height of the squall that our sail jibbed violently, and threw the boat over until the sea poured in green over the gunwale. Of course the native crew were paralysed with fear and could do nothing; indeed, how the boat ever righted herself again is a mystery to me. We were all glad when we made out our little vessel through the blinding spray, and not many seconds afterwards were safely hauled in under her quarter.

CHAPTER XI.

THE BANKS' AND TORRES' ISLANDS.

> "One show'd an iron coast and angry waves;
> You seem'd to hear them climb and fall,
> And roar, rock-thwarted, under bellowing caves,
> Beneath the windy wall."—*Tennyson.*

WE next visited the Banks' Islands which lie to the northward of the New Hebrides. These islands, less known than their neighbours, constitute a small group discovered by Captain Bligh in 1789, during his wonderful voyage to Timor after the "Bounty" mutiny.[*]

On our way between Opa and the Banks' Islands we called at Merelava or Star Peak, a little volcanic island precisely resembling Stromboli, but which has not been active within the memory of any of the natives. Mota was the first island we visited in the Banks' group. It is the headquarters of the Melanesian mission in these seas, and is chiefly remarkable on account of its language, which is probably the most perfect of any dialect in the Western

---

[*] The following paragraph, taken from Captain Bligh's 'Voyage to the South Sea,' London, 1792, refers to the discovery of the Banks' Islands:—

"The sight of these islands served only to increase the misery of our situation. We were very little better than starving, with plenty in view; yet to attempt procuring any relief was attended with so much danger that prolonging of life, even in the midst of misery, was thought preferable while there remained hopes of being able to surmount our hardships. For my own part, I consider the general run of cloudy and wet weather to be a blessing of Providence: hot weather would have caused us to have died with thirst; and probably being so constantly covered with rain or sea protected us from that dreadful calamity."

Pacific. The Mota language has been adopted as the vernacular for the schools at Norfolk Island, and all the boys, wheresoever from, are taught Mota, not English. The people on shore were very glad to see our vessel, and came down to the rocks in hundreds to welcome us when we landed. There is no water on the island, which is the greatest drawback to its advancement, and although the mission has visited it for the last seventeen years, the appearance of the people is exceptionably disreputable.

Upon Mota Lava, a larger island a few miles away, we found a white trader living. The place is healthy and pretty, the soil being of light sand. This trader had been some months on shore collecting "copra" and seemed very contented and happy, having with him his Samoan wife, who kept a neat little house where I had some tea. My hostess could talk a little English and gave me a fan from her own island, the handle of which was made from the butt end of a ramrod, as a memento of my visit. In the adjacent village I found nothing especially worth mentioning, except, perhaps, that the chief seemed to be so big a swell that the club-house literally could not hold him, so he had erected, at the end of the long low "gamal," a small but very elevated little shrine for his own individual use!

I will put down here a few notes of Banks' Islands customs, which are very similar to those prevalent throughout the New Hebrides, gathered from time to time from my companions.

A marriage is generally arranged between the relatives of the pair interested, a payment being made to the father, who will then give up his daughter when it is thought desirable. There is no ceremony, but sometimes a feast is arranged at the time of the settlement of the affair amongst the relatives. When the day arrives for the bride to leave her father's house a present is usually made to the son-in-law.

In cases of a serious criminal character the offender is usually punished by death. It is generally customary for a man to have two wives. A man will not name his wife's father, but will sit and talk with him; he will not come near his wife's mother nor mention her name, they avoid one another but if necessary will talk at a distance. A man will not name his wife's brother, nor his son's wife, and hardly any one in any of the islands can be induced to mention his own name. In Fiji and also at Opa in the New Hebrides brother and sister are strictly tabooed and will not even speak with each other. If people from old age or sickness are lingering in misery it is usual (of course except where the missionary influence has made itself felt) to bury them alive. This is sometimes done when relatives are tired of nursing the sick, who are, not unfrequently, buried with their heads only uncovered; their friends going from time to time to ask if they are still alive. Cannibalism is utterly unknown in the Banks' group, although so universal throughout so many of the other islands in these seas. There are regular terms upon which property may be borrowed; the rate of interest is cent. per cent. without any limitation as to time.

We called at Vanua Lava, an island with the same name as the second island of Fiji, and also at Santa Maria, the most southern of the group. This last place is interesting in many ways. It is almost circular in shape and about twelve miles in diameter. In the centre, some two thousand or so feet above the sea is a beautiful lake, lying, as it were, in the old crater of a volcano. The people have been long known as treacherous and warlike, but of late years have behaved themselves more peacefully. An outlying reef runs round the island, through which we ran in one of the ship's boats.

On the weather side is a pretty little village to which I walked through a mile or less of beautiful forest. On account, they said, of the number of pigs kept by the people here, the houses are built upon massive foundations of stonework, and are really of imposing appearance. The pigs certainly are numerous, and this place is celebrated for its boars' tusks, which are used so largely for armlets amongst the Banks' and New Hebrides. Scattered about the village were small storehouses raised some feet from the ground upon piles, and identical in every respect with those used by the Maoris of New Zealand. The feature of the village, however, consists of a long stone wall running right through the group of houses, and ornamented at intervals with large wooden images carved from palm trunks. Other similar images were grouped about near the houses. They are very grotesque and rude, and are said not to be idols, but monuments in honour of deceased chiefs. The arrows of this place seemed to be more than ordinarily deadly, as on several occasions when I wished to buy some, my boy from the ship, who spoke a word or two of English, warned me with the statement that they "makee kill allsame musket."

Coasting round to the leeward side of the island we passed some very pretty scenery, notably a point known as "Cocksparrow point," how and why I did not learn. Here it was almost always usual for the boats to be shot at until quite lately. Upon this promontory is a curious cave, shaped like a short bottle, with only one outlet, namely at the top, resembling in this respect the cells constructed upon Norfolk Island for exceptionally dangerous prisoners. Concerning this cave is an amusing native legend which was told to the bishop and runs somewhat as follows:—

THE LEGEND OF THE GREEDY BIRD-CATCHER.

Once upon a time many warriors went out from the village to shoot birds and fish for their families and themselves. Some wandered by the shore, and some upon the hills, and so, each pursuing his own course, they became scattered and separated. Presently one chief walking by himself came upon a hole in the ground which he discovered to be a cave, and in which were many hundreds of birds. This chief was a greedy chief and did not call to any of his friends but went back home and told nobody. In the evening when no one was watching he stole away to the cave with a rope, determined to let himself down and catch many birds. This he very successfully did but on reaching the bottom the rope fell down after him, having come unfastened from above, and he was made a prisoner. It was useless to call to his friends now, for all were at their homes in the village and no one was at all likely to be within earshot. Thus he remained in the cave many days, and his friends thought he had been killed by a shark or by some hostile tribe. Then, thinking he must surely die, he became very despondent. Presently an idea struck him, and he set vigorously to work pulling the loose rope to pieces and making it into a great number of short strings. When this was done he took his bow, and with some blunt arrows he had, soon knocked over many of the birds, which were so plentiful that he could almost catch them with his hands. These birds he tied to his limbs in all directions, leaving their wings free. Then, when he had got a great number tied to his arms and legs, and all the string was used up, he made as great a noise as he could, and plunged and kicked about as much as his exhausted strength would allow him. This so frightened the birds that they all at once made a dash for the hole in the roof of the cave, and so strong were they and so much frightened with the noise that he made, that they flew right out through the hole, taking him with them, and so the unfortunate but selfish man, after a severe warning, was saved!

We glided away from Santa Maria upon the most peaceful of evenings, and in two more days were at Lo, one of the smaller of the Torres' Islands. This group consists of four little low-lying islands to the north-west of the Banks'. They are, geologically speaking, of recent origin, and strikingly resemble the Loyalties in outline. We called at only one of them, the vessel not having been here more than once previously. I believe it is the intention of the mission to pay more attention in future to the group. We made two visits, one on the way north, and the other on our return, when we left Bishop Selwyn behind to stay two months with the people, who were suffering most acutely from horrible sores aggravated by want of water and careless treatment.

The islands of the Torres' group as well as several of the Banks' are practically altogether without water. The soil consists of crumbled coral through which the rain percolates as it would through sand: the natives are accordingly dependent upon coco-nut milk as their sole beverage, and of course do not wash. At Mota in the Banks' Islands, as I have mentioned above, the effect of this want of what we consider a necessity of life was very distressing, but upon the island of which I am now writing it was positively appalling.

The men wear a short stick, generally about three-quarters of a inch in diameter and an inch and a half long, through the cartilage of the nose, which presses the sides of the

TORRES' ISLANDS NOSE ORNAMENT.

nostrils upwards, giving a most hideous expression to the face. These little blocks are of polished black wood and have a small mother-of-pearl disc let into them at each end.

We found a very large number of people on the coral rocks which surround the little inlet where we determined to land. Their appearance was far from inviting, as they were very well armed with bows and arrows; on further acquaintance, however, they proved to be amongst the most amiable and merry people we had met.

There have evidently been many labour vessels here from time to time, for we found that several men could speak a little "sandal-wood English" as it is called; none of them, however, appeared at all pleased with their experience of civilisation. The place they had been to was Port Mackay in Queensland, the centre of the sugar district. One man was very communicative, and had a long sentence such as the following, which he repeated continually—poor fellow, it was the only thing that remained to him of his three years' wages: "Me speakee English, my name belong Black John, me been Porter Mackai, too muchee wark, my word, me no sleep all er time, plenty wark, big fellow wind he come, me plenty sick, my word, me no likee Porter Mackai, plenty sugar he stop, me carry him plenty time, me get one feller bokus (box), one feller gun, plenty tambacca, me stop three feller year, my word too muchee wark, me no sleep, me carry sugar, my word, me no likee him, now you give me tambacca, you come England? me savvy England, plenty far, good feller man he belong England, feller man belong Porter Mackai he no good," and so on over and over again.

When we landed on our way south seven or eight weeks later, we found the condition of things very deplorable. We walked up to the village with a long string of natives carrying the bishop's boxes, &c. They had promised to build a new house, but had been unable to do so. The terrible sickness was striking them all down. The usual straggling hamlets are to be found here, also connected by a winding path through the woods; at certain places all the women and girls filed off down a different pathway from the one we took, ours being tabooed for women. They were a bright and merry lot, but it was terribly sad to see their little villages in the state they were. The houses are simply semicircular arches built upon the ground. I have nowhere else seen the semicircle taking the place of the gable before in native architecture. Outside almost every hut we saw a little temporary shed, and here lay the sick from the house. I have seen nothing more horrible. The disease generally attacks their legs, and flies and want of water soon produce mortification, and the sufferers die, and yet the wonder in most cases was that they *lived*, for so awful was their appearance we really could not look at some of them. All the time, as we walked along, our communicative friend kept pointing to little graves with the words: "Here two man he stop. Here three feller man. Here woman stop," and so on. The malady seems to be contagious, and there was some little difficulty about our visit, for these people are very superstitious, and would easily persuade themselves that the white men had brought the disease.

We tramped along for a short distance towards the centre of the island, surrounded by the usual crowd of wondering natives. Many of them had doubtless never seen white men before, for such labour vessels as have been here would not have sent any one inland. The young girls and boys were very pretty and affectionate, holding our hands as we walked along. Nothing seemed to strike them so much as our *nails*, men and women being called up repeatedly by the more courageous ones to look at and feel them. When I first pulled up my sleeve there was quite a stampede—that any one should be white all over seemed to them something quite fearful! Towards the end of our visit we discovered an amusing fancy which we had not understood before; it was that the people were all most curious to know our names. I had been asked some question a hundred times, and at last some one guessed what it was that they wanted. After that Bisopé (Bishop) and Kooti (my name) were passed round with huge delight, and much pointing at the possessors of these titles!

The Torres' Islands people, although I fancy thick-headed and merry, have at least the art of making very beautiful arrows, which are small and of a light-coloured wood, highly ornamented. Their bows are perfect pieces of workmanship too, and they also make tortoise-shell knives, like paper knives, for eating their food with, but this is about the sum of their industries.

One really needs to visit some such place as this to appreciate the value of water. Here were many hundreds of men, women and children, of whom I suppose but a few had ever known what it was to wash. Natives will not use salt water to wash in, although they will bathe in it while fishing or even perhaps for pleasure. On the whole, however, these dirty Torres' folk seemed to me more merry than any people I visited, and the noisy crowd that came down to see us off was evidently none the less happy for being so unclean. It was only when we saw the poor, dying wretches lying in dozens outside their houses in miserable little sheds, that we realised how awful a thing it is to be the prey of disease and flies and loathsome insects, in a tropical country, and without the all-purifying element.

We sailed from Avava, as the Torres' group is called in its own language, northwards to Santa Cruz, leaving these poor creatures in great spirits at the prospect of the Bishop's return, when we were to leave him behind us on our way South.

CHAPTER XII.

THE SANTA CRUZ ISLANDS.

"The Capitana and the Galiot being near the north coast of Santa Cruz, there came from the shore a small canoe with a sail, followed by a fleet of fifty other canoes, the people in them calling out and waving their hands; but they approached the ships with great caution. When the canoes drew near, it was discovered that these people were of a dark complexion, some more black than others, and all with woolly hair, which many among them had stained or dyed with white, red, and other colours, and some had half of the head shorn; other distinctions were observed, and their teeth were stained red. . . . Most of them were stained or painted black, so as to make them blacker than their natural colour. . . . They continued for a time irresolute. At length they set up a loud shout, and sent a flight of arrows at the ships. The Spaniards, who had kept themselves prepared, fired their muskets in return, and killed one Indian and wounded many others."—*Discovery of Santa Cruz*, 1595. '*Burney's Travels*,' vol. ii.

In 1567 Don Alvaro de Mendaña sailed westward from the port of Callao to find still more New Worlds, to carry still farther the Castillian standard, to add if possible still more to the already so long list of Spanish discoveries and conquests.

The expedition crossed the great Pacific ocean, steering always towards the setting sun, and for months the bold navigators sailed doggedly westward, always hoping for a reward. Their voyage was even longer than the journey from Europe to the New World, but with the memory of Cortez and Pizarro in their minds they were nothing daunted. At last they discovered a group of large and beautiful islands, and finding at the southern end of them, a well-sheltered bay, they anchored and commenced an examination of their newly-acquired possession. We are told that "the discoverer of these islands named them the Isles of Salomon, to the end that the Spaniards, supposing them to be those isles whence Solomon fetched gold to adorn the temple at Jerusalem, might be the more desirous to go and inhabit the same."

Mendaña's published descriptions of the islands were full of magnificent exaggeration. The land was of unparalleled wealth, even Peru was not comparable to it. Here were not arid mountains and forbidding deserts; here was a very Paradise, where every kind of valuable wood abounded as in Central America, where Nature was most prolific in her gifts, where gold was plentiful and water plentiful. We can well imagine the descriptions those ancient mariners would give when they returned to the simple country folk of their native land; all their hardships were then forgotten, and nothing remained to them but vague memories of the distant islands, so often enlarged upon that now even they themselves would not know truth from falsehood.

The outcome of these extravagant stories was what might have been expected. Volunteers were soon found willing to venture even so far as to these Solomon Islands, in the very uttermost part of the earth, and twenty years or so after his return, Mendaña again started from Callao at the head of a small band of adventurers, who had determined to settle in these newly-found Pacific islands. Westward steered the great navigator as he had done before, and in due time picked up an island which at first seemed both large and beautiful, and which no doubt was thought by all on board to be one of the group. Mendaña, however, soon discovered that there was some mistake; this was not one of the Solomons, nor had he even sighted this land on his previous voyage.

A discontented mood, however, was upon his followers, who insisted upon staying where they were, and, as this land seemed a pleasant and fertile one, settling here. The group, thus accidentally discovered by Mendaña, was given the name of Santa Cruz, and here an attempt was made at forming a colony. Mendaña himself died on the main island in October 1595, and partly on account of his death, and also, doubtless, from the hostility and ferocity of the natives, the grim conquerors who had faced so much, abandoned, apparently for ever, all idea of extending the Spanish power so far afield. They returned disheartened to Callao, and the Santa Cruz group of islands was no more seen or heard of for over two hundred years.

They were rediscovered and visited by both Carteret and d'Entrecasteaux at the end of the last century, and a few names were given to them, and the principal bearings of the islands were laid down. Nothing however of interest beyond the ferocity of the natives and the excellence of their canoes, was recorded until ten years ago. In 1871 the group was brought conspicuously before the public on account of the terrible tragedy on the small island of Nukapu, where Bishop Patteson and others were killed. The incidents of that murder are too well known to require repetition here: there is little doubt now that the affair was carried out in deliberate revenge for the kidnapping of five natives which had taken place some time before. In 1875 the English public were again startled by the news of the murder of one of the most popular commanders in the naval service. On that occasion, as I believe has always been the case, the natives seemed both good-natured and friendly until a moment before the party left the shore, when, without the slightest previous warning, an attack was made upon the party, and Commodore Goodenough and two seamen were wounded with poisoned arrows. The commodore died of tetanus on the ninth day, and both the sailors who were struck, also lost their lives. Since this sad event the islands have been left almost unvisited, no attempt whatever having been made to land.

Towards this group of so curious and fatal interest, we directed our course after leaving the Torres' Islands, and soon found ourselves in sight of Vanikoro, the southernmost island. The group takes its name from the large or main island which was first called La Isla Granda de Santa Cruz, and whose native name is Nitendi or (as in some dialects) Ndeni. It consists of about a dozen islands, some eight of which are quite small, and lie to the north in a cluster known as the Swallows or Reef Islands; next to these lies Nitendi, and to the south again Tapua and Vanikoro. It was upon this last-named island that the celebrated expedition of La Pérouse—the Franklin of the Southern Seas—was lost. One could hardly conceive a more dangerous piece of land, for from every corner of it run great reefs, giving the coast a most forbidding appearance. As we sailed along I watched the breakers from the fore-top-gallant yard and they seemed to stretch away in every direction like the feelers of an octopus. Although the island is itself quite small, the circumference of the reef is estimated at no less than thirty-five miles.

Many European traders have been at this place during the last few years, mostly attracted by the report that there were still valuable remains of the La Pérouse expedition upon the reef to the south-west of the island. The ill-fated Capt. Ferguson, who was murdered this winter in the Solomon group, succeeded only a year or so ago in obtaining an amount of salvage in the way of brass cannons, &c., that was, I believe, sold in Sydney for as much as £600. The natives are reported to be friendly, and no doubt white men will be attracted here before long.

It was not our intention to call at Vanikoro, so we stood away after running close to the reef and brought up the following morning off Tapua, which lies some twenty miles to the northward and westward. Here we intended to call, as H.M.S. *Basilisk* had been in some years before and had found a good harbour. We stood off what was evidently the harbour's mouth early in the morning, and even lowered a boat to try and find an entrance through the reef. After several hours, however, we were obliged to give up the attempt, for the wind did not serve so as to secure us a good retreat, supposing we got into any difficulty. We stood away again, therefore, that night, and passing to the eastward of the main island, brought up in the morning off Nufiluli, one of the Reef Islands, which the bishop had visited two years before.

These Reef Islands of Santa Cruz are small low coral patches, I suppose nowhere more than thirty feet above the sea level. They lie in a very labyrinth of reefs which have never been explored. We backed the main yard in a narrow channel between the islands of Nufiluli and Pileni, and allowed the fleets of canoes which were paddling from the two islands to come up to us. The natives came alongside quite fearlessly, for they knew the vessel—as well they might, since the bishop had brought back to them in 1878 a man from here who had been blown away as far as the Solomon Islands, and whom he found a prisoner there. They were very excited, for no vessel had been seen by them since the bishop was here before, over two years ago. This man was amongst the first on board, and very glad he seemed to see his old friends. Before long the vessel's deck was crowded with the natives, who swarmed up the sides like monkeys. They were finely-made fellows of a dark copper-colour. Through their noses they wore a thick tortoise-shell ring about an inch and a half in diameter, and in their ears were from ten to as many as twenty thin tortoise-shell rings of about the same size. A very fine and neatly-made mat was their sole article of clothing, passed between the legs and tucked in before and behind in the same manner as those worn by the natives of Opa in the New Hebrides. For ornaments the usual armlets were worn, and also in many cases

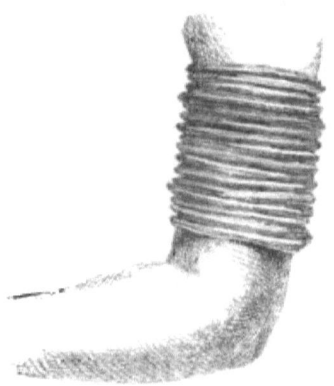

SANTA CRUZ ARMLETS.

a round, flat, shell breast-plate was hung round the neck. Most prominently of all, however, they carried, always and without exception, large red wood bows, and from a dozen to twenty long and highly-ornamented poisoned arrows. Their canoes were quite laden with sheaves of these arrows, which are certainly the most terrible and deadly weapons I have ever seen. They are not (indeed no arrows in these seas are) feathered like our own, but are made of a simple cane shaft four or five feet long, and carved with some care, the designs upon them being coloured with red and white pigments. The points are long and thin, and of a light brown colour, the tips being made of human bone.

The canoes of this group of islands are as distinctive in character as the people themselves. They are almost always *built*; that is, are not carved out of a single log as is usual in the canoes of less ingenious races. They are, moreover, stained white, and in addition to the usual outrigger, have a counter-balancing platform on the other side, on which may be carried bundles of arrows, coco-nuts, breadfruit, and other necessaries. Their dexterity in the management of these canoes is most remarkable. We saw several of them upset and swamped, but the owners swimming up to them would, in less time than it takes to write of it, shake the water out with a swinging motion, jump in and bale them dry with the greatest ease.

After an hour or so, during which we ingratiated ourselves into the good opinions of the natives as much as possible, we resolved to go ashore. The bishop had landed on the small island of Nufiluli before, and we had but little fear of hostilities here, the only element of danger lying in the jealousy which exists between the natives of Nufiluli and the island of Pileni a few miles to the north. Whenever any attention was shown to a chief of the former island, the natives of the latter seemed displeased, and vice versâ.

We pulled up in the whale boat to the opening in the reef, surrounded by many canoes. There was but little water in the lagoon, and dozens of natives had waded out waist-deep fully two miles to meet us. I never saw a more beautiful reef formation than exists at this place. Outside, the sea is profoundly deep, say eighty or ninety fathoms, and one can look down through the sapphire-coloured water into an apparently infinite profundity. From these depths the coral wall rises perpendicularly, as though built by human labour.

But what human labour could compare with this? Walls of Baalbec or Saracenic traceries, or Campanile of Giotto, or Roslyn Chapel pillars—the greatest or most beautiful of man's creations, what are they to such a work of Nature? I have seen a thousand wonders of human skill, patience, and ingenuity, but this little island wall, built by the never idle though short-lived coral architect, puts every one to shame. There is no describing it; no conceiving its wealth of beauty. There it stood perhaps five hundred feet from base to summit, faultlessly pure and beautiful. Through a narrow cleft, I know not how many hundred feet deep, in this wall we steered our boat, and soon were in shallow water, among the coral patches of the lagoon. We were pushed and towed through the shoal water for about two miles before we finally ran the boat upon a sandy beach and waded ashore.

Drawn up upon this beach were some splendid canoes, fitted with spars and sails, and reserved for long journeys. They were over forty feet long and were decked in, so that such cargo as they might carry could be battened down and kept from wet. Upon the platform between the main hull and the outrigger was a small house in which a fire could be lighted. The sail, which was of matting, was of the usual heart shape, with a semicircle cut away from the top. These vessels will not sail near the wind, but attain a very fair speed when running free. The natives of Santa Cruz do not hesitate to make cruises far out of sight of land, their knowledge of the stars being very considerable. I have noticed the elder of the three boys whom we subsequently brought away with us from here, teaching the names of various stars to his younger companions, and was surprised at the number he knew by name. Moreover, at any time of night or day, and in whatsoever direction we

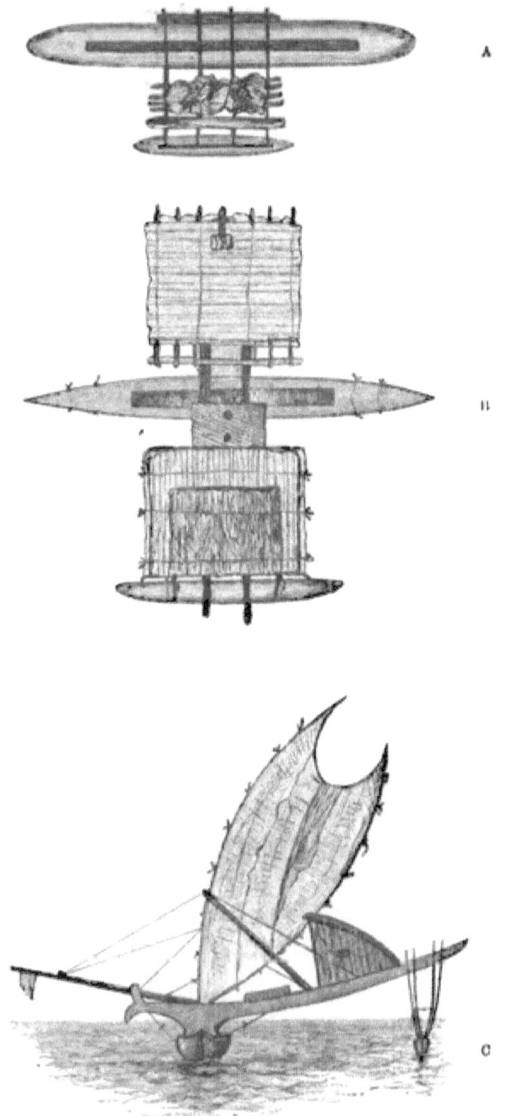

A, ordinary coast canoe; B, plan of sea-going canoe; C, view of sea-going canoe, showing sail.

might happen to be steering, these boys, even the youngest of the three, a lad of ten or twelve, would be able to point to where his home lay; this I have found them able to do many hundreds of miles to the south of the Santa Cruz group.

Upon landing we found a number of natives on the beach with eager and curious faces, but as yet there were no women visible, and we were taken up at once from the shore to the club-house of the village. There appears to be no great difference between the club system here and that of the New Hebrides. The house, however, was larger and better built than any I have seen in the more southern islands. The floor was covered with mats, and a finely-plaited one was brought for us to sit upon. The leading men of the village sat all around, and hot breadfruit and yams were brought for us to eat. We had with us a Loyalty Island native who had been left here for a few months two years before, and he was able, to a certain extent, to act as interpreter. We were perhaps an hour in this house undergoing a sort of examination, and being looked upon with immense delight by the less dignified of the community. My beard was so generally admired that friends were continually brought in to gaze at and even to stroke it, after which they would depart in great glee, and communicate the result of their experience to small knots of idlers outside. From the club-house we were taken by a chief to his private residence, where we again were seated upon mats, and brought presents of breadfruit, &c. This house was one of a small cluster, and a stone wall ran round it. Here we saw for the first time many women and children. The girls were finely made and of strong and healthy appearance, the children very shy, but with the invariable bright, pretty eyes. They were laden with tortoise-shell ear-rings, and all the men and boys wore the thick ring through the centre of the nose. In this chief's house were four divisions, boarded off by partitions three or four feet high, and having the appearance of stalls in a stable. Each of these loose-boxes, as they may be called, was the sleeping-place of one of the chief's wives, who, when a stranger enters, promptly repair to their quarters, and remain until wanted. In some houses we saw as many as six of such divisions.

After a tedious repetition of the process of being stroked and admired, we walked about a mile along the shore under a fiercely-burning sun, to another small village, and here went through some more sitting in state, being presented, moreover, with bags of nuts, kits of breadfruit, coco-nuts and yams. Whenever any gift was made a return present of very much greater value was evidently required. Blue beads are the rage in these islands, and with them practically everything the natives have may be bought; also small pieces of iron eight inches long, and one and a half wide are in great request. These pieces, the value of which is about a penny each, are preferred even to finished axes, and I think the reason of this must be that they can work the raw material into whatsoever tool they may find most suited to their purpose. But what labour it represents! Grinding by hand upon a rough stone, short sticks of iron into useful tools!

Of the things to be bought, mats are the chiefest, and some of these are very beautifully executed, being made almost exactly in the way so-called "sword mats" are made in civilised countries. We also bought some of their money, which is curious. It consists of coils, resembling a very old leather strap an inch wide, which are covered with scarlet feathers neatly sewn on, and are worn round the waist upon state occasions. I was unable to obtain a new one, nor indeed did I see such a thing. Such as we bought were evidently of great age, the scarlet colour of the feathers being visible only when they were lifted up. Models of canoes also were offered us for sale, and one that I saw was almost large enough to hold a boy. They are evidently made as toys for the children.

After a very wearisome day we managed to get clear of the beach; getting away is always the difficult thing in such cases as this, for every one wants to come in the boat, and when ordering them out or pushing them over the side, one may very easily commit some breach of etiquette and get into trouble. At last, however, we succeeded in launching the boat into deep water and pulling away.

We had accomplished the object of our visit, which was to induce some of the natives from here, who were known at a village upon the main island, to come over with us and, as it were, introduce us to the chief there. Elated with our success, we pulled off to the ship in good spirits accompanied by dozens of canoes, which however, by hoisting our sail, we soon were able to leave behind. I remember that one white-haired old ruffian, with the most diabolical countenance and not a rag on his body, stood up in his canoe and shouted so pathetically to us that we lowered our sail for a moment and waited for him. He came paddling up breathlessly, trembling with excitement, and seizing the bishop's hand with great fervour, he rubbed it carefully with his nose, then he very formally presented me with the oldest and most disreputable poisoned arrow I ever saw, and paddled quite contentedly away! There are eccentric characters evidently even at Santa Cruz, and we laughed very much at the grotesque behaviour of this veteran. To be on board the old ship again was a great relief, it seemed so home-like and safe. Never on shore for a moment had man or boy laid down his bow or bundle of arrows, and we could not but feel that it would have required very little at any time to have occasioned a disturbance.

With six natives of the Reef Islands on board, we made our way during the night towards Nitendi, the main island of Santa Cruz. We kept well away from the shore in order to avoid being seen by the coast-tribes, until we believed ourselves to be opposite the place at which we hoped to land, when we bore directly down upon it. It is a bold high island, this of Nitendi, very different in appearance from the newly-formed coral islets to the north, and appears to have no outlying reefs whatever. We got up steam in our little "coffee mill," so that in case of any trouble with the natives we could at any rate insure the vessel "staying," should we require to beat off the shore, and also to a certain extent retain command of the ship if the wind fell light. Passing the place where Commodore Goodenough was killed, we stood in towards an open bay a mile or so to the westward, where is a small inlet and a village known as Lelouova. For some time we had noticed canoes paddling about even as much as four or five miles from the land, but none ventured near to us, and we stood on our course, steering straight in towards the little bay. As we got nearer, the number of these greatly increased, and at last we sent our Reef Island natives, who knew some words of the language of this island, into the rigging to shout to the men in the canoes. These natives who had in their own boats visited the place for trading purposes, soon made themselves understood, with the result that a few of the more bold spirits ventured alongside. No sooner had this been accomplished, than, leaning over the bulwarks and enticing them with beads and "turkey red," we induced a few to come up on deck. By this time we were as close in as was deemed wise, and therefore backed the yards and lay to. Hundreds of natives soon swarmed up the side, and they seemed even a wilder and more uncouth-looking lot than those of the islets to the north. I can conceive of no more repulsive objects than were some of these men. Let a copper-coloured savage shave his head in parts. . Let him gather up such of his crisp woolly hair as is not cut, into long, frizzly tails, which will stand out like spokes from the boss of a wheel. Let him dye some of these white and some scarlet, as his sweet fancy may direct. Let him smear his face with charcoal, relieving the monotony of soot, however, with scarlet or yellow streaks. Let his body be scaly like a

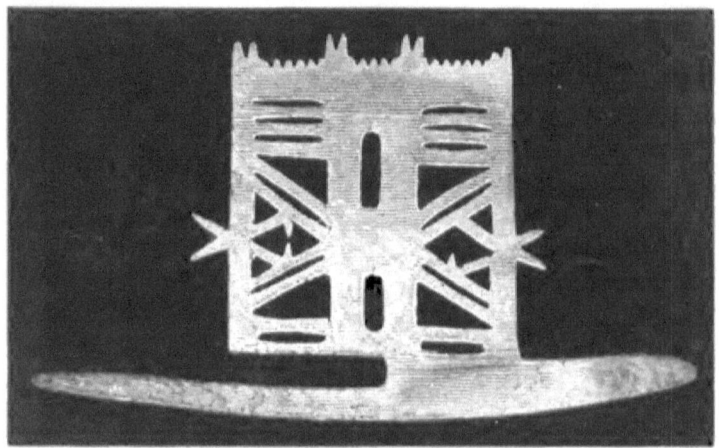

NOSE ORNAMENT, SANTA CRUZ.

fish's, from skin disease, and yellow in parts from the wearing or carrying of turmeric-coated mats. Put a thin mat between his legs and a large round shell plate upon his chest; squeeze a dozen pearl shell bangles upon the upper part of his arms, and hang a ring through his nose, and twenty in his ears, not forgetting to smear his big, ugly mouth with the red juice of the betel nut; let him carry always and everywhere some twenty thick arrows, highly carved, tipped with poisoned human bone, and painted red and white; add to this interesting bundle a long red bow, and perhaps a richly ornamented club—and you have the makings of a pretty considerable ruffian ! Not one whit less terrible in appearance than this description implies were many dozens of the men that now swarmed upon the decks of the *Southern Cross*. Some of them were fine, good-looking young fellows, gorgeously arrayed in pearl armlets and tortoise-shell earrings, and wearing elaborately fretted mother-of-pearl plates fastened into their noses, which partly hid the centre of the face. There were also white-headed and closely-cropped old villains, with countenances little short of demoniacal in their ugliness, and all were in a state of excitement, which I should have thought beyond possibility. Every canoe was well stocked with bundles of poisoned arrows, some of which we were able to buy with beads and iron.

There is something about the appearance of these bundles that is more terrible, I think, than that of any other weapons. Their colour and high ornamentation; the smooth, long points of human bone which, presumably, are steeped in some deadly juice so that the faintest scratch shall produce tetanus and death; the horrible stories connected with these arrows; the universal fear of them resembling that of hydrophobia—all these things lend a ghastly fascination to the arrows as we see them in every man's left hand and piled up in dozens upon the outriggers of the canoes.

Nearly every man carried a small sack resembling the "old clo'" bag of the London streets, although not so large, and in this he kept the little stores which he brought off for barter. We were offered more mats than anything else, and some of them were perfect in taste and workmanship. Clubs also were brought, not the polished hard ones that one ordinarily sees, but a curiously-shaped white kind, with designs upon them painted in red and black. The eagerness to sell was something beyond all describing; at times, seeing in one of our hands something they would like, perhaps half-a-dozen men would leap from their canoes, and struggle up the side, so overcome with excitement that they could hardly even shout, their faces being absolutely awful to look upon.

This kind of thing lasted an hour or so, and then Mesa, the chief of the place, and probably also of this part of the island, came off in some state. The bishop received him in the cabin, and resolved to accompany him ashore. A boat was therefore lowered, but it was not thought safe for any one to go except the bishop and the Loyalty man who had spent some weeks upon the Reef Islands two years ago. Twenty natives jumped into the boat as soon as it touched the water, and then the bishop squeezed himself into the stern in the midst of them, and shaking out the little sail steered towards the land. We arranged meanwhile to keep as many natives on board the ship as possible, and to signal if there were any sign of them clearing off for the shore. It was very nervous work, for no one had been here since September 1875, when punishment was administered to the natives on account of the murder of Commodore Goodenough.

In half an hour or so we made out the boat coming off

ORNAMENTED CLUB, SANTA CRUZ.

again to the ship, and soon the bishop was alongside and reported that every one on shore seemed friendly, and that he proposed leaving the Loyalty Island man here for a time, calling for him again in about two months. This man, whose name is Wadrogal, is one of the elder Bishop Selwyn's earliest pupils, and possesses a large share of the bravery for which all the natives of the Loyalties are celebrated. He expressed himself quite willing to stay, and even to take his wife on shore also; such things as he might want therefore being put into the boat, the bishop sailed in again, and this time I jumped in among the wild naked crowd and was taken ashore also.

We landed upon a steeply shelving shore, consisting of iron sand such as is found on the west coast of New Zealand. There was a good deal of surf breaking upon the beach where our boat grounded, and into this we immediately plunged, waist-deep, hoping to steady the boat, by holding on to the gunwale. A great many natives were on the shore, standing by the bows of the boat, and we expected these would have helped us to run her up out of the breakers: they did not lend us a hand, however, but merely shouted and gesticulated. This was rather an awkward moment, and I began to wonder what would happen next; we could not haul the boat up ourselves, and the natives did not seem willing to help, but surrounded us in great numbers vociferating and making signs, we all the while not understanding a syllable, but struggling to keep the boat from bumping,*

After a few rather anxious moments, the mystery was solved—a long line of women appeared; here were the labourers; these lords of creation could not stoop to pull or carry. We soon got all we wanted done with the help of the women, although they seemed very frightened.

* Vide frontispiece to Part II.

Mesa, the chief who on board had evinced much partiality for my society—partly I fancy on account of some turkey red on my helmet which, however, I had deemed advisable to leave behind me, now that the boat was well out of the water, led me affectionately away from the beach, evidently with the desire of showing me something.

We passed by some splendid canoes, even larger than the ones we had seen on the other island, and so away from the beach along a small pathway through the forest. This took us after a short time to a village in which was a fine club-house (called an "ofilau"). Here I went through

CLUB-HOUSE, SANTA CRUZ.

the usual sitting in state and eating hot breadfruit and being admired. There were not many people about, as the ship had attracted a large number and many more were with the bishop by the boat. Several men, however, sat down with me, and numbers of boys peered in at the low doorway. We were intensely jovial and noisy, talking and laughing a great deal, although not understanding a word of each other's language. Unbuttoning my shirt

I caused the most unbounded delight by the exhibition of a white chest, and when I kicked off a shoe and displayed a foot of the same colour, the excitement and astonishment knew no bounds. People flocked in to see and touch the strange creature, and their wonder and curiosity rose higher than ever. I had brought with me no presents or valuables of any kind—nor indeed any clothes beyond the plainest shirt and flannel trousers, as it was most desirable not to excite their cupidity, but I found, fortunately, a small bundle of fish-hooks in the pocket of my shirt, and these I distributed, amidst great enthusiasm, amongst my crowd of admirers. It was a strange experience, indeed, to sit there, where I suppose no white man had ever been, amongst that crowd of savages, perhaps the most treacherous in the world. The light was dim, for there were only two or three square holes for doorways; a fire burnt in one corner, and in the centre of the house was a large arrangement like a four-post bed, upon the top of which were stowed bags of nuts and stores of spare arrows and other treasures. Every one had his bow and arrows, and would not so much as cross the house without them, and I could not resist a suspicion once of foul play and quickly roused tempers; it was therefore pleasant to see through the little doorway the waves dashing against the rocks outside, and in the distance the ship with the canoes still round her. After some time we went out again, Mesa still indefatigably attentive, and walked through the village, which consisted of a great number of houses built closely together. The women here were very shy and had an ill-used appearance; I saw one rather pretty girl, but she slipped away timidly as I came near.

Walking back through the forest to the little bay where the boat was, I passed a woman leading a child by the hand, and carrying on her head a black wooden bowl containing mashed yams. She stepped aside and covered her face with some native cloth that she wore around her, much as an Arab woman would have done. The child shrank away from me in fear, and another one that followed ran crying into the forest. Mesa and his companions laughed contemptuously, but they themselves had been but little less frightened a few hours before on the ship. I walked in front, not, perhaps, without a feeling of nervousness, as I was quite unable to watch the movements of my savage escort. It was a narrow moss and fern-covered pathway; there was a little stream of water, and across it natural stepping-stones. The rocks were black, and tree-shadows were thrown across the path with little bright circles of light sprinkled everywhere. It was like a glade near Bolton Abbey or in Derbyshire, and, but for the loud talking of the natives who followed me, I could hardly realise that this was indeed the main island of the Santa Cruz group, and I almost the first white man that had visited that village, and walked along that little pathway.

We found a great crowd upon the beach, and they did not seem at all to like our leaving, but evening was now upon us, and delay would have been most unwise. Amidst great excitement and noise, we struggled away from the shore, bundling as many natives as we could into the water, and "casting off," when possible, those who clung on to the gunwale of the boat. These people never seem to realise that there is a limit to the number even a white man's boat will carry.

In an hour or less we had cleared every one off the vessel with the exception of our six friends from the Reef Islands, and were standing away north-west again, to pay a second visit to Nufiluli and Pileni, and return these men to their homes. I have seldom been more utterly tired—not from actual bodily exertion, but from sheer excitement—than when I got on board the ship again. There was a feeling of relief amongst us all that night; the anxiety of the last few days was taken off our shoulders now, for the experiment was over, and had proved satisfactory. With such terrible precedents we could hardly have expected so successful an experience. Our best hopes had been realised, and a beginning at least had been made upon an island that had been considered almost hopeless. It is impossible to say what the people thought of our visit, but, as we carried no arms and took practically nothing from them but gave away a considerable amount of, to them, inestimable treasure, one may presume they considered our intentions were friendly. Our success undoubtedly lay in the fact that we came, as it were, with introductions, that is, we brought natives with us who already believed us to be harmless and even useful. This very scheme was attempted by Bishop Patteson ten years ago. He had been shot at here on the main island, for his motives were misunderstood. He crossed over, accordingly, to the small islands to the north, where he thought the people were more friendly, and landing there in hopes of first making himself known to them, met with his death.

We landed our Reef Island friends at their homes on the following day, and made several visits on shore, the most important result of which was that we succeeded in getting three boys to come away with us. This was as great a triumph as landing at Nitendi, for no one had yet been taken from this group. The youngest boy soon became a great favourite on board. His name was Nawen, and a more bright, sharp-witted youngster one could hardly imagine. He wore thirty ear-rings, some of considerable size,* and a nose-ring,

---

* The natives of Santa Cruz all use head-rests, many of which closely resemble in shape and size those found in Egypt. These wooden pillows are also common in Fiji and New Caledonia; they are not, however, in these cases used to preserve the hair, as in Japan and possibly in Egypt,

and although very sea-sick at first, soon recovered, and was for the rest of the voyage, the merriest and happiest of all the boys on the ship. His great accomplishment was the ma-

"HE WORE THIRTY EAR-RINGS."

nipulation of a piece of string into what, I believe, are called "cat's cradles." It is interesting to notice the wide-spread prevalence of this amusement. The natives are very clever at it, and can carry out very numerous combinations, taking and retaking the arrangements from each other for hours together.

We lay off Nukapu, the island where Bishop Patteson was killed, on a calm, beautiful evening, but no canoes came off, and no signs of any kind were made by those on shore. This island has not been visited for nine years, the last occasion being when H.M.S. *Rosario* called after the bishop's death, and an engagement with the natives took place.

---

but on account of the number of ear-rings, which make it impossible for these people to sleep with their heads on the ground or upon any other kind of pillow.

We made no attempt to land, as it was threatening a calm, and we thought it wiser not to incur any further risk amongst these people for the present.

In the morning we were out of sight of Nukapu and off a little island called Nupani, where the people are apparently friendly, as many canoes came off, and their occupants after but little hesitation were induced to come on board. They seemed even more excited about "turkey red" than their neighbours of the other islands, and I shall never forget the frenzy of delight that was shown when we tied pieces round their heads. They trembled in an agony of expectation before receiving them, and when they had them on, danced and hooted, and yelled like maniacs.

Almost all the time during our cruise in this group the volcano of Tinakolo was visible. It is a perfect cone, rising without any fault from the sea level, and while we were in its neighbourhood, sent forth a thin and beautiful column of white smoke. On one occasion at night a brilliant stream of fire issued from the crater, and ran down the sides of the mountain into the sea, producing a very grand effect. From Santa Cruz we stood away to the westward, steering for Ulaua in the Solomon Islands.

CHAPTER XIII.

THE SOLOMON ISLANDS.

" Larger constellations burning, mellow moons and happy skies,
Breadth of tropic shade and palms in cluster—knots of Paradise.
 * * * * * *
Droops the heavy-blossomed bower, hangs the heavy-fruited tree,
Summer Isles of Eden lying in dark purple spheres of sea."

AFTER a pleasant sail from Santa Cruz we sighted the high land of San Christoval, the most southern of the Solomon Islands.

"The Solomon Archipelago extends N.W. and S.E. for the space of two hundred leagues. It is composed of eight or ten principal islands, and many others less considerable, but the number of which is not yet properly known. The structure of these islands is throughout the same; it is a long chain of mountains, often very lofty, which form their axes in the general direction of the group." *

Our first calling-place was at Ulaua, a small island lying between Malanta and San Christoval. We landed upon a rocky coral shore on the western side, and scrambled up to the village. It was very beautiful, the vegetation being distinctly more Malayan than anything we had seen in the southern groups, the trees larger and the undergrowth if possible more prolific. It reminded me of the country round Penang on the Malay peninsula. The village is long and straggling, and where the "bush" has been cleared away, a

---

* Finlay's 'South Pacific Directory.'

very beautiful avenue is formed, down which the little houses are built. This clearing is perhaps a mile in length, and the houses are dotted here and there all the way along. They are better houses than we have been accustomed to, having sides four or five feet high and a somewhat flat roof, in fact they resemble the poorer chalets of Switzerland. Everything, indeed, is different in this group of islands, the people are very distinctly Papuan, being much darker than the Santa Cruz or New Hebrides natives; both men and women, however, are splendidly formed and in many cases very handsome. They have no clothes here whatever, even the women not

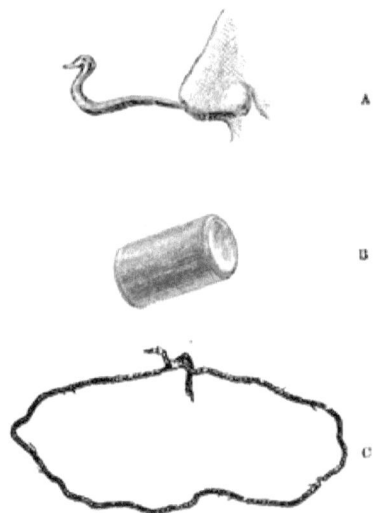

A LADY'S COSTUME, ULAVA, SOLOMON ISLANDS.
A, mother-of-pearl ornament worn in the nose; B, block worn through the ears; C, waist string.

getting beyond a string round their waists. The decorations they wear are more than ordinarily various, and we noticed armlets and anklets formed of very prettily arranged native beads which were made from shells and dyed blue and red and yellow. Some of the girls wear a little mother-of-pearl bird which is fixed into a hole in the extreme tip of the nose and has a most singular appearance. These people are ingenious, and carve handsome bowls, which they inlay with mother-of-pearl and other shells. They are also noted canoe makers.

Perhaps the Solomon Islands are more celebrated for their canoes than for anything else, and if so I think with

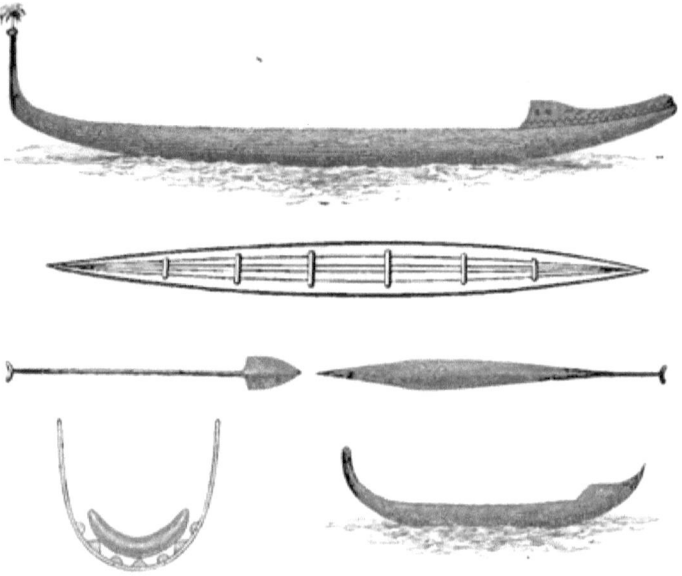

SOLOMON ISLAND CANOES.

reason. Not even the gondolas of Venice are more exquisitely graceful than these little boats. They are made of bent planks of wood held together with strong thwarts and cemented with a kind of gum obtained from a tree. The stern is always carried up to a considerable height like the bow of a gondola, and in large canoes both bow and stern are of the same graceful shape. They are narrow and have no outrigger, but sit on the water literally "like a duck." When

the bow is not carried up in the gondola form I have
mentioned, it is often made to represent a shark's head, and
always in a canoe of any pretensions whatever there is a large
amount of inlaying work, the designs being quaint and con-
ventional, but certainly not without merit. I suppose these
canoes are the most "crank" craft in the world, yet the natives
can take them out in fairly rough weather and always
manage them wonderfully. The paddles are short and thin,
and are used indifferently on either side, two or three strokes
on one side, then two or three on the other and so on. In all
the villages that we visited in this group we found one or
two canoe houses, where those not in use were kept, and
almost every chief of note had a state canoe, usually in a
house by itself. The work expended on some of the more
magnificent ones surprised me very much, in some cases
there being many thousands of pieces of pearl shell, all carefully shaped and let in in accordance with a quaint design.*

The Melanesian Mission has had a native teacher at Ulana
for some years, and it has been visited several times by the
clergymen themselves. I was present at an examination of
the natives, which was very amusing, the little naked urchins
enjoying it all immensely and exhibiting much pride when
receiving any praise.

On our second visit to this place a month later
we very nearly got into trouble, and as an example
of the character of the natives, I may as well mention
what took place. A house had been built for the native
teacher, which could be used as a school and also as a
sleeping house, when any of the missionaries wished to
stay on the island. During the past year the chiefs of the
village, thinking, I suppose, that the house was too good for
its purpose, took partial possession and used it as a village

* Vide illustration, page 187.

club-house. When some objection was raised to this by the bishop, the excuse was that there had not been a sufficient sum paid for the house in the first instance. An extra payment to the extent of a few axes and fish-hooks was accordingly determined upon, and the bishop began handing these to the leading people. Upon giving one rather sullen-looking ruffian an axe he became intensely angry, and threw it upon the ground before us all in a great rage. This is always a sort of declaration of hostilities, and in a moment every one began shouting at once, angry words seemed to be passing, and none of us could make out what it was all about. The people were quite unarmed, or I fancy we might have got into some trouble here, for it seemed impossible to discover what was the matter, the native teacher being too excited or frightened to interpret properly. After a time, however, it appeared that some man of minor rank to the one who had thrown down the axe, had been given a present before his position entitled him to one, and his superior was in consequence highly indignant at the insult. The incident seemed to show me how easily a hostile feeling can be aroused amongst these people, and also how difficult it must be, unless one's knowledge of them is really very great, to avoid giving offence unintentionally.

We visited two or three places on the island of San Christoval, watering the ship at a charming little river on the northern end, and also calling at Wango, which in the old days when whaling was more common was often used as a watering place. The natives of this island have been utterly ruined by traders and whalers, and their condition now is really most pitiful. It is the old story: in Japan, in China, in Africa, in the Sandwich Islands, where you will, the white man seems for a long time only to change the vices of the natives. If he suppresses cannibalism he introduces drunkenness. If he improves the laws of humanity he makes more lax those of morality. I do not uphold the native *au naturel*, I mean the savage native. I do not believe in the noble savage, but I often feel that the difference between his wickedness and our wickedness is to a great extent one of kind. If we teach him not to kill, we teach him to cheat, which is the more wide-spreading and insidious crime of the two. If we are astonished at his neglect of mercy, he would often be no less astonished at our neglect of morality.

These Solomon Islanders have some fine traits and some honest healthy laws for all their ferocity: but to go to a place like this, and see how we have completely overthrown their better parts, and only partially substituted our wiser customs, is indeed a sad experience.*

Wango is a large place, prettily situated on a river bank; the houses are well built and in front have balconies, if one may call them so, like the huts of the New Zealand Maoris. The people themselves are handsome, the girls singularly, and I may add fatally pretty; indeed, with the exception of the Sandwich Islanders, they are the best-looking natives I have seen. In most cases they wear no clothes, but are elaborately decorated with bangles, and I counted on one girl no less than twenty on each arm, all above the elbow. On the other bank of the river is another village, also of considerable size. Here I saw some really magnificent bowls, one in particular, being over five feet long; they are conventionally designed to represent ducks, the bowl forming the body, an elaborately-wrought head and tail being added. In front of the duck's bill a fish is generally

---

* The Melanesian Mission has no station in this immediate district now; the harm done by the traders is indeed so wide-spread and deeply rooted that, with his present staff and means, the bishop considers it an almost hopeless task to attempt to grapple with the evil.

attached and the whole is highly ornamented in mosaic fashion with pearl and other shells. The people are

ORNAMENTED BOWL, WANGO, SOLOMON ISLANDS.

losing their art, both in bowl-making, and canoe-building, and we noticed in the village a ruined canoe house, which in its day must have been a really fine building. The pillars are standing, each one being carved to represent sharks in the act of swallowing men. They are all different; in one the man going down head first, in another he is caught sitting, in a third, the shark has him by the legs, and so on.

After leaving Wango we called at a place called Mwatta, which is less frequently visited perhaps, but here, too, the natives are utterly demoralised, and took no interest in us. The whalers and traders have done their work effectually, and the missionaries feel it impossible to make any stand against their influence. At this place when we went ashore no notice of us whatever was taken. They seemed to know all about white people, and to want to have nothing to do with them. They are not, however, to any great extent emancipated from their old customs, if we may judge from the canoe house, in which were hung twenty or thirty human skulls; one also was stuck outside, and the flesh was still upon it. The bishop went and saw a sick man or two, and some sort of interest was shown in us after that, but the people seemed to be glad when we went down to the boat and pulled away.

UNFRIENDLY NATIVES.

The next island we visited was Malanta, but only called at two places, the most southerly one, Saä, being usually visited; the other, Pululaä, only having been called at once. The people of Malanta are undoubtedly most out and out ruffians. In the South Pacific Directory they are called "the most treacherous and blood-thirsty of any known savages," and I think with some truth.

We went ashore at Pululaä one morning, pulling into a small estuary round which mangroves were growing in great quantities. When we arrived at the mouth of the little river itself we were somewhat surprised that no canoes came off, and that there were a great number of natives on the shore. On getting nearer in we noticed that these natives were all men, and all armed with an unusual number of long spears and bows and arrows. Something was evidently about to take place, but what we could not tell. They did not shout or show us any welcome; they merely drew themselves up in a line along the shore, their long spears standing up far above their heads, and having a most formidable appearance. There was no turning back now, however, so we pulled on until the boat grounded, and then jumped into the water and waded ashore. At first no one seemed to know us, nor could the bishop remember any face amongst the wild crowd, but he kept repeating the chief's name, and so we waited for some time, hoping for a friendly face. These men were evidently strangers, and did not know quite what attitude to assume. They made no actually hostile demonstration, but holding themselves aloof, shouted vociferously and seemed to be ready for anything that might turn up. There were no women and children near, and this little army was far more elaborately equipped than is usual in ordinary times. Their ornaments in some cases were most beautiful, one or two men wearing wide sashes, one might almost call them, of native bead-work, fringed with human teeth. The more elaborate of these were worn over

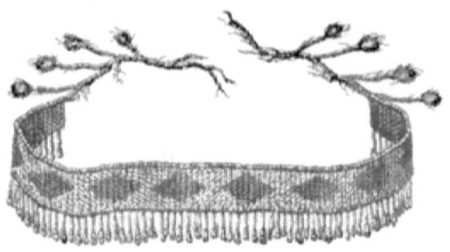

SOLOMON ISLAND SASH.

the right shoulder, and round under the left arm. The colours were, as always in native workmanship, quiet and rich in tone and harmoniously arranged.

After a rather awkward delay of twenty minutes or so, during which we laughed and talked amongst ourselves, and endeavoured to appear quite at our ease, a merry old fellow arrived, who turned out to be the chief whom the bishop had seen on his former visit. This man spoke a few words to the crowd, evidently assuring them that he knew who we were, after which they were willing to trade in bows and arrows and spears and ornaments. This old chief had been kidnapped when a boy and taken to Fiji, where he had worked for several years, and had learned a few of the more common English oaths, with which he now besprinkled his conversation. His son was sick, and he succeeded in making the bishop understand that he should like him to be doctored. We also made out with some difficulty that the assembling of these armed ruffians was on account of a feast to be given that night at the village; natives from far and wide had been asked, and were coming in all day long from the neighbourhood. The customs at these feasts are very curious. No part of the food provided, for instance, is *eaten* at the entertainment. Each guest, on the contrary, brings such provisions as are necessary for his own use during his stay, and takes his share of the feast away with him when he goes. Our idea of "eat what you can, but pocket none," is exactly reversed, and "pocket what you can, but eat none," is the Solomon Island practice. This custom is necessitated by the "taboo" laws, which are so severe in this group that at a public feast it would be almost impossible to avoid some infringement of these complicated regulations; the difficulty is therefore avoided by the food being taken away and eaten at home. Without attempting any entrance upon so wide a field as the question of tabooing, I may illustrate the sort of complications that arise when the food is eaten on the spot by a single example. If after a meal a visitor should purposely or accidentally retain a morsel of the food, he is enabled thereby to exercise a mysterious influence over the giver of the feast. The host considering himself thus charmed will redeem the lost fragment at as high a figure as he can afford. A piece of betel nut was, at a feast on a neighbouring island, carried away by a guest a few weeks previous to our visit. The chief fell ill, and imagined something was wrong; at length he discovered what had taken place, and, although the man with the piece of betel nut was living far away, upon another island, sent across to him, and redeemed the fragment for forty dog's teeth, which is an equivalent for four thousand coco-nuts!

While doing a brisk trade in ornaments and spears with the rough crowd on shore, I bought a bow and a bundle of arrows from one ill-looking native, for a good-sized knife. He seemed very eager to close the bargain, and I was no less anxious, for both bow and arrows were very fine of their kind. When I handed him the knife, however, he slipped the arrows into my hand and disappeared through the crowd with my bow! One can do nothing on such an occasion, for it is obviously unwise to initiate a disturbance.

ORNAMENT WORN ON FOREHEAD.
Tortoise-shell fretwork upon a shell disc; about ⅔ actual size.

On the other hand, if the natives imagine you can be quite easily cheated, their opinion of you does not remain very high. As a rule, in such cases all trading is stopped until the stolen article is returned, but in this instance, there being so many strangers present, and their whole aspect being so far from reassuring, we deemed discretion the better part of valour.

I have said nothing of the spears used by the natives of the Solomon Islands. They are certainly the finest weapons in the South Seas, and I secured one that was as much as sixteen feet long, a single black shaft, highly polished and ornamented at the "business end" with an elaboration of human bone and coloured fancy binding, that defies all description. The spears more usually carried are about ten feet long, and also made of black polished wood, and tipped with human bone. There are, near the extremity of these weapons, ten or a dozen barbs resembling the tip of the spear, which are fastened to the shaft by a binding of coloured canework, the whole being held together and strengthened with the same resinous substance as used in canoe-building. The price of such spears as the ones I have last mentioned is from one stick to a stick and a half of tobacco, equivalent to about three-halfpence.

Leaving these people to their evening feast, and let us hope there was to be nothing on the "menu" worse than pigs' flesh and yams, we sailed down the so called Indispensable Strait to the little group of islands known as the Floridas.

Indispensable Strait lies between the two long and mountainous islands of Malanta and Guadalcanar. The Floridas close it at the north-west, and the island of San Christoval at the south-east end. It is accordingly almost land-locked, and about a hundred and fifty miles long by forty broad. The mountains of Guadalcanar are as much as eight thousand feet high, and of exceedingly picturesque outline. Whilst sailing amongst the islets of the little Florida group we did experience the typical and usually-accepted enjoyments of South Sea Island cruising. The weather was, at least for a day or two, almost perfect—the sea blue, the islands green, the waves upon the reefs like snowy foam. Behind this foreground were the great purple mountain-peaks of Guadalcanar, curiously fascinating to us on account of their never having been visited by white man or black. The poor superstitious natives report the existence of hairy men and giant crocodiles, and I know not what terrors beside, but even the so-called hill tribes have not probably explored beyond the more accessible passes, and there is every reason to believe the higher country is quite uninhabited. Between the mountains and the sea on Guadalcanar is some fine-looking flat country which resembles in appearance that of the Rewa district in Fiji, and will doubtless some day grow sugar and cotton for the markets of Europe.

We went ashore to shoot pigeons one day upon a little uninhabited island in the Straits. It was well wooded and very beautiful. Remains of huts were found upon the shore as though some fishing parties had temporarily lived there. I also found a native oven of smooth round stones, and by it a human skull and a few loose bones: the story of that poor creature's death needs no telling.

The Florida group, lying at the upper end of this Indispensable Strait, is but little known, and is set down on the Admiralty charts with the wildest inaccuracy. We slept ashore one night at Gaeta upon the most southern island of the little archipelago. The place had been literally rescued from heathenism by Mr. Penny of the Melanesian Mission within the last two years. The village at which we stopped was a few miles from the shore and in a high and picturesque situation: we struggled up to it along the swampy forest path, escorted by twenty or thirty natives, on a beautiful and quiet evening in August. Near the village, through a steep ravine, ran a fairly broad stream, in which we had a pleasant bathe—no ordinary luxury in these South Sea Islands. The houses in this district are mostly of the kind known as "platform houses"; they are, that is to say,

PLATFORM-HOUSES, SOLOMON ISLANDS.

elevated some four feet from the ground, and have a balcony in front upon which one can sit and enjoy the fresh air and lovely view to one's heart's content. I enjoyed my evening here more than any other during my cruise. The natives were kind and cheerful, we were all in good spirits, and the air was cool and even invigorating. Whilst I sat upon the balcony the bishop held a service in the house, and gave, through an interpreter, a short address. I suppose there were over fifty natives crowded into the little room, and a curious congregation indeed they were. Old white-haired warriors with strange thoughts, doubtless, concerning these new times, so different from the days of their youth and manhood; scraggy old hags with shrunken breasts and careworn look crouching in corners with grim attention; finely-made, healthful Florida beauties with bright eyes and clever faces; upon their arms some, doubtless to them, coquettish ornament, and round their waists an ample fringe, which stood out in a droll manner like a ballet-girl's skirt. Young lusty warriors, too, in the prime of their youth, who laid their bows and spears outside the door, and listened quietly to the strange news the mighty white men had to tell. Lastly, and these in greatest numbers, stowed away amongst the rest and covering the matted floor so thickly as not to leave a foot of space, the invariable, quaint, old-fashioned little boys and girls—always the same, their bullet heads so loosely fixed on, their long thin limbs, their bright and gleaming eyes, their funny, playful ways, so pretty, and yet one cannot help feeling, so painfully monkey-like. Negro or Indian or Arab or Malay, how alike they are—as everywhere, so too not a whit different, here in Melanesia. I sat outside listening to the little songs they sang, and watching the fireflies flitting to and fro among the trees, and the great sago palms looming weirdly overhead, and the dark hill beyond above which the evening star was setting—nothing could have been more quiet, solemn, peaceful.

This house, in which we slept, has an uncomfortable notoriety, which I confess during the night dispelled much of the romance of our situation. It is the resort, from time to time, of divers predatory centipedes, which in this island are conspicuous for both ferocity and appetite. I believe their bite is not fatal, but it is sufficiently serious to make even the natives as frightened of them as of alligators. "Always there is a black spot in our sunshine"—in these tropic climes snakes, alligators, mosquitoes, sharks, centipedes! truly Nature gives us no rose without its thorn; for my part centipedes were simply feeding on me the night through, and the few occasions when we had a scare and lit a candle were the only moments of relief!*

Savo is a pretty island of this group, and we called there upon two occasions. I had looked forward to this place with great interest as the chief had been on board with us ever since leaving Norfolk Island.

This Lord of Savo, as an Eastern dragoman would say (*vide* Kinglake), this Scorner of the Solomons and Suppressor of Florida, had quitted his government, and left his enemies to breathe for a moment, and had crossed the waters in the strict disguise of a shirt and pair of trousers, with a small but eternally faithful retinue of followers, in order that he might look upon the overpowering magnificence of the Melanesian Mission headquarters! He was a friendly and good-natured old fellow, and we had spent many hours together trying to exchange ideas in the usual pantomimic manner. I had, moreover, corrupted him by countless

---

* Eight weeks after our visit to Gaeta the terrible massacre of Lieutenant-Commander Bower, of H.M.S. *Sandfly*, and four seamen, occurred. The actual site of the attack was a small uninhabited island, off which our vessel lay during the inland excursion described above. It is somewhat remarkable that this place, where we were so cordially welcomed, and where I spent my only night on shore during the entire cruise, should in such a short time become so fatally notorious. Some further particulars and comments upon this massacre will be found in the following chapter.

donations of tobacco and other treasures, in return for which I was given to understand that when I set foot upon the land of his inheritance I should be overwhelmed by hospitality and curiosities. How was my faith in the nobility of the savage chief overthrown when, at the end of my second visit, I became aware that the only return I had received for my generosity consisted in a well-rifled bunch of very inferior bananas! I even found myself bargaining hotly with one of this nobleman's retinue for a spear just as we were leaving, and in desperation, by the assistance of an interpreter, pleaded that he, the chief, would intercede on my behalf. He was equal to the occasion. "It's not *my* spear," he cried with feeling; "if it were mine I'd give it you, I could'nt *sell* you anything. It belongs to the people on shore!" I left Savo with an entirely new opinion concerning the nobility of Melanesian chieftains!

There was nothing of special interest in the other places we visited in the Floridas. Here was a fine harbour; here the *Dancing Wave* was cut out several years ago; here a man-of-war punished the natives for some atrocity or other. Such were the distinguishing marks of most of our places of call. After a few days cruising in and out amongst the intricacies of the group we steered northwards once more and were shortly at anchor in the very beautiful harbour of Santa Ysabel de la Estrella, as Mendaña called it three hundred years ago. Here is a pretty little anchorage within a great gulf, known on some charts as "Thousand Ships Bay." The native name of the district is Bugotu, and, it being the Ultima Thule of our cruise, we lay here several days.

The curse of the northern Solomon Islands is an institution known as "head-hunting" The more savage tribes make collections of heads with which to adorn their houses, and are as assiduous in their search for these articles of vertu as any collector in Europe is for old china. The mere acquisition of such old heads among their own people as may turn up in the natural course of things, does not satisfy these zealous hunters. They go far afield for their highly-prized ornaments, and organise extensive expeditions, sweeping down on weaker tribes and carrying off all they can seize. The southern end of the island of Ysabel is a favourite hunting-ground for the more northern tribes, who come down in great force, bringing large canoes full of warriors from the islands of Choiseul and New Georgia. The more peaceful southerners make no attempt at resistance, but have built themselves strongholds into which they retire and, if possible, defy their enemies. These places of refuge are of two kinds—tree-houses and hill-fortifications. The tree-houses possess the greatest interest, and in some parts of the island are quite numerous and even used as ordinary places of residence in times of peace. The people attain almost the agility of monkeys by continually climbing up and down these trees and walking along their branches.

At the village near which we first anchored there was but one tree-house; but it was very good of its kind. The tree in which it was built, was a magnificent one growing upon the cliff by the shore; all the lower branches were cleared away, and its peculiar appearance made it most conspicuous amongst the surrounding palms and smaller growth. There was a cleared space around the foot of this giant, and from the branches hung a slender rattan cane ladder. The ascent is certainly not a very enjoyable affair, the ladder seems of the very weakest, and swings about unpleasantly; the rounds, moreover, are merely bits of stick lashed on to the cane rope, and afford practically no foothold to the booted European. On reaching the top I was surprised to find a large well-built house, quite level, and fixed in among

TREE-HOUSE, YSABEL, SOLOMON ISLANDS.

the branches with the greatest ingenuity. The floor is covered with mats and scrupulously clean. It is twenty-six feet long by eighteen wide, and the ridge pole is ten feet from the floor. The strength and solidity of the whole structure is most remarkable, and I suppose at a pinch nearly all the inhabitants of the village might find refuge here. At either end of this house are pleasant balconies, one of which seemed literally to overhang the sea which lay more than a hundred feet beneath. The height of the house from the ground is between seventy and eighty feet. Arrayed along the sides are numbers of small heaps of stones for defensive purposes. When a raid by the head-hunters is reported, the people all retire to this curious fortress, and drawing the thin ladder up after them can defy their enemies. If the invaders come near to try and cut down the tree (no light work, for the trunk is hard as iron), the besieged party pelt them with stones from above, and unless the enemy were armed with rifles I should say these tree-fortresses were quite impregnable. Other fortresses there are upon this island, as I have said, and these are but little less curious; they are perched upon bold rocky peaks, and the approaches are in some cases cut off by the construction of large dykes or fosses, upon which a most surprising amount of labour must at one time have been expended.

I enjoyed the few days we spent amongst these people immensely; they are certainly ingenious in their various arts. The houses are quite models of workmanship, neat, prim, and clean, and are all of the "platform" kind which in so damp a climate is almost a necessity.

Some of the canoes belonging to the village were more magnificent than any I have seen, one in particular being simply covered with shells and decorations of all sorts; they are kept more for show than use, however, and are the pride of the chief and the envy of all visitors. I do not think the people here are at all industrious, for they possess but few weapons and make native cloth only in small quantities;

their yam plantations are by no means admirable, and their chief delight seems to be in sitting on their hams upon the

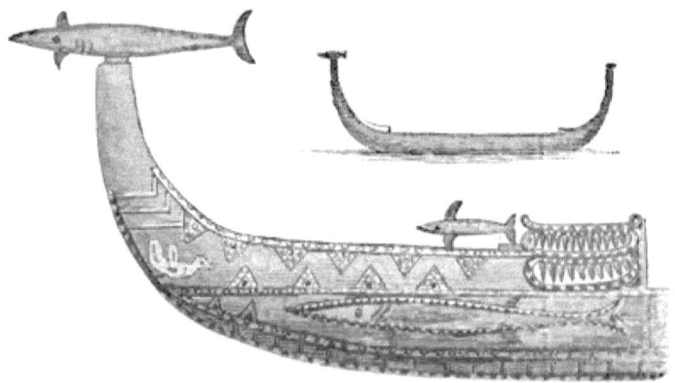

SOLOMON ISLAND STATE CANOE.

shore, with their shields and tomahawks beside them, gazing vacantly into space.

Traders call frequently, and almost every man has an axe mounted upon a black wood handle of his own manufacture. The name of this weapon is "mattiana" which signifies "his death," and the possession of one is every young Bugotu man's ambition. In the evenings the more enterprising men will do a little fishing, perching themselves upon high tripods which are erected on shallow patches near the shore, and working a large net between four of them. The island abounds in cockatoos, toucans, and both green and scarlet parrots. Whilst bathing in the little stream one morning, the cockatoos became so enraged at our intrusion, and withal so curious to know more of who or what we were, that they assembled round us in scores, screaming with anger, and we could have knocked them down with sticks; it was a most amusing experience.

The money used in the Solomon Islands is interesting, and

I am tempted to give a rather detailed account of it. The general currency, consisting of strings of shell beads about the size of a shirt button, very well made, and strung in fathom lengths, is of two kinds, known as red money and white money. Above this in the scale of value, come dog's teeth, which are the gold of this coinage. Only two teeth from a dog's jaw can be used as legal tender, and their value is very considerable as will be seen from the table I give below. A hole is drilled in each tooth, and when a man has a sufficient number, he sets them on a band of suitable width and wears them as a collar; I have seen a collar of this kind which would be worth perhaps not less than £20 of our money. Porpoise teeth are also used, but are only one fifth as valuable as dog's teeth. One other coin obtains which seems to be a ring of *marble:* it is worn upon the chest, and is looked upon as a charm as well as a legitimate coin. The value of these different moneys varies but little throughout the group, and may be roughly estimated as follows :—

10 coco-nuts	= 1 string of white money, or 1 flat stick of tobacco
10 strings white money	= 1 string red money, or 1 dog's tooth
10 strings red money	= 1 "isa," or 50 porpoise teeth
10 isas	= 1 good-quality wife
1 "bakiha" (marble ring)	= 1 head among the head-hunters
1 bakiha	= 1 very good pig
1 bakiha	= 1 medium young man

From this table it will be seen that a wife such as would be considered a suitable match for any rising young islander is worth about ten thousand coco-nuts. This price is of course a very variable one, depending however far more upon the social position of the father, than upon the good looks or qualities of the girl herself.

The customs in connection with marriages possess some

thing of interest. When a man proposes for the hand of a girl he strikes a bargain with the father, who of course rates his property as highly as possible—say at ten thousand coco-nuts. This the wild aspirant is perhaps unable to pay; but he goes round to his friends and in consideration of so much work to be done when required, succeeds in borrowing from them the necessary sum. The girl is then engaged, and an indefinite time elapses before things are brought to a conclusion. At the marriage a feast is given, and the relatives and friends who advanced money to the bridegroom are of course asked. To these presents are made in proportion to the magnitude of the loans. For instance uncle A., who gave two white strings, gets fifty yams. Friend C., who gave some dogs' teeth, gets a pig, and so on, the amount thus returned being about fifty per cent. of the original donation.

Not an unnatural consequence of this custom arises, and that is, the men who put too high a value upon their daughters do not get them married.

Takua, a great Florida chief, has three daughters, all unmarried. One rash wight last year did propose for the youngest, but discovered that her price was sixty thousand coco-nuts! The man struggled to raise the sum, but failed. Then the chief Takua rose up in his wrath and fined him a thousand coco-nuts, for daring to propose when he had not the necessary wealth. The poor fellow employed a professional pleader to try and obtain a reversion of this sentence, but he lost his case and has been a disgraced man ever since.

These Solomon Island beauties are by no means to be thought lightly of; they are short but well-made girls with pretty hands and feet. Their faces are covered with a very delicate tattooing, which is colourless, and only visible when seen quite closely. The process, an important event in every girl's life, is somewhat thus: A number of people are hired (for a porpoise tooth apiece) to sing and howl for a whole night round the girl's house, thus keeping her from sleep. The next day the artist arrives—his pay is high, often many thousands of coco-nuts (or of course their equivalent), and the operation is proceeded with. A pattern is carved all over the face, and consists of a number of sets of concentric circles or polygons, the outer ones of which are about the size of a sixpence; the entire design resembles cells of a honeycomb. When the operation is completed, the girl, overtired from pain and want of sleep, is left to rest for many hours, at the end of which time the smarting will have considerably diminished.

After a few comparatively uneventful calls at various points on the islands of Malanta and San Christoval, we started away from the Solomon's, laying a southeastern course towards the Torres' Islands. For *thirteen* miserable days we beat against a strong south-east trade-wind, making in all that time only 360 miles, and experiencing terrific squalls at the rate sometimes of thirty or forty a day. Any one who wants to know how uncomfortable a sailing vessel can be, should try a fortnight's beating under double-reefed topsails against fresh gales in a hundred-ton vessel. At times the motion for hours together was so violent that we could neither sit nor lie without holding on. Before we started upon our actual course from the one group of islands to the other we had had bad weather, and it lasted until we were down to the south of the New Hebrides, so

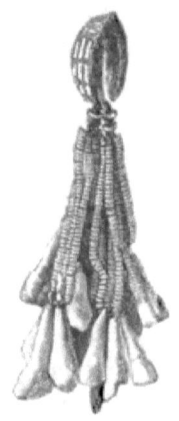

EAR PENDANT.
Inlaid black wood, native bead-work, and human teeth.

that in reality our ill-fortune in the matter of wind and waves continued for fully a month. During that time we had no relief for even so much as a few consecutive hours. Twice we were obliged to lay to; the ship the whole time was drenched from stem to stern; everything below was damp and mouldy; the crew were sick, the natives were sick, and we ourselves were bilious and cross. It was now almost three months since we had tasted fresh meat, or other vegetables than yams, and even bread was almost an unknown luxury; we felt that we had some right therefore to grumble at this additional burden of adverse weather. I must not, however, forget to add that our little vessel behaved through it all most admirably. I felt there was no limit to her endurance; we had only to trim two little sails and lash the wheel and there she would have ridden for a month if need had been. Whilst struggling to reach the Torres' Islands, it is true that our forestay was disabled, but it only necessitated some six or seven hours' delay, and I may here state as a somewhat wonderful fact, and certainly an encouraging one to timid landsmen, that although I have travelled by sea a distance of over a hundred thousand miles, this seven hours' halt for repairs upon the little sailing vessel *Southern Cross* was the longest detention on account of a mishap, that I have experienced.

At the end of the fourth week of head winds we obtained a slant from the eastward, and so, having held on for as much as two hundred and fifty miles out of our course, in hope of such a change, we were at last able to bear down without any further tacking to the Loyalty Islands.

CHAPTER XIV.

NEW CALEDONIA AND THE LOYALTY ISLANDS.

"Or see the white town flush with dying day,
And the red mountain fire the glimmering bay."—*L. Morris.*

On the tenth of September I was put down on Nengone in the Loyalty group, and the *Southern Cross* proceeded on her way south to Norfolk Island. I felt more sorry than I had thought possible, to leave the little vessel on which I had spent three months, seeing so much that was new and strange. I had made many friends amongst our native passengers, who, notwithstanding the barbarity of their early surroundings, were in the main a good-hearted, merry lot. From this island I hoped to find some means of crossing to Noumea in New Caledonia, from which port a steamer runs fortnightly to Sydney. Mr. and Mrs. Jones of the London Missionary Society received me with great kindness, and made me much at home during the few days I spent with them. They were quiet, restful days, after cruising for so long in the little Mission vessel during, for the most part, not too peaceful weather. Mr. Jones has a large house, and all the surroundings and conveniences such as one sees on an Australian station; he has been on the island now for twenty-five years, and I may add is one of the most popular, alike among missionaries, traders and adventurers, of all the white men in the South Seas.

There had been a "war" on the island since we called on

our way north, and the excitement consequent upon this state of things was as intense as it was natural. The decisive battle was fought only a few days before I landed, and twenty-one persons were killed, eleven of whom, however, I am afraid, were children! It was a battle of revenge for injuries received by the Protestants at the hands of their Roman Catholic neighbours.

The French took possession of this island more or less formally in 1866, their hold upon it previous to that being merely nominal. Shortly after the introduction of a Resident, certain Roman Catholic priests were sent to convert the natives, and these, I need hardly add, did not co-operate very amicably with the Protestant missionary. From that time, indeed, to this, a feeling of hostility has existed between the Romanist converts and the Protestants. On several occasions outbreaks have occurred, one, indeed, resulting in the removal of the Roman Catholics and their entire flock to the Isle of Pines.

The feeling is now hostile beyond all mending. How strange it seems that a people, but now rescued from cannibalism (it is not ten years ago that a boy was eaten at this very village where I stayed), with hardly a conception of Christ other than that instead of being a great warrior chief he was the Prince of Peace, should have their very worst passions aroused in a religous contest! The whole island is torn up with the passion of this quarrel. It burns in their breasts as no heathen feud has ever burned. It cannot be laid aside. The very boys and children are interested, and their hatred of the rival creed knows no limit. This state of things appeared to me the more sad because in all other respects I found here a model community. The people, apart from this disastrous quarrel, seem more benefited by missionary work than any I have seen. Their enthusiasm in religious matters is most remarkable. They have built themselves a large and handsome church, they buy dresses and European costumes, in which, however, they look entirely hideous, as all savages in civilised habiliments do. They give five or six hundred a year to their missionary society and are in very many respects models of generosity and religious zeal. Through all the South Seas, moreover, no men are more noted for bravery than those of this group, so that if there is any reckless expedition or voyage of discovery on hand, the promoter always endeavours to obtain a Loyalty Island crew. I cannot say that I think the French rule here other than pernicious—their policy being one of interference and aggression; seeing that the natives are quiet and well-behaved enough, the motto of their political governors should be " Ça ira "; instead of which the authorities take the exactly opposite course, and are continually meddling where interference is inexpedient and even fatal. These people have their own hereditary chiefs and native customs, but the French come in, set up other chiefs of their own creation, and make laws that violate the traditional habits of the islanders. The result, as can only be expected, is continual ill-feeling, insubordination and even rebellion.*

I spent five very pleasant days with Mr. Jones, the missionary, and found his people were models of kindness and

---

* The French are here most cordially hated by the natives; they are not even admitted to be white men. Such conversation as this I have held with the more educated, who speak a little English:—

" What feller that boat belong? He belong white man?"

" No, he no belong white man."

" What feller he belong then?"

"Oh, he belong oui-oui-man."

" Well, then, he belong *white* man?"

"Oh, no; oui-oui-man no belong white man; oui-oui-man belong all same devil." (I need hardly say "oui-oui-man" is sandalwood English for Frenchman.)

good manners. He had brought up the men to many useful trades, so that one could build, another do joinery, a third make boats. The women were no less useful, waiting neatly and well at table, keeping the house clean and in good order, milking the cows, making butter, cooking and the like.

There are two traders on the island, who collect from the natives such fungus, copra, &c., as they may have, and give them in exchange tobacco, calicoes, and so on. One of these men had built himself a small cutter of about six tons burden, in which I arranged to go to Noumea. I rode across the island to the bay where we had landed from the *Southern Cross* some months before, and embarked on my tiny vessel at sunset on a lovely evening. We had three natives to help in working the little cutter, the owner and myself occupying the toy cabin aft. There was a heavy sea in the passage between the Loyalty group and New Caledonia, but not much wind; the result was we knocked about in a manner that was positively awful. When daylight broke in the morning we were out of sight of land, and in a very unsatisfactory position. For the greater part of the day we tossed listlessly about on the open sea, but a wind springing up in the afternoon, we made the high land, and steered up towards the entrance known as Havannah Passage. The tide running through this pass was very strong, and as it met the easterly wind, formed a curious sea resembling a whirlpool to which I remember having seen nothing similar, unless it were the Niagara river below the falls. To steer in between this curiously-broken water and the raging breakers on the reef required no small amount of skill, and once or twice it seemed as though one of the great waves would surely break on the weather side of us, in which case our little cutter would have fared indifferently well, I fear!

The reefs of New Caledonia, like those of Fiji, are very extensive, and run out many miles from the shore, forming beautiful lagoons, inside which even large steamers may sail, but also constituting a considerable source of danger in these seas where the charts are far from accurate.

We ran for fifty miles round the south-east end of New Caledonia amongst small islands, and under great headlands that reminded me of the coast of Greece; it was a lovely sail in the bright light of the full moon, and although the mountains were gaunt and barren in reality, their appearance that night was very beautiful.

New Caledonia is the largest of the so-called South Sea Islands, being, independent of the Isle of Pines and outlying reefs, as much as two hundred and thirty miles long and between thirty and forty broad. A range of mountains runs along the entire length of the island, leaving but a narrow margin of useful land on each side. This will always prove a great hindrance to any opening up or extensive development of the country. Internal communication will be but indifferent for many years to come, and it may be doubted if the island will ever become of great value, unless its mineral resources turn out to be what some sanguine New Caledonians predict. It has most certainly the appearance of a mineral country. There are indications of iron upon every hillside, the mountains presenting much brilliant colouring. We passed close under Mont d'Or, a very fine headland, supposedly rich in nickel and other metals, but whose title is a misnomer. Late at night we pulled into Noumea harbour; the wind had entirely dropped, the moon was full, and the water like a mirror as we rowed slowly in through the shipping.

I had expected to find the mail steamer from Sydney lying in Noumea, as her day of sailing was the following one. Passing under the stern of a small schooner, I accordingly shouted to a native who was leaning against the bulwarks, "Steamer, he no come?"

"No," was his answer; "steamer he no come—steamer he stop on a stone—all man he go saltwater—plenty man he die—steamer he finish."

This was serious news indeed, and it seemed true enough, for we found the French man-of-war getting up steam, and making all haste to start in search of the missing packet.

I went to bed at once, being tired out, and determined to leave the question of the steamer's non-appearance until the morrow. The alarm proved a false one, as appeared the next day, the vessel's departure from Sydney having been delayed forty-eight hours by the San Francisco mail, with which this one runs in connection.

Noumea, capital of New Caledonia and its dependencies, is a hot, dusty, squarely-planned town; the streets, broad, and straight, and shadeless; the houses, low and wooden, with corrugated iron roofs. Billiard saloons and drinking bars seem more general than shops, and billiard playing and drinking seem more popular pursuits than working. There are no trees in the streets; there is nothing pleasant to look upon wherever you may turn. There is nothing Frenchlike beyond the long thin lettering of the shop-signs; I do not speak of the people, I speak merely of Noumea. It is twin sister to Port Said, than which I suppose one could say nothing less flattering.

Noumea, blinking in the sunlight—Noumea, sunburnt, scorched, dried up—great heaven, what a place for light-hearted Frenchmen to come to! And yet they are here, surely enough. At the bars drinking syrups, and in the saloons playing billiards, and at their little shop doors, here they indeed are, with low-cut waistcoats, and narrow black ties, and sallow, moustachioed faces. The women too, tripping up the street or sitting in their shops, are no less unmistakable, so daintily shod, so neatly dressed, with such good figures and bewitching airs. They all seemed out of place though, men and women too, with their bowing and shoulder-shrugging and hat-raising, and energetic conversing; the tropical sun and the shadeless, long, unlovely streets seemed unsuited to them.

Busy English merchants are to be seen also in Noumea in fair numbers, and lazy sea captains such as are never seen on shore more than a mile away from wharfs and landings, and who have about them a general feeling (in the sense in which a modern upholsterer talks about a cabinet with a Chippendale "feeling") of oakum and Stockholm tar. More noticeable, however, than any other class of people, are the convicts who are to be seen in considerable numbers everywhere. These that walk freely about the streets are "libérés," or as we should call them "ticket-of-leave men." Others, also at liberty in the streets, are exiles serving a term of banishment. Here are even stately Arabs in fez and turban and long white skirts—political offenders from Algiers. Lastly, I must notice the gangs of hard-labour convicts passing through the streets to their work with armed escort.

There are now about eight thousand prisoners in New Caledonia, the great majority of whom are quartered on the island of Nou which lies within the harbour, and upon which are large prisons, barracks, workshops, &c., &c. One or two smaller prison stations are situated on the main island, but these are of but little importance compared with the establishment at Nou. A ticket-of-leave system is in force, land being given in a way which I find rather obscurely described as "conditionellement et dans une proportion raisonnable." These libérés now amount to about two thousand; they form small settlements amongst themselves, and mix but little with the immigrants.

To free settlers this French colony does not apparently present any attraction, some few hundreds, at an outside estimate, constituting the annual immigration from France. The fact is, New Caledonia has not succeeded in becoming much more than a penal settlement. All the people in Noumea are government people; all the talk is of appointments and promotion, and of prospects of being removed to Réunion, or to Saigon. Frenchmen in New Caledonia do not ever look upon the place as a home, they do not even look upon it as an adopted home. The spirit here is similar to that of the military community at Aden, or some similar station. Whether or not it was owing to my recent visits to Australia and New Zealand, and the consequent strength of contrast, I do not know, but when in New Caledonia I felt more than ever the truth of the assertion that Frenchmen will never make good colonists.

I had a long and interesting drive one afternoon in the country. The roads are magnificent, being the result of convict labour. Passing the outskirts of the little town (Noumea has only three thousand inhabitants), where are barracks and "departments" without end, and villas that are not pretty or attractive, but *mean* in appearance, we get out into the country, or, as all English-speaking people call it, the "bush." They may well call it bush, for what do I see? surely not—yet—yes it *is*, the old universal, everlasting, omnipresent, never-green gum, the same stunted, white-barked, shaggy, gnarled, ugly eucalyptus that one sees everywhere in Australia, from Cape York to King George's Sound. This New Caledonia, then, belongs evidently to the Australian continent, and not to the South Sea Islands.

The immediate country is as like that around Adelaide as anything could well be, but the high, finely-shaped mountains, they have not on the Australian mainland. We passed a few native houses with foolscap-like roofs, reaching to a

NATIVE HOUSE, NEW CALEDONIA.

great height; there are not many natives round Noumea, however, as since the late insurrection they have been driven far back into the mountain districts. It is supposed that there are still between twenty and thirty thousand in New Caledonia, but that they have decreased over fifty per cent. during the last half century. The only thing of special interest that occurs to me in connection with them is that they adopt the same extraordinary costume, if one can call it so, as that worn by some of the tribes of South Africa.

It was cool and pleasant as we rattled back through the now almost deserted streets; but more pleasant still was it when, an hour or so afterwards, I found myself—after a more than three months' entire ignorance of such things—seated at a prettily set table with ladies passably fair and gentlemen presumably brave, discussing dinner in a cool, open room, whilst native servants glided noiselessly about—everything so comfortable, so pleasant, so luxurious!

The business of Noumea is practically all in English hands. The shipping, although obliged to sail under French colours, is also English. The steamers on the coast are English. The mail contract with Sydney (£6000 a year) is with an English company. What is French is only the administration, the red tapeism, and the management of the convicts.

I was sorry not to be able to see the northern part of the island, which indeed would justify more eulogies than I am able to pass upon the Noumea district. It is no doubt a rich country in places, and capable of growing sugar to some extent, although I firmly believe the mineral interest is the only one to which one can reasonably look for any great amount of success. I sailed for Sydney on a Sunday morning, the whole settlement, consisting of not an inconsiderable number of well-dressed ladies, and perhaps a hundred idle lookers-on, assembling upon the quay to see the steamer away. We were two hours steaming across the wide lagoon, then passed the light-house and out through the reef. It is perhaps the last South Sea Island reef I shall ever see, and I watched it with great interest, stretching away as far as eye could reach to right and left. The old, now so familiar sound, the well-known, ever-beautiful, tumbling, snowy surf—I was quite sorry to see the last of it.

CHAPTER XV.

LABOUR AND TRADE IN THE SOUTH PACIFIC.

... "En sorte que partout òu on reconnaît la civilisation et les faits qui l'ont enrichie, on est tenté d'oublier le prix qu'il en a coûté."—*Guizot.*

OF the labour traffic carried on so largely between the islands and Queensland, Fiji and New Caledonia, I may perhaps say a few words now. I do not wish to make invidious comparisons between these three centres of labour importation. I will merely say that in my own opinion the abuses are greatest in New Caledonia, for the reason that the French Government has not taken even so much as the insignificant interest in the subject that our own authorities have indulged in. The labour trade is in a bad state everywhere, whether under French flag or English, and what is said here on the subject applies equally to all the colonies to which natives are taken. The question is a very difficult one to approach, chiefly because the moment any one attempts to point to the abuses that take place, he is put down as belonging to the sentimental and so-called "Exeter Hall" party, with whom truly one cannot have much patience. For my own part, I believe that we, as a civilised nation have no right to hire native men until we have first made them clearly understand what our terms of engagement are. At present the labour trade is merely a disguised slave trade. It is said the islanders are paid. Yes, but what does the pay amount to? Even if the "trade" given as wages were honest stuff, it would be no payment to them. They give it all away as soon as they land at their homes, and have not, nor can possibly have, any conceivable use for it. I have myself seen quite new corduroy trousers, the value of which must have been nearly a sovereign, sold back to white men for a few pence worth of tobacco. I have seen flannel shirts, boots, hats and such things sold for a few knives or beads. What, in the name of fortune, do these poor creatures want with trousers and shirts? I admit that if a man, knowing where he is going and what his work is to be, want some harmless article of European manufacture, there may be some excuse for letting him work for it, but I fail to see what excuse we can give for allowing ignorant captains and so-called "government agents," who know no word of the people's language, to go wherever they please and entice the natives on board their ships with red cloth or tobacco, and then carry them off to countries of which they know absolutely nothing. As to the much talked-of three years' term, after which they are taken back to their homes, it is hardly necessary to point out that the natives have no more idea of what we mean by three years than a child in the nursery.

The whole labour trade system, therefore, I believe to be distinctly wrong as at present carried out, and very probably wrong however it were to be carried out, for we take the strongest men away from their homes at the best period of their lives, and as a rule we return them again demoralised and diseased, so that the whole social organisation of the native tribes is corrupted, and their numerical strength most alarmingly diminished.

The condition of the trade carried on in these seas in such articles as copra, bêche de mer, vegetable ivory,

&c., &c., is no less unsatisfactory. There are, no doubt, some honest traders and respectable captains engaged in this business, but there are also, it must be confessed, some of the biggest scoundrels in creation. These fellows no less than the labour trade people want carefully watching or their conduct is certain to produce trouble. Our men-of-war have hitherto spent a great deal too much time in the harbours of Sydney, Melbourne and Hobart Town, and when they have gone down to the islands, it has, since Commodore Goodenough's time, been the custom merely to visit a few well-known places, and then return to some civilised settlement. There has, indeed, been practically no surveying done in this quarter of the Pacific for a long time, and to this day even the general bearings of a great part of many of the groups are not so much as approximately known. The charts are all antiquated and faultful, and I am certain that in very many places the French navigators of the last century were as well off in the matter of sailing directions as we are to-day.

It is satisfactory to know that Her Majesty's ships have been ordered to visit the islands more frequently than in the past, and to check as much as possible all acts of violence whether committed by white man or black. This order was given none too soon, the cause of its issue being the news of a more serious massacre than any that has occurred since the attack upon Commodore Goodenough at Santa Cruz in 1875. The catastrophe to which I refer is the murder of Lieutenant-Commander Bower of H. M. schooner *Sandfly* and four seamen, who were killed in the Florida group in October 1880, without, apparently, the slightest provocation. The reason for this attack is in my judgment, however, simple enough. The natives have begun to disbelieve in the English war vessels; to quote the words of a native called Hailey,* chief of Coolangbangara, in the Solomon Islands. "White man allsame woman, he no savee fight, suppose woman plenty cross she make plenty noise, suppose man-of-war he come fight me, he make plenty noise, but he all same woman—he no savee fight." This is their feeling. They see traders not unfrequently and labour ships pretty often, and they are told of the mighty vessels we possess which will destroy them all if they misbehave themselves. Many of them, however, have never seen these vessels at all, and at last believe the whole story to be a fabrication.

The murder of Lieutenant Bower is a terribly pertinent example of the state of things now existing in these seas. It happened, not at some place like Santa Cruz, where white people are unknown, and the temerity of ignorance might be expected, but amongst islanders who were comparatively well informed concerning Englishmen and their power, but who, at last, had begun to discredit altogether what they had heard about our ability to administer punishment. I have in the last chapter given a short account of the evening I spent at Gaeta. I was a night and part of two days, only a few weeks before the occurrence, in the very place from which these murderers came, and I do not hesitate to say that had this district been visited once or twice in the year by a man-of-war, the natives would have been convinced by actual knowledge of what hitherto they had only learned from hearsay, and would not have dared,

---

* This man, in his message to Captain Ferguson announcing the Esperanza tragedy, from which a quotation is given above, introduces himself as follows—"The Hailey, king belong Coolangbangara, big feller fighting man; me speak you; me kai kai (have eaten) ten one (eleven) feller man belong Esperanza; me take him altogether trade—musket, powder, tobacco, bead, plenty; me take everything; me make big fire, ship he finish."

therefore, to have made such an attack upon a crew of white men. If our men-of-war had been even reasonably active on their island cruises, and had merely hovered about these islands, their presence would have been known by every tribe of natives, and their power by that means felt. Now, we shall doubtless chastise them severely enough,* but no such chastisement would have been needful if these seas had been in any way regularly or thoroughly visited.

This is not the place to enter upon the question of the relative positions of the Commodore of the Australian Station and the High Commissioner of the Western Pacific. I need only say, that nothing could be more unsatisfactory or even disastrous. The attempts that are made to punish the natives for their murderous attacks upon white men have so far been very often either utterly insignificant or alarmingly unjust, and the result is that things are going daily from bad to worse. It is my intention to leave the whole subject with the simple statement, that the existing state of affairs requires the attention of the Imperial Government with as little delay as possible. If my readers care to form an opinion for themselves upon this subject, I would ask them to peruse the following incidents, which have occurred in the islands during the last few years.

* I extract from a Melbourne paper received in August, 1881, the news of the satisfactory punishment of these savages.

"Information has been received from Lieutenant King, commanding H.M. schooner *Renard*, regarding the arrest and punishment of the natives implicated in the murder of Lieutenant Bower and the boat's crew of the *Sandfly*. It seems that Bishop Selwyn has been a valuable auxiliary in the business, which was carried out without bloodshed or acts of hostility, and only by threats of punishment. The Florida chiefs are all in a great fright, and are doing their best to catch the two other men. Bishop Selwyn says they will have them alive or dead soon. The Bishop is living at Florida Island, and apprehends no more trouble there for a long time to come."

January 1875. The brig *James Birney* was taken by natives of an island in the Lord Howe's group. Captain Fletcher, together with eight white men and two coloured men, was killed.

August 1875. The boats of H. M. S. *Pearl* were attacked at Nitendi, the main island of the Santa Cruz group. Commodore Goodenough and two seamen were killed, three others were wounded.

July 1876. The *Lucy and Adelaide* of Brisbane, labour vessel, was attacked at St. Bartholomew, an off-lying island of Espiritu Santo, New Hebrides. Captain Anderson was killed, and the boat's crew all wounded.

February 1877. The schooner *Douglas* was attacked in the Louisiade archipelago. Two white men killed and five wounded.

November 1877. A white trader named Easterbrook was murdered at Sulphur Bay, Tanna, New Hebrides.

1878. The great rising in New Caledonia took place during this year, and over a hundred and fifty white people were killed. Since this occurrence the lives lost in desultory engagements between settlers and natives have been too numerous to mention.

April 1878. The schooner *Mystery* lost a boat and crew at Opa, or Leper's Island, New Hebrides. The government agent and four natives were killed.

May 1878. A white trader named Halgett was murdered at San Christoval in the Solomon Islands.

June 1878. A white trader named Morrow was murdered near Marau Sound, Guadalcanar, Solomon Islands.

September 1878. A boat's crew of the *May Queen* was cut out at Pentecost (Aragh), New Hebrides. The mate and a Tanna sailor were killed.

November 1878. The *William Isler* of Cooktown was

attacked at Brooker Island, Louisiade archipelago. A Mr. Ingram, white crew, two Chinamen, and three natives were killed.

As many as six parties of shipwrecked sailors are reported to have been murdered in this group alone.

November 1878. A white trader named Provost was murdered at Langa, an off-lying island of Guadalcanar, Solomon group. Three natives were killed with him.

July 1879. A boat's crew of the *Agnes Donald* was cut out at Pentecost (Aragh), New Hebrides. The mate and native boat's crew were murdered.

March 1880. A white trader named Johnston was murdered at Opa (Leper's Island), New Hebrides.

May 1880. The schooner *Esperanza*, of Sydney, was attacked off New Georgia in the Solomon group. Captain Mackintosh, the mate, a white sailor, and four natives were killed.

July 1880. The schooner *Dauntless*, labour vessel, lost a boat's crew at Api, New Hebrides. Fraser, the mate, and Nicholl, the government agent, were killed.

September 1880. The auxiliary screw vessel *Ripple* was attacked at Bougainville, Solomon Islands. Captain Ferguson and five natives were killed. Two white men seriously wounded.

September 1880. The brigantine *Borealis*, labour vessel, was attacked at Ugi, an off-lying island of San Christoval, Solomon Islands. The crew, consisting of five white men and a Fijian, were killed.

September 1880. The cutter *Idalio* was attacked at Espiritu Santo, New Hebrides. Captain McMillan and part of crew were killed. At the same time one of the boats was cut out, and all but two of its crew were killed.

October 1880. The *Hongkong* attacked at Leveade

Island to the south of New Britain. The crew were overpowered and killed, but the captain escaped.

October 1880. The schooner *Zephyr* attacked at Wonda (? Wango), Solomon Islands. The captain and crew were massacred in native fashion.

October 1880. The *Annie Brooks*, of Cookstown, attacked off Brooker Island, Louisiade archipelago; Captain Foreman and crew of eight whites and three Chinamen killed.

October 1880. A boat's crew of H.M.S. *Sandfly* attacked at a small off-lying island named Mandoliana, near Gaeta, Floridas, Solomon Islands. Lieutenant-Commander Bower, R.N., and four seamen killed.

November 1880. The *Jabberwock* attacked at Tanna, in the New Hebrides; several lives lost.

November 1880. Some boats' crews of the *Prosperity* cut out in the Louisiade archipelago: nine Chinamen killed.

I may also mention the following instances concerning which I have not been able to collect further particulars. The *Pearl* and the *Marion Rennie* were both cut out at Rubiana in the Solomon Islands. The *Dancing Wave* and the *Lavinia* were attacked and taken in the Floridas. Three whalers' boats' crews have been captured by the natives of the Treasury Islands, and four by those of the Lord Howe's group. A Captain Blake was recently killed at Simbo near Rubiana in the Solomon Islands, and a party of French naturalists were massacred at Basilisk Island in the autumn of 1880. Many other disasters have doubtless occurred in these seas during the last six years, but the above are those which have come more immediately under my notice.

As a corresponding subject for reflection I would ask my readers to notice this second list of island tragedies contributed to the Melbourne *Argus* by Mr. Neilson, one of the oldest and most universally respected of South Sea Island missionaries. The following outrages are all the work of white men, and give a very fair idea of the kind of treatment the islanders are receiving from our countrymen in the South Seas. Mr. Neilson writes—

"Allow me to give a few instances of the kind of things that are done in the islands.

"I knew a white man who employed some natives to work for him; in a fit of drunken recklessness he shot one of them dead. He underwent no trial, and received no punishment.

"I knew another white man who called out to some natives who were in his employ to come and assist him quickly in something he was doing. He thought they were not coming quick enough, fired at them, and shattered the foot of one of them, so that he is a cripple for life. The white man was unpunished.

"I knew another white man who had a number of natives labouring under him, whom he used to follow in their work with a large whip, with which he flogged them when they were not giving him satisfaction. After a time this same man had bad sores on his feet, which prevented him from walking. He then got a litter made, on which he was carried round, and from which he flogged the natives.

"I knew a vessel in the labour trade that visited an island. The boat pulled in to the beach, and the sailors in her commenced dragging the women by force into the boat. The natives thereupon attacked the white sailors, killed them, and afterwards ate them. A ship of war went to punish the natives, who explained the state of matters to the captain. He exacted a fine of twenty-five pigs, and as this was not paid, he set fire to the natives' village and destroyed their property.

"I knew of a native on board of a ship who, for a trifling act of insubordination, was tied up to the mast and tortured to death, and no one was punished for it.

"I knew a white man who went ashore on an island, and said that he wanted to purchase a concubine, and offered a musket for one. A young man coveted the musket, dragged his own sister by force to the boat, and sold her into banishment. This white man and his concubine lived for a time close to me. Afterwards he left the island, but before doing so, he sold his concubine to another white man for a case of gin.

"I knew another native woman who was taken by force as the concubine of a low white. At a game of cards she was gambled for, and won by another low white. The poor woman afterwards grew sick, and was not able to work for him, and he murdered her. The white man was not punished.

"The white man who began the labour traffic, and who was, I think, the greatest scoundrel I ever knew, told me that on a great many islands, natives had destroyed their canoes, and went no more on sea voyages, as they were afraid of being kidnapped.

"I knew well a captain in the island trade who used to maintain that natives had no souls, and that it was no more harm to take their lives than to take the life of a dog. On two separate occasions I had considerable difficulty in dissuading captains of British ships of war from attacking natives, who had been guilty of no crime but that of justifiable self-defence against the violence of white men. On both occasions I was happily successful.

"I knew a white man who in a fit of anger shot his native concubine dead. He pretended that his gun had gone off by accident, and was never even brought to trial.

"I knew of a party of eight natives who were taken to work on a plantation; they were so oppressed that at last they stole their master's boat and made their escape. On their way to their own island they were driven by stress of weather to another, where six of them were killed and eaten. The two others were rescued by a missionary at the risk of his own life.

"I knew of a party of eleven natives taken to Fiji, who were so ill-used by their master that they stole a boat and escaped, made their way to the New Hebrides, but did not reach their own island, and, having fallen into the hands of heathens, one was killed, cooked, and eaten every evening until the whole were finished.

"I knew a white man who began a plantation and imported twenty-five natives to work it. He was unable to supply them properly with food, and before they could raise it for themselves, eight out of the twenty-five had perished from famine.

"I knew a white man who forcibly obtruded himself into a piece of land belonging to a native chief, and threatened that if the natives attempted to drive him away he would get a man-of-war to punish them. The natives, being alarmed at this threat, allowed him to remain.

"Attention having been directed to the character of the government agents on the labour vessels, I have to state that I have seen a few of them, and knew pretty intimately two of them. One was a broken-down, unreformed drunkard. The captain of a ship of war said to me, 'I do not know what the Queensland Government mean by appointing a man like that. For a glass of whisky he would sign anything.' The other was a captain who had been engaged in the labour traffic, and who, for irregularities, had been removed from his command. He also was a drunkard, and a man who in addition was extremely reckless in the use of firearms. He was appointed government agent in a Queensland vessel, and on his first voyage in that capacity he was wounded in the leg by a native spear. He died in consequence of his wound. On his death-bed he bitterly repented of his misdeeds, denounced the labour traffic as an abominable one, and wished that his life might be spared that he might expose its iniquities.

"I have known a considerable number of white men who have been killed by the natives while engaged in this trade, and while deploring their sad end, and regretting that they should have been cut down in the midst of their wickedness, I have in sober seriousness to express my decided conviction that most of them were men, the cup of whose iniquity was full, and that they suffered the due reward of their deeds.

"Others again were men who had done no injury to the natives themselves, but upon whom the natives took revenge for the evil deeds of their countrymen, for the principle of national or tribal responsibility is held the whole world over by tribes and nations both savage and civilised.

"I beg, then, in conclusion, to call upon all Christian men, when they hear of massacres and outrages committed upon white men in the South Seas, not hastily to jump to the conclusion that the natives are invariably and chiefly to blame, and to state my firm conviction, as one having had perfect knowledge of this labour traffic from the very beginning, that ten natives have perished from the cruelty of the white man for every white man that has perished at the hands of the natives.

"I have abundance more of similar facts that are at your disposal should you wish for more. In the meantime allow me to subscribe myself—Yours, &c."

PART III.

THE FAR EAST.

"Other men are lenses through which we read our own minds; each man seeks those of different quality from his own, and such as are good of their kind; that is, he seeks other men, and the *otherest*."—*Emerson.*

A WINDY DAY IN JAPAN.

CHAPTER XVI.

THE CHINA PORTS.

"If there is a man who does not work, or a woman who is idle, somebody must suffer cold or hunger in the Empire."—Saying of a Chinese Emperor.

CHINA and Japan constitute the globe trotters' paradise, and Yokohama is as a rule their "Ultima Thule." Travellers merely take *trips* to India and the Nile, but if they continue their journey to China or Japan, they very frequently come home "the other way," and feel to some extent followers of Drake or Cook. When the newly-fledged wanderer first sets his foot on shore at some such place as Penang or Hong Kong, he has some right perhaps to consider himself a traveller. It is at Penang, for instance, that the ever-increasing army of round-the-world tourists first see something of the Far East, and certainly no subsequent feelings are to be compared with those experienced during the first hour ashore at this port. One then realises the meaning of Thackeray's statement, that if a person wants really to appreciate the novelties of France or the East, he should go in a yacht to Calais or Smyrna, land for two hours, and never afterwards go back again.

I landed in the Straits Settlements after a run of twenty-one days from Suez, and I confess that the island of Penang seemed to me an earthly Paradise. I still think it one of the most beautiful places in the East.

We lay two or three days in Penang harbour on our way out to China, and nothing could be more enjoyable after three weeks' unbroken monotony. The programme is always the same at such ports of call as this; we go ashore in great haste as soon as the anchor falls, anxious to lose no time now we are in a country new and strange to us. We call at the office to which our letters of introduction are addressed; when once in the cool back room of such an office, we relapse into gossip and the imbibing of cooling drinks. It then occurs to us that after all there is nothing to see, and that it is better to chat quietly with men whose knowledge of the place is considerable, than to wander about in the streets under an oppressive tropical sun. So the day passes, and in the evening some excursion is arranged, such as to the most delightful baths and beautiful waterfall, or on horseback to the governor's bungalow on the hill. At the waterfall is a little primitive hotel where I have spent more than one delightful evening. Matilda, the maid of this inn, as every Eastern traveller knows, makes curries second to none, and within a stone's throw of the house one can see almost primeval Malayan forest scenery with all its wonders of orchids and sensitive plants, and even monkeys. The vegetation is simply marvellous, the growth being indeed so dense that there is a story of one governor firing dollars from his guns into the jungle to induce the natives to go in and clear the ground in search of them.

The Malays are lithe, active, calfless fellows; but it is difficult to know what they do beyond catching beetles from the trees, or seeking employment as house or stable servants to the Europeans. They engage themselves in neither trade nor profession, and have yielded all but the very simplest occupation, such as I have named, to the Chinese. Chinamen in these settlements are ubiquitous, and, indeed, almost omnipotent. All the European firms use them for clerks and compradors, and all the trades and industries are carried on by them. On the mainland, in the Province of Wellesley, the sugar plantations are supplied almost entirely with Chinese labour, and in the tin mines upon the high lands of Perak, no other workmen are employed.

Singapore is less interesting than Penang; the novelty of everything has slightly worn off when you reach this port, and the place is very ugly and common-place, being merely a European town with Chinese inhabitants. I was surprised to find in Singapore a capital museum and library, and above all, most beautiful public gardens. It was not quite pleasant to find such things existing in the Far East; I felt a sort of dread that they would want me to see a Town Hall, and thought of the colonies and shuddered. It takes away something from one's idea of the Malay peninsula to find these common-places of civilisation; but one is glad enough during subsequent visits that there is comfort and even luxury at the main stations of the Eastern route.

Six or seven days after leaving Singapore we sighted the Gap rock at the entrance to Hong Kong, after some horribly unpleasant weather in the China Sea. Of all weathers I think a combination of high wind and sea and intense heat is the hardest to bear, and this somehow or other seems the normal state of things in these waters.

I had no idea that Hong Kong harbour was so picturesque, and therefore was pleasantly surprised. Steaming in soon after sunrise on a glorious clear morning, the panorama was exquisitely beautiful. We anchored amongst a fleet of steamers and sailing vessels, and were immediately surrounded by some scores, perhaps hundreds, of "sampans." These are handy little boats, made of varnished or well-oiled wood, and looking more like South Kensington models than anything else in the boat way. Over the stern is a small circular bamboo awning, enclosing a cosy apartment in which are generally a few doll-like children. A long steer-oar projects from the stern through a hole in the after part of the house. These are clean and comfortable little habitations after all, and I think are infinitely preferable to the dirty and squalid dwellings of a narrow Chinese street. Some thirty thousand people live in sampans at Hong Kong, and more than double that number at Canton. They are small dwelling-places surely enough for a man with a family, but then we must remember that Chinese children are good beyond the conception of an European. These little people have been for so many generations taught to look upon filial devotion as the primary sentiment of their hearts, that it has now become almost an instinct. There is no parallel amongst other races to the moral relationship which exists in both China and Japan between parents and children, and I cannot help thinking that the peaceable and happy condition of these thousands of tiny floating houses is largely due to that state of things. The children are astonishingly *good* from earliest infancy, and nowhere is this more noticeable than in the house life of the floating population of Chinese cities.

Hong Kong is a place where one can spend a week most pleasantly. It is not very characteristic of China, however, and were it not for the princely hospitality of the English residents one would soon get tired of the little island. A long street runs along the foot of the hill, and in it are some scores of curio shops, which to the newly-arrived European prove most seductive. I cannot say, if I except the store of Ah Feng, the Japanese curiosity merchant, that I look back with much pleasure upon my visits to these emporiums of Chinese art. One learns after a few weeks' experience, that it is not from the bland, English-speaking, prosperous merchant that he makes the most valuable purchases, but rather from little out-of-the-way curio venders in the great Chinese cities, where the white face of the European is but seldom seen. Hong Kong, perhaps even more than Singapore, is an English city in which the serving class is Chinese; it is an enjoyable resting-place, with houses of the finest, and merchants who thoroughly deserve the name of princes, but for views of China proper we must go elsewhere. There is a pretty race-course in a little natural amphitheatre, known as the "Happy Valley," and there are gardens and one or two pleasant drives. I should also mention a suburb, known as Pokefullum, which is worth visiting, lying round on the windward side of the island, where some of the most fortunate residents have cool summer retreats.

My visit was brought to a close somewhat sooner than I had intended by an invitation from a friend in Foochow, asking me to go up to that port, and stay a few weeks previous to and during the great event of the year, the opening of the tea season. This was too good a chance to lose, so I threw over my contemplated visit to Canton for the present, and started away on the first coast steamer, together with a company of tea-merchants and bankers.

On our way northwards we called at two of the leading intermediate ports, namely, Swatow and Amoy. Swatow is the port of the city Chao-chow-foo, far inland in the province of Kwang-tung. It possesses a thoroughly good and useful harbour, but one that is in no way picturesque, resembling indeed, more nearly than any other place I know, the harbour of Aden—the jagged rocks are bare and scorched, and the sun beats down upon both rock and sea most pitilessly.

Upon the smooth cliffs that stand perpendicularly out of the water in many places, are cut out names of some hundreds of Chinese snobs who visited the place centuries ago.

We spent several hours rambling through the narrow and dirty streets of the city. It is very unlike Hong Kong, being quite native and squalid and filthy beyond all redemption. Almost the only thing of interest that we saw was an amusing theatrical performance. The company was of the kind usually termed "strolling," but it was in their method of erecting their stage that the originality lay. A platform was flung across a leading thoroughfare, from the balcony of one house to that of the opposite one, and upon this the entire stage was placed and the play enacted. The audience, which was very large, stood in the street and gazed upwards open-mouthed. The traffic of the street was almost entirely suspended, and as the play would probably take many hours, and perhaps even days to represent, one might have imagined that some inconvenience would be felt, but it appeared not to be so; the greatest good humour prevailed, and passers-by, stopping for an hour or so, contributed their infinitesimal offering, and ultimately went their ways, I presume, edified and refreshed.

The local industries of the place are chiefly the manufactures of pewter-ware of all kinds, and of fans. In the production of these articles a very considerable amount of artistic skill is displayed; the rapid free-hand painting of the fans, and the no less admirable engraving of the pewter pots and boxes, were most astonishing. After a long and tiring day we went on board, and sailed away at sundown.

The entrance to Amoy, our next port of call, is pretty, is even beautiful, but a few miles up the harbour we came upon the same kind of barren and decomposing granite rocks and parched hillsides, as we had seen at Swatow. Amoy is, however, a place of considerable importance. It is the port of departure for Formosa, and for the last hundred and fifty years has been the seat of a large foreign trade. The city is undoubtedly picturesque, being divided into two parts by a ridge of rocks along which a fortified wall runs. A fine road, paved with large blocks of stone, connects the two divisions of the city, which are enclosed in a circumference of probably not less than eight miles. The population of Amoy is about half a million. We were fortunate during our short stay here to be present at a large review of native troops. The men here are renowned soldiers; they were the last to hold out against the Tatar invasion, and still wear a kind of turban, supposedly to conceal the fact that they, too, are subject to the indignity of the queue. I have seen no more comical sight than this great assemblage of Chinese soldiers; the uniforms were gaudy but not unpicturesque, and nearly every other man carried a long flag-staff with a tiny banner at the top; the rest were armed with bows and arrows, or long spears, or oldfashioned flint-lock guns. There were only one or two regiments of well-equipped soldiers, and these were archers, who seemed to be the best troops in the field. I could not make out any definite line of parade, and there was no formal march past, the principal feature of the day being a successive drawing-up into line of the various regiments, who after standing for some time at what I suppose corresponded to "present arms," retired rather confusedly to more remote parts of the ground, and there indulged in target practice and various trials of skill and strength. It was quite clear that for any purpose of modern warfare such troops as we saw at Amoy that day were utterly useless. They had not a stand of arms amongst them that would have been seen at an European review any time during the present century. I think, of the few rifles which they possessed, the greater part must have measured from ten to twelve feet from butt to muzzle, and although they might be very interesting objects in a museum, would be ludicrously out of place in modern warfare.

After leaving Amoy, the only port I visited with the exception of Foochow, which will be dealt with in a separate chapter, was Shanghai. This is the most European of all the Chinese settlements. Quite apart from the native city, Shanghai is an imposing and important place. Its "bund," or esplanade as we should call it, is a splendid street, running parallel to the river, and having on one side a row of houses, banks, and offices, that would be a credit to any part of London. Two rows of trees are planted along the road, and there are broad and shady sidewalks. Behind the bund one finds several other streets of European houses and offices, there being generally a small garden and yard, known as a "compound," attached to each residence, reminding one of the suburbs of London. Behind these streets again are the quarters of the Chinese hangers-on. As many as a hundred thousand Chinamen have elected to live here, rather than in their own city which is less than a mile away. Here they, moreover, have to pay rates and taxes, and to submit themselves to the somewhat tyrannous restrictions of a municipal board.

I paid several visits to the large native city which adjoins the European Shanghai, and is surrounded by a fine wall; it is a very interesting place, and the people are much more polite and civil than in the Fukien province. The streets are, as always in China, narrow and tortuous, and the houses overcrowded and badly built. I noticed no European produce to speak of in the city, but saw purely native manufactures everywhere. The people, too, seemed quite untouched as yet by the "white progress," the reason of this being that all who have any knowledge of, or love for Western things, go and live at the back of the European settlement. I visited many of the best tea houses and gardens, most of which are situated within, and form part of the grounds belonging to the various joss houses. There is one more noteworthy than the rest, being built on an island in the centre of a small lake, and approached by several fanciful bridges, which make it the very realisation of that most familiar of objects, the house and bridge of a willow-pattern plate. We passed a pleasant hour at this tea-house, sitting upstairs by a tiny latticed window overlooking the smooth but rather yellow water, and sipped little cups of tea, and watched the Chinese refreshment seekers coming in and out.

The "curio" shops of Shanghai are good, but the shopkeepers charge fabulous prices, and are hard men to deal with. The Chinese are such inveterate curio hunters that, unless you hit upon something that they themselves do not appreciate, you are beaten by endless sharp collectors with whom you stand no chance at a competitive sale. Their love of jade stone seemed more astonishing to me here in Shanghai than before. I saw several pieces the prices of which were ten and twelve thousand dollars.

The shops are now overstocked with modern productions, which are very worthless, the contrast between the old work and the new being most striking. The Chinese no longer originate much that is beautiful, or, in a true sense, artistic. Their old works of art are truly priceless; and if they copy faithfully the designs of their ancestors, they can produce valuable things, but this is so seldom done. They make cheap and faultful imitations nowadays, and rarely, perhaps never originate. European taste has, as in Japan, so no less here, almost destroyed the ceramic art; the Chinese now make only for sale, and even amongst themselves sacrifice quite everything for the acquisition of dollars. I do not know whether it is England that has made such a nation of shopkeepers of them, but a nation of shopkeepers they certainly are. Every man of them, from the lowest coolie to the highest mandarin, is a merchant at heart, and concentrates his whole soul on some commercial "pidgin," from which he hopes to make his "leety präfit."

From Shanghai I had hoped to go to Pekin, but the country was suffering so terribly from the famine, and the condition of the people was so disaffected, that our consul strongly advised me not to attempt the journey at that time.

I learned that upwards of five millions of people had perished from the famine up to the end of May 1878, the condition of things being thus described by the Roman Catholic Bishop of Shansi:—"Jusqu'à présent l'on se contente de manger ceux qui étaient déjà morts, mais maintenant l'on tue aussi les vivants pour les manger. Le mari mange sa femme, les parents mangent leurs fils et leurs filles, et, à leur tour, les enfants mangent leurs parents, comme l'on entend dire presque chaque jour."

Can any conceivable state of things be more terrible? The government have done practically nothing, complaining that they have no money and can raise none, and yet there was at the very time of this statement's appearance in the Shanghai papers, £37,000 worth of timber lying in the Soochow creek on its way to Pekin, where it was to be used in repairing the portal of the Temple of Heaven. Thus, to satisfy the pride and vanity of a few priests and mandarins, the Chinese Government will spend vast sums of money, while their people are dying literally by millions for the want of a few grains of rice.

A CHINESE COOLIE.

CHAPTER XVII.

FOOCHOW AND DISTRICT.

"The rocks are of that sort called Primitive by the mineralogists, which always arrange themselves in masses of a rugged, gigantic character, which ruggedness, however, is here tempered by a singular airiness of form and softness of environment. In a climate favourable to vegetation, the gray cliff, itself covered with lichens, shoots up through a garment of foliage or verdure, and bright cottages, tree-shaded, cluster round the everlasting granite. In vicissitude, Beauty alternates with Grandeur; you ride through stony hollows, along straight passes traversed by torrents, overhung by high walls of rock, now winding amid broken shaggy chasms and huge fragments, now suddenly emerging into some emerald valley, where the streamlet collects itself into a lake, and man has again found a fair dwelling, and it seems as if Peace had established herself in the bosom of Strength."—*Sartor Resartus.*

FOOCHOW is the most delightful of the Chinese settlements; in natural attractions even Hong Kong cannot be compared with it: as a purely characteristic native city it is probably even more representative than Canton; and as a central point from which to make excursions to tea districts or temples or convents, it has no rival. There is also an amount of agreeable social intercourse in Foochow, which would be almost impossible in a larger place, and which is no doubt to a great extent due to the absence of strangers and visitors. People are not driven to exclusiveness by the number and importunity of travellers, and there are, moreover, none of the burning questions, political or otherwise, that so often in other communities give rise to ill feeling.

The entrance to the Min river is magnificently picturesque, and will compare favourably with the Hudson or the Bosphorus. On the north side of the river's mouth lies Sharp Peak, which is a kind of summer resort for the merchants of the Foochow settlement, and where are also the large summer residences of the missionaries.

We were able to steam about thirty miles up the river, coming at last to anchor at a bend in the stream, where is a small settlement and a fine government dockyard, in which both ships and engines have already been constructed. There are now two establishments of this kind in China, both of considerable importance. This one, when in full work, employs over two thousand men, and at the time of my visit there were only six Europeans in the place. A training school has been established in connection, where are two French and two English instructors, and, with the help of these gentlemen, quite an enjoyable day may be spent at this Chinese Portsmouth. Only one ship was on the stocks at the time of my visit, but of late more spirit has, I believe, been shown by the government, and larger grants are to be made in the future. The Chinese are gradually acquiring greater technical knowledge, and will very soon, I have no doubt, be able to take the management of the whole of this dockyard and arsenal in their own hands.

A fine pagoda stands on the point at the bend of the river, and has given the place the name of Pagoda Anchorage. We left our ocean-going steamer just below this point, and were taken some fifteen or twenty miles farther up the river in a steam launch, thus reaching our destination after about three days' passage from Hong Kong.

The Min river at Foochow is about as large as the Rhine at Coblentz, but has a long narrow island lying in midstream. On one side of the river, a mile or so from the shore, lies the city of Foochow with its magnificent walls and towers, and on the other side, upon a rather steep and very picturesque hill, the little European settlement of twenty or thirty houses is situated. As I sat on my balcony in one of the higher of these houses on the afternoon of my arrival, I thought I had seldom seen a more exquisitely beautiful view. In front of me lay the great city of Foochow, stretched out upon a sloping plain, its actual shape, although well marked by a wall with high towers at intervals, being almost lost in the wilderness of low buildings which stretch right down to the river edge, where they are indeed even more dense than in the city itself.

Hardly a greater distinction exists between the river and its banks, than between the city and its suburbs. The houses appear to be carried right out upon the water on account of the number of large sampans, which are moored in rows like barges on the Thames, only in infinite number. In this way the city stretches across to the island and covers it, and again, with but a narrow passage for river traffic, across to the mainland, where, being now several miles from its original centre, it becomes somewhat straggling and broken, dissolving itself at last into green hills on the one side, and into the European tea "hongs" and private gardens and houses on the other.

Then, standing out clearly, because it is the only straight line in all the landscape, I notice the great Foochow bridge "of a thousand ages." This magnificent work crosses, through a literal forest of small masts with thick underwood of sampans, from shore to island, and beyond again from island to shore. It is over a quarter of a mile long, and is built of enormous blocks of gray granite. The piers are straight and square, and the bridge itself is also straight and square; it is the simplest conceivable structure, and, on account of the immense weight and size of its materials, has proved most thoroughly durable. It has withstood the floods and storms of nine hundred years, and is practically as strong and good as the day it was completed. Some of the granite blocks are as much as forty feet long. The floor of the bridge consists of huge slabs, and there is a parapet about four feet high on each side. Beyond all this, and beyond the bright green fields of the sloping plain, stands a stately range of hills, which, as the valley of the river winds away, closes in on every side so that the city seems to lie in the arena of a great amphitheatre.

The houses of the European residents here in Foochow are, I think, not to be beaten anywhere in the East; they are so large and comfortable, are surrounded by such pleasant gardens, and command so glorious a panorama. All around the house in which I stayed were deep verandahs, and in front a terrace with flowers, below which was an admirable lawn tennis-ground, and below again, upon another terrace, kitchen-garden, stables, kennels and so on. The whole place, curiously enough, is built upon an old Chinese burial-ground, every square foot outside the gardens being occupied in that way. Any unpleasant feeling one may have about the graves soon wears off, and I learnt in a very few days to prefer Foochow to any of the Chinese ports. There is a pleasant little club, and there are good racquets and fives courts. The charm of a visit to Foochow does not, however, lie solely in the attractions of the settlement itself; the places of interest in the neighbourhood are most numerous.

The first excursion that I took was to the Paeling Hills to see the tea plantations. We started early one morning, in chairs of a lighter kind than are usually used in the settlement, for a trip to these hills, our party consisting of three Englishmen, a tea boy, and seventeen coolies. We crossed the long bridge, and, skirting the city walls, jogged along for many miles through the densely populated suburbs. On all sides was a maze of narrow streets, in which were to be seen thousands and thousands of Chinamen, passing to and fro and working in the shops. We pushed our way at a good round trot through all this for more than two hours, obtaining from our elevated position a most admirable view of Foochow street life.

At last we arrived at the outskirts of the city, where the houses were less closely packed, and soon afterwards were out upon the flat plains, threading our way through the paddy fields upon narrow stone paths. The paths are in places as much as six or eight feet above the fields, and being only two feet or so in width, it is no easy matter to pass the strings of heavily-laden coolies that one meets flocking in towards the city. Having reached the foot of the mountains, we began slowly to ascend a well-made stone pathway. We were some hours making the ascent, walking ourselves most of the way to save our tired-out bearers. It was intensely hot, and we were glad to reach a level spot where there was a little resting house, at which we waited some time enjoying the glorious view. The great Min valley now lay at our feet, with the shining river, like a thread of silver, winding its way through the centre. To our right the valley divided, and stretched away westward into dim distant hills on which the clouds were resting. In front lay the sloping plains, like a vast garden, dotted over with hamlets, and broken up into an infinite number of little fields; beyond this the rugged mountain ranges, cutting the clear sky with their bold and finely-shaped peaks.

Immediately on reaching the crest of the hills we found ourselves amongst the tea plantations. On all sides of us were men, women, and girls stooping over the little shrubs and gathering the leaves into large bamboo baskets. They only pick certain young and green leaves, which must be selected with some care, and they do it with wonderful quickness and dexterity. From these plantations we passed on to the little farmhouses, where we found them carrying on the various other processes for preparing the tea for the city market. On being brought in from the fields it is spread out on large mats in the sun for a short time, after which it is put into flat trays of four and five feet diameter and rolled by men's feet. The coolies use their toes like fingers, and curl the tea up into a large ball, rolling it in that manner round and round the circular tray; by this process the first curl is given to the leaf. Then it is spread out again in the sun for a little while, and then curled once more, this time more carefully and by hand. At last the tea is dried a third time until almost all the green colour has left it, when it is ready for firing. Very little firing goes on in the tea districts, that little being done over red-hot charcoal in the peasants' cottages. The final operation consists of packing it tightly into bags weighing half a picul or sixty-seven pounds, in which state it is sent down to Foochow.

We met scores of women and young girls on our way up, carrying these bags down the mountains. They hang one on each end of a bamboo pole, which makes their load at least a hundred and thirty-four pounds apiece. This enormous weight they will take ten, twelve and fifteen miles in the day. Many of the girls were not more than sixteen or seventeen years old, and more healthy, merry, and even pretty young women no one could wish to see. They were all neatly dressed, wearing wide and very short blue trousers, which covered only a very little of their brown round sturdy legs. Above these garments was a loose blue tunic, which covered, though failed to hide, their well-proportioned figures. Their hair is always deepest black and shiny, I am afraid, with grease, but ornamented with bright silver hairpins and scarlet or white artificial flowers. People who have only seen the yellow, sickly, washed-out women of the Chinese cities, can form no idea of these rosy-cheeked, chubby wenches of the Paeling Hills; down they came in files of eight or ten or twelve, singing a little grunting tune to which they kept step, in order to make their loads more easy.

The wild flowers, amongst which such familiar ones as azaleas, rhododendrons and violets were conspicuous, excited my surprise no less than these bright pretty peasant women, for I had no idea that China produced such homely objects.

On our way home in the late evening we passed through a large agricultural district in the lower part of the hills, and there I found the rice farmers as happy-looking and apparently prosperous as the tea-growers. The hills were all terraced to hold the water, without which rice cannot be grown; and when no stream is to be found, the labourers are obliged to irrigate their fields. This is generally done by means of long slanting chain pumps, worked by men or women who stand upon a sort of scaffold, and raise the water by treading rapidly on little perches, which are inserted in the horizontal cylinder that drives the pump. Another method of irrigation I noticed which was no less amusing. Two men would hold a shallow wooden bowl across a small pond or well, by means of a couple of ropes. They would then swing the bowl over the pond and deftly dip it in, flinging the contents on to the surrounding country. The water was as it were *flicked* up, falling in a spray in whatever direction the men wished.

It was night before we reached the city again; and the

gates being shut, we skirted the walls once more and threaded our way through the densely-crowded suburbs that line the river bank. I have seen nothing anywhere more weird than these streets at night. Great Chinese lanterns everywhere, and, by the dim light, yellow faces might be seen peering in all directions from the dark houses, curious as to who it was passing along with such loud shouts, and such a string of servants. The quaint vertical sign-boards with their huge gilt characters shone conspicuously against the dark overhanging roofs; all below us—for we rode, of course, on our coolies' shoulders—was glittering, bright with the light of thousands and thousands of lamps, and above us all was dark and still. The tradesmen in the poorer quarters were still at work making lanterns and sandals and hats and pots and pans, or tailoring or working with leather, or cooking or what not. It all seemed for work and profit; there was no rest anywhere; even those who ate or drank did so standing, as though in a hurry to be off; only now and then the insidious smell of opium rose, and, lurking in some dark corner, we could see the half-naked forms of men stretched out on shelves with the little lamp beside them, and the heavy mist of smoke hanging round the room. I have no word of admiration indeed for anything I saw here in the city—it was all dirt and squalor, worse in its utter filth and overcrowded misery than anything I have seen in Cairo or Constantinople or London. It was a weird and wonderful sight, and yet so depressing as almost to do away for a time with the pleasant remembrances of our visit to the bright, happy tea districts of the Paeling Hills.

Another object of great interest in the neighbourhood of Foochow is the Ku-shan monastery. Our route this time lay down the river, in the direction of the Pagoda Anchorage. We steamed for seven or eight miles in a launch, and then took to our chairs and coolies, and crossed the paddy fields to the foot of the hills.

The monastery of Ku-shan stands at the top of a very steep ascent, 2,500 feet in height. It is reached by an enormous flight of granite steps which stretches from the foot of the hill to the summit, and nothing could be more utterly wearisome than the ascent of this gigantic staircase.

The monastery is very large and beautifully situated in a little valley of its own. It consists of the usual three buildings, one behind the other, which are of no architectural merit, but are quaint and barbaric, very costly doubtless, and of great antiquity. In the first building are four colossal figures of Buddha; these are the guardians of the temple, and are truly ugly enough to frighten any one from committing an act of desecration. In the second building is a very ornate and elaborate shrine, in front of which at four o'clock every day a service is held. The monks were the only attendants beside ourselves, and the ceremony was chiefly musical, consisting of weird chanting. In this second building are various relics of Buddha, a great attraction to the numberless pilgrims who come immense distances to see them. The one that was shown to us with most reverence was a tooth of Buddha, which I examined with great care, and was allowed to measure. It was roughly five inches by four, and six inches long, from which I judge that the illustrious Prophet was about the size of the Albert Memorial.

The third building is the monastery proper, where are about two hundred priests in residence. By far the most interesting episode in connection with my visit to Ku-shan was an interview we had with one of these priests, who, during the previous night, had deliberately held his finger in a flame and burnt it slowly away. Dr. Osgood, of Foochow, was present the whole time and saw it done but was not allowed to interfere either during or after the operation. This man held his finger for an hour and a half in the flame, and burnt it down to below the second joint. The wound was very bad when I saw it, and the room actually smelt of roasted meat. I held his hand and examined it, but was not allowed to bind it up in any way. The poor fellow seemed exhausted and ill, but smiled faintly when we came in. His ambition is to burn two more off, during the next two years. In another part of the building we saw men having their heads branded with red-hot irons. I could not learn what the special occasion was, but suppose it must have been some annual festival at which this particular kind of self-mortification is practised.

I was glad to get away from the scene of these horrible barbarities, and to ramble away through the beautiful grounds of the monastery. We came to a small temple a mile or so away, situated in a lovely little glen, and had luncheon outside a small Buddhist shrine. Here was a deep-toned bell, which was sounded automatically every second by the action of water from a stream; its sound had never died away for many centuries—indeed they said for over a thousand years. The scenery everywhere was very beautiful: on all sides were rocks and ferns and quaint grottoes and shrines and small waterfalls. Everywhere, too, the marks of great antiquity, old hieroglyphics cut on stones, and granite steps worn almost into inclined planes. Our day at Ku-shan was a most delightful one, and will always live in my memory as the pleasantest of all the excursions I made in the valley of the Min river.

I spent a fortnight in Foochow, and almost every day had some fresh experience of the beauty of its neighbourhood and the kindness of the European settlers. All is so different here from Europe, being so full of life, the great quaint city with its mediæval towers and walls, and its bridge and shining river and myriads of people swarming like bees.

The English merchants have "houseboats" here, as also in Hong Kong and Shanghai, which are a kind of Chinese "dahabeeyah," thoroughly comfortable, and even luxurious. In these we spent many delightful evenings, the custom being to go up the stream at sundown, ten miles or so, and then drop anchor and have dinner in the cool and pleasant country air. I cannot describe the peaceful beauty of such evenings. We would lie out on the deck in the soft evening light, and watch the sun go down behind the hills, and see them change in colour, from green to gold, and from gold through a hundred rare tints, to sombre purple at last; then the dark cloud of night would drop swiftly down, as it does in those low latitudes, and shroud the hills almost at once in gloom and mystery, and we would watch the stars peep out and the fireflies drift lazily by, and then a light or two would glimmer on the bank, casting long streaky waves of reflection across the river, no sounds to disturb our peace but the insects chirping upon the banks and the soft ripple of the river against our boat. At last comes a great break in it all as the Chinese crew burst forth into a wild barbaric chant, and haul away at the anchor and start to row us down the stream.

I have purposely avoided in these short chapters any details of Chinese customs or institutions. I feel that in the standard works on the country, there has been said on all these points perhaps even more than enough. If any of my readers will take up Williams's 'Middle Kingdom,' or Archdeacon Cobbold's 'Pictures,' or the 'China' of Bohn's series, he will realise how absurd it would be for a visitor of but a few months' experience to touch on any subjects but those of superficial interest. I have therefore attempted to do no more than rapidly describe the principal incidents of a few pleasant weeks in that part of the world.

From China one naturally passes to Japan, which we always look upon as the sister kingdom, notwithstanding its infinite differences. In Japan, one can go amongst the people, and live in their houses, and walk through their country, and learn to know them and love them. How different in China, which, indeed, the ordinary Englishman only sees from the shoulders of his coolies, and which, although now so intensely interesting to visit, would be quite unendurable were it not for the delightful houses of the settlers and the strong arms and legs of the coolies, who, when you have seen enough, can hurry you back to your English homes.

CHAPTER XVIII.

THE JAPANESE PORTS AND KIOTO.

"What do we see? Peace, plenty, apparent content, and a country more perfectly and carefully cultivated and kept, with more ornamental timber everywhere than can be matched even in England."—*Sir Rutherford Alcock.*

AFTER a few hours upon the broad yellow waters of the Yang-tse-Kiang we crossed the bar at the river's mouth, and turning our backs for the time upon China, sailed away to the sister kingdom of the Eastern world. I have approached no country with so much of impatience and curiosity as Japan: it is the traveller's paradise, and has placed China in the shade as a country for "globe trotters" and others to rave about. Japan, indeed, if the sister kingdom of China at all, is sister in all that makes her more gentle, beautiful, and good than her companion, to whom she is inferior only in strength and size. There have been attempts of late to take away from this country something of its fair character, and one traveller has gone so far as to dispute almost all that has hitherto been said about the Japanese themselves. For my part, I am amongst the admirers of both Japan and the Japanese, and consider that no writer, from Thunberg to Sir Rutherford Alcock, has said too much in their admiration.

Japan, like most islands that lie off great continents, is subject to more than ordinary storms and bad weather, and on our passage from China across the mouth of the Yellow

Sea, we had our full share of adverse gales. We were on board one of the oldfashioned American vessels that, after many years trading across the Pacific, and up and down the coast of California, had at last been taken over by the Mitsui-Bishi (Three Diamonds) Company of Japan, and was at that time carrying the mails between Shanghai and Yokohama. I confess to thoroughly disliking these "top-hampered" steamers in bad weather, and yet, having been in several of them during severe storms, and in one, the old *China*, during a moderate typhoon, I am bound to say that, except in the matter of personal discomfort from the groaning and creaking of their timbers, and the unpleasant sensation, that the upper stories must presently be washed overboard, they have always proved themselves thoroughly trustworthy sea boats.

Having, therefore, experienced considerable discomfort during my short voyage, I was the more delighted with the glorious panorama of Nagasaki harbour as we steamed into it one May morning. I was wonderfully struck with the European character of the scenery as it appeared to us from our vessel's deck. The hills slope pleasantly up from the water's edge, and are as green as those of Westmoreland, whilst the tall dark pines and brightly-coloured undergrowth reminded me of Northern Europe. On landing all possibility of comparison soon disappeared, for right in among the houses of the town were growing palms and pomegranates, and camellias and bamboo. Turning away at once from the more Europeanised portion of the city, we rambled through the native streets, finding new sights and sounds to amuse and surprise us at every turn. Every one coming from China is, immediately on landing, struck by the width of the streets, and the comparatively few people in them; and even here, although Nagasaki is far from a model

Japanese city, one must also notice the tidiness and cleanliness of the place.

The most interesting feature of this capital of Southern Japan is its tea-houses. Temples and streets and shops we saw in thousands and of better quality elsewhere, but I found few such pleasant resting-places in any other part of the country as these tea-houses in the suburbs of Nagasaki. Those to which I refer are situated amongst some temples

SCENE AT A TEA-HOUSE.

and groves upon the steep hillsides at the back of the town. They command an extensive view of the harbour, which lies like a great island-studded lake some hundreds of feet below.

No traces of the strong winds and heavy seas that were raging outside could be discerned; the ranges of hills form a complete shelter to this peaceful haven, and small polished wood boats were skimming the smooth water as if upon a river.

Of the delight of being waited upon by pretty girls in costumes, such as one had so often seen in pictures but had never before properly realised, I must not stop to write now; we were only at Nagasaki en route for other places of interest, and the business of telegraphing to Yedo for passes to be sent to us at Kobe, of consulting our consul upon many subjects connected with these passes, of making sundry purchases of Saga ware and other specialities of the district, &c., &c., took up too much of our limited time for us to experience anything particularly notable or worthy of record.

We started after a stay of something like forty hours for the Inland Sea, one of the most talked-about objects of interest in Japan. It is certainly a magnificent piece of water scenery; the surface is studded with little green islands of which there are said to be as many as three thousand. Great numbers of fishing and trading junks may be seen plying from port to port, or anchored in shoal water, and beyond all to the north is a glorious background of finely-shaped mountains. There is one port of importance in the Inland Sea, namely Shimonoséki, which has attained some notoriety on account of the bomboardment of September 1864, by an allied force, consisting of the war vessels of four nations. Our steamer stopped off the town for an hour or two, and although the port is quite closed to Europeans without a passport, I succeeded, in the absence of some high functionary, in sneaking ashore with a fellow-passenger in a native boat. I think that my hour's ramble through Shimonoséki was as enjoyable as anything that I experienced in Japan; perhaps on the principle which causes stolen fruit to be proverbially sweet. The place contains some ten thousand or more inhabitants, and is as clean and pleasant a city as one might wish to see. We climbed a hill at the back, and obtained a glorious view down the Inland Sea and of the Shimonoséki Straits. There was a pleasant little temple here, surrounded by a garden which possessed the attraction of a shooting gallery. The range extended down a well-kept gravel path twenty or thirty yards long, with a rack of bows and arrows at one end, and a target at the other. A jolly old priest with sleek smiling face emerged from a small building near at hand, and after regarding us for some time with ill-disguised curiosity, handed us each a bow with the intimation that we might try our skill. We spent a quarter of an hour most pleasantly learning from our reverend friend something of the Japanese fashion of using the bow; he was an excellent shot, and seemed highly amused at our incapability to so much as strike the target. Descending the hill again we found ourselves in the more busy parts of the city. The streets are broader and more clean than those of Nagasaki, and in the shops I noticed a great quantity of pretty pottery, and the usual chaos of Japanese manufactures for consumption and domestic use. After the invariable visit to a tea-house, where we were refreshed by tea and sweets, we sculled off to the ship again, and gave glowing accounts of all we had seen to our less enterprising fellow-passengers.

In about twenty hours, after passing through the beautiful straits that lead from the Inland Sea to the ocean, we entered the harbour of Kobe, and were soon at anchor off the settlement. The native name for this place is Hiogo, but the European "concession" has now assumed such formidable dimensions that its name, Kobe, is more frequently used by travellers than the other. The place itself is in no way attractive, but the harbour and its vicinity are beautiful.

A few miles from the town is a waterfall surrounded by an uncommon combination of natural beauty. It is almost shut in by steep cliffs, covered with most luxuriant vegetation, on the sides of which pretty little zigzag paths have been cut leading to the various points of view. Along these little paths at closely recurring intervals, are neatly-built tea-houses with white matted floors and polished wood verandahs, looking for all the world like models, and entirely too spick-and-span for actual use. One soon discovers, however, that these little hostelries are not only for ornament, for the most fascinating tea girls, in brightest coloured garments and shining black hair, come hobbling out on their high clogs at the approach of a stranger, and do their utmost to entice him in. The rain came down in torrents during our excursion to this beautiful valley, and so we selected the most delightful-looking tea-house, and taking off our boots, went in prepared to amuse ourselves as we best could until the weather improved.

After drinking a considerable amount of tea, and eating a great many of the rather sickly sweets which are generally brought with the tea, we prevailed upon some of the girls to sing, which they did in the quaint and jerky fashion peculiar to them. After this we saw one girl dance a somewhat melancholy measure, consisting almost entirely of supposedly elegant "poses." The fan played a very conspicuous part, but there seemed to me to be but little of beauty or picturesqueness in the performance. A second girl accompanied the dancer upon a three-stringed instrument something like a banjo, called, I believe, a *samisen*. With but one or two exceptions all the married women I saw in this district had black teeth and no eyebrows, and although this custom is now being discontinued, an enormous majority still submit to it. I think it is almost the only absolutely untasteful custom peculiar to the Japanese. Their idea in adopting it is, that a woman, when once betrothed, is better without any attractive features, and must not be looked upon any more with admiration by the opposite sex.

After spending several days at and around Hiogo, I started by rail for Osaka which is commercially one of the most important cities in Japan. It is situated upon a labyrinth of rivers and canals, and has often been compared to Venice; it much more closely resembles Stockholm, however, in respect to the network of water-ways by which it is intersected. This was the first large Japanese city I had visited, and the extent of the place and the crowds of people thronging the streets impressed me very much.

Osaka is built entirely of wood, with the exception of the Tycoon's castle, the modern Mint, and a few other public buildings. I have seen nothing out of Egypt so enormous as the stones employed in the construction of this stronghold of the old Tycoons. One that I measured was forty feet by ten by six, and I was informed that some were as large as forty feet by twenty. They were not as truly adjusted by any means as the monoliths of Egypt, but they have had a changeful climate as well as earthquakes to contend against, from both of which influences the temples of the Pharaohs have been free. We spent several hours in going over the Imperial Mint, which is an entirely European construction, furnished with the most approved machinery from England and France. All the old quaint native coinage is being converted into modern pieces corresponding to "quarters," dollars, five dollar gold pieces, &c., &c.

The bronze manufacturers of Osaka are renowned throughout the world, and in this kind of national art-production they are more nearly following the old lines, and submitting with less servility to European taste than in anything else. That is to say, even now one can buy in Osaka bronzes finished the day before yesterday, that will do credit to the national taste, and are not spoiled or in any way tainted by the innovations which, in order to meet the requirements of the English and French markets, are being now introduced into almost all the native arts of Japan.

From Osaka I travelled by railroad to Kioto, the ancient capital. Our way lay through a rich agricultural district,

A JAPANESE PEASANT.

plentifully sprinkled with farms and hamlets. Peasants were working in the fields, and men and women trudging along the little roadways, the whole presenting a very pleasant picture.

Kioto is a purely Japanese city; as yet no Europeans are living there, and compared with Tokio, for instance, there is little of European custom or influence noticeable. It is the stronghold of the conservatives of Japan, and here, perhaps more than anywhere else, the feeling of resentment with reference to the new regime prevails. For a thousand years, for twenty-five centuries indeed, according to native tradition, the Mikados of Japan had held their court in or near this sacred city. It is then a little excusable that something of discontent should prevail when they find themselves left out in the cold, and Yedo, Tokio forsooth, a mere upstart city, made the centre of attraction and the home of the Mikado!

The temples, gardens and palaces of Kioto are justly celebrated, and we spent many days in regular sightseeing, much as a stranger would do in London or Paris. The prettiest resort in all the city is, I think, the temple of Chiomin, where a splendid view is obtained, and which is altogether perhaps the most attractive place of its kind in Japan. It is exquisitely situated among gardens and groves and rockeries, and approached from under an enormous wooden portico, which is itself a marvel of constructive genius. Behind the temple proper lies a large suite of rooms, which are set apart for the Mikado's use during his visits, as yet very few and far between, to the native city of his ancestors. These rooms are very simple and uncostly; everything seems of the best of its kind, but there has been no reckless throwing away of money on extravagant or useless display. On the hill immediately above this temple stands a very handsome pagoda, and above that again is another temple, built on the side of the rock, and supported from below by strong wooden piles of great height, the whole looking wonderfully picturesque among the green vegetation.

In an out-building near the grand portico we saw the big bell of Japan. It is eleven inches thick, eighteen feet high, and eight feet in diameter. A great log hangs horizontally from a beam at the side of the building, and this, being pulled back with a rope by two men, is allowed to swing against the bell, striking it upon its outer rim with enormous force, and producing a marvellously soft though powerful tone.

Of other gardens and temples I hesitate to write lest there should be no end; suffice it to say, that in all was something tasteful, quaint and original.

One might spend weeks, no doubt, in a city like Kioto, and see new sights every day. The shops themselves are almost all little museums to travellers from the West, and with time and patience one might pick up valuable specimens in them yet. The enormous collections that are to be seen in the London shops to-day, are not typical to any great extent of Japanese art; these things are made for the European market, and are made to sell. Even if you go to any leading curiosity shop in Kioto itself you will not see much that is old or really beautiful. It is only after repeated visits, or when you are backed up by some good letter of introduction to these Attenboroughs of Japan, that you see the valuable specimens. Then it is, after much persuasion, that you are taken with great ceremony and some mystery, into the sanctum sanctorum behind a maze of screens, and from out some ancient chest is brought, carefully swathed in paper or silk, an antique gem which puts all that you have seen before into the shade, and makes you realise in what the real wealth of Japanese art consists. For such things as you are in this manner shown, no true estimate in money value can be made. These have been the work of years, made with no view of sale; labour has been squandered, or rather lovingly bestowed upon the most insignificant details, and one does not know which most to admire, the marvellous dexterity of execution in detail or the charming general effect.

A few months before the date of our visit to Kioto, some European travellers discovered a series of rapids in a river amongst the hills, fifteen miles or so from the city. We received such glowing accounts of the place that we determined to make up a party and go there, and accordingly five of us started early one morning in jinrikishas, with two boys and sixteen coolies to make the excursion. After a run of about three hours we came to the river, and found a cluster of houses and some boatmen waiting for such travellers as might wish to descend. Their boats were not large enough to take us all, as the general order of passengers came on foot, and in parties of not more than three or four at a time. After some delay, however, we were packed into a boat which had been brought from somewhere higher up the stream, and our little carriages being put into two other boats, we started off, the watermen punting with their long thin poles. The stream soon began to carry us along without any assistance from our boatmen, who had now to exercise all their skill in steering the light craft and keeping her off the rocks. We shot along at speeds varying from three to perhaps twenty-five miles an hour for ten or twelve miles. At times the excitement was intense as we dashed down a swift fall, apparently right on a projecting rock, which at the last moment would be avoided by a skilful piece of steering. There were about sixteen separate rapids, corresponding almost exactly to the "gates" of the Nile; one or two, however, were even more formidable than the main channel at the first cataract, which can only be taken by dahabeeyahs descending the river. Here also, as on the Nile, a different course is taken when the boats go up again, in many places the rush of waters being too great for the men to attempt returning by the way they descend. The scenery is of the finest during the entire distance; the river follows a gorge in the hills, the sides of which are covered with glorious foliage—foliage of that rich variety of colour which can be seen nowhere in such perfection as in Japan. At the foot of the rapids we found a small village with a more than usually clean and large tea-house, and after a comfortable though late luncheon out on the balcony of the pretty little cottage, we started once more in our jinrikishas, and in a few hours were rattling through the streets of Kioto again.

From Kioto I started by way of Lake Biwa to make the journey of the Nagasendo or central mountain road of Japan, but of the pleasant weeks spent in the interior of the island, and of my visit to Nikko, I propose to write in the following chapters, and will therefore pass over them here, and take up my story a month later on after reaching Yokohama, whence I visited the better-known watering-places such as Myanoshita and Hakone.

I spent a week or so in Yokohama before starting for a tour through the lake districts and watering-places which lie around the base of Fuziyama. It is not an attractive place, although very wonderful as showing how quickly the merchants of England and America can create for themselves a home, and surround themselves with European comforts and luxuries. The main street of Yokohama is as good as that of any ordinary English county town, and contains hotels, banks, stone-fronted stores, and a club. Another astonishing feature in Yokohama is its suburb known as the Bluff, where are some really beautiful houses and gardens, and where dinners or dances or lawn tennis may be enjoyed to one's heart's delight.

Of such experiences as one can gain in Yokohama, however, I had had fully enough in China and elsewhere, and accordingly as soon as I had rested a little after the long overland journey, and recruited my stores, I started along the first part of the Tokaido or coast road of Japan for Myanoshita and its district.

Early one morning my boy informed me that a carriage and pair was at the door! Such a thing I had almost imagined did not exist in Japan, and so, although I had heard that about fifty miles of my route was along a good wide road, I was unprepared for such luxury as this. It turned out to be a very comfortable little victoria, drawn by two sturdy ponies, which pulled us over the first forty-five miles to Odawarra in capital style. I was almost sorry, however, to give up the universal jinrikisha, which one always looks upon as the correct vehicle to use when travelling in Japan. It being terribly wet I stayed as short a time as possible at Odawarra, which at the best is but a flat, uninteresting fishing town. Leaving my grand equipage behind, I was here transferred into a kango, and thus was carried for ten long miles, in pouring rain, over very mountainous country. The discomfort that an European experiences when riding in a kango is certainly very great. It is not a reasonable seat like the Chinese "chair," but a dreadful thing slung *under* a pole. The Japanese being all small people, the kangos are made to fit them as it were, and consequently for a European measuring anything like six feet to ride in such a thing is nearly impossible.

It was late at night before I reached my destination, and glad enough I was of a change into dry clothes, and

KAGO RIDING.

a stretch upon the clean tea-house mats after sitting so long in a doubled up position. The tea-houses in this

KANGO RIDING.

district are far larger than any I had before seen, and moreover have certain European luxuries wherewith to overwhelm the home-loving Englishman. At Myanoshita I found both a looking-glass and soap, and after a time, when supper was brought in, they actually produced a table. These kindly efforts to supply my supposed requirements were well enough, but my amusement was rapidly changed to disgust when, a few minutes later, the boy brought in some rice—not on the usual neat little lacquer tray, but upon an enamelled ironware plate! On inquiring into the subject I found that they had given up using their native utensils in most cases, and had adopted the hideous, coarse earthenware and metal goods of England and Germany. Here was a problem for political economists; at the next house they could have bought beautiful and serviceable utensils at the lowest conceivable price, and yet they were using dishes and cups from Europe, whilst we in England are filling our houses with the ordinary household pottery of Japan!

At Myanoshita there is a natural hot spring, which is carried through the leading tea-houses, and led into square baths. These baths are delightfully refreshing after a long day's rambling in the neighbourhood. The place has been a favourite resort of Japanese tourists for many years, no doubt, but has of late been so given up to Europeans that I fancy the people who go there now, are more frequently hawkers or travellers, on definite errands, rather than mere holiday makers and pleasure seekers.

One afternoon I walked to Kiga, a neighbouring village, and one of the prettiest in the district. It lies away up a well wooded valley, and as one looks down upon it from the hillsides, he might easily imagine it to be a little cluster of Swiss chalets, the shingle roofs and dark brown timber sides of the houses giving exactly that impression. There are hot springs also at Kiga, and the same kind of wood-work shops as at Myanoshita. In all the villages of the neighbourhood wood-turning and working are the main industries, and the model tea-houses and endless ingenious boxes and trays made here have long since found their way to England, and become familiar to every one.

When the weather had improved a little, we packed up our modest allowance of baggage, and started to walk to Hakone, the Keswick of the district. On our way we passed the very pretty village of Ashinoyo, where are sulphur streams reputed to cure all diseases whatsoever, and much frequented by sufferers from every kind of skin affection.

I must notice here one of the most abominable specimens of what I suppose was intended as a practical joke, that I have ever known. Two Frenchmen had recently been through the district, marking the most pretty girls in each village with some indelible ink or caustic, which they had persuaded them by various absurd stories, to apply to their cheeks or foreheads. The marks had developed in some cases to nasty scars, and the poor girls with much bashfulness came to us for advice. The condition to which these village belles were reduced was truly lamentable, and I felt thoroughly ashamed of belonging to the same race as the perpetrators of this disgraceful piece of folly. We found several of the victims here at Ashinoyo trying the effect of the sulphur springs.

After a walk of three or four more miles we came in sight of the lake of Hakone and were soon resting ourselves on the cool balcony of the leading tea-house in the village. The lake, which is of great depth, is three thousand feet above the sea, and is said to lie in the basin of an extinct volcano. One of the best views of Fuziyama may be had from here. It is a grand mountain, and exactly like the invariable pictures with which we are all so familiar. There was a good deal of snow on the summit when I was at Hakone, and in the morning as the clouds lay upon the lower hills and over the upper end of the lake, we could see the curiously-shaped cone standing out against the sky, just as one sees it on a thousand tea trays and saki cups, and indeed on almost everything Japanese.

One of the interesting excursions from Hakone is to the burning springs on the hills at the north end of the lake.

The easiest way of reaching this place is by rowing down the lake for about four miles, and then striking up the hillside on foot. This we accordingly did, hiring a punt for the purpose. We went along at a fair pace in our highly polished plain wood boat, being propelled by four oars, used like sculls from the gunwale, this being the universal practice in Japan. From the landing-place, where is a single hut, we walked up a narrow winding path for perhaps half an hour, and then reached a village, through which ran a small stream. The place consisted of a quadrangle of wooden houses with a square bath in the centre, in which were some twenty or thirty men and women all together as is the national custom. The water here is supposed to cure all kinds of ophthalmia. All the houses in the place are tea-houses, and in the off season they are entirely shut up and deserted.

After walking for another mile or so we reached the top of a steep hill, where was a small pass between two spurs of the range. This was the spot we had come to see; it is known as "Big Hell," and indeed is a very terrible place. In all directions were vent-holes, from which steam or water was issuing; in some places the steam was at a high pressure, threatening to burst open the surface of the ground. Very little water comes from any of the crevices, but there is much noise and yellow sulphurous smoke. One could not help feeling that at any moment the ground might burst open, and a volcano be created. It is a far more extraordinary phenomenon in most respects, than the sides of the lake of Rotomahana, to which, however, it bears a greater resemblance than to any other place that I have seen.

We returned from Hakone by the celebrated pass of that name, which forms part of the Tokaido road. The path by which we descended was no doubt originally one gigantic staircase, from base to summit; it is now a narrow roadway, paved with huge broken stones, polished to a dangerous degree of smoothness by the tread of so many thousand bare or straw-shod feet. We could not realise the full extent of the magnificence of this pass, which, as well as being one of the oldest, is perhaps the most beautiful in Japan, for it poured with rain from the time we left Hakone

RETURNING THANKS.

until we reached Odawarra in the evening. All that we could admire was the beauty of the forest that flanked the path on either side. At times the trees overhung so as to

s

form a complete arch, which would have kept off any less tropical rain than that to which we were subjected. Below the pass we came upon a grove of tall and stately cryptomeria, where we noticed a little temple, approached by stone steps, in which peasants were kneeling at a shrine, returning thanks for a good harvest, perhaps, or for safe passage of the Hakone pass; then out again through the lighter trees, where the underwood was composed of camellias and azaleas, amongst which the dark stones of this staircase of a thousand years wound their way in a score of turns and curves—so descending lower and lower, we at last reached the village at the foot. The roadway was first opened in A.D. 802, and both in historic and natural interest, is amongst the most attractive sights of this part of Japan.

At Odawarra I had appointed the carriage that had brought me a week or so before to be in readiness, and on the following day, after a pleasant drive, found myself once more in Yokohama.

CHAPTER XIX.

THE NAGASENDO ROAD.

> "Agriculture, which the Japanese consider as the most necessary and useful science for the prosperity and stability of the empire, is in no place in the world so much esteemed as here, where neither foreign nor civil wars nor emigrations lessen their population, and where they never think of encroaching upon the territories of other nations ... but where their whole care is directed in the highest degree that not a single sod shall lie fallow, nor the revenue of the earth be unthriftily employed."—*Thunberg's Travels*, 1779.

THERE are two main roads running between Kioto and Tokio. One is known as the Tokaido, and passes for the most part along the coast; the other is called the Nagasendo, and runs through the very centre of the island, over and amongst the great mountain ranges. The former road is the better of the two; with the exception of a few miles one might take a jinrikisha from one end of it to the other. In fact, the only part not fit for the light wheels of these little carriages is that in the neighbourhood of, and across the Hakone pass about which I have written in the last chapter.

The Nagasendo is, in my opinion, immeasurably the finer route of the two. At the time of my visit it had been traversed only by a few tens of Europeans, whilst the main army of globe-trotters and tourists from the Chinese settlements have for some years passed over the Tokaido at the rate of hundreds a year. As I wished to see as much as possible of the un-Europeanised side of Japanese life, and also wanted fine mountain air and good scenery, I chose the Nagasendo.

I was fortunate enough to come across a young traveller in China, who had resolved to take the inland trip from Kioto to Tokio, at about this time, and so, feeling that union would be strength, we decided to join forces and start together.

Having made all necessary preparations, and provided ourselves with a jinrikisha each, and two for the native boy and the baggage, we rattled off one lovely afternoon upon our first stage to Otzu on Lake Biwa. We had been a little troubled before starting as to what we ought to take in the way of provisions. One cannot make up his mind to live on rice, and rice only, for a month, and yet the trouble of purchasing and packing into a small compass such things as tinned meats and soups and biscuits, and more especially the difficulty of knowing how much of these articles one would be likely to want, is very great. Our minds, however, were quite at rest when we were once fairly off; it was no use troubling ourselves any further about such matters, for all possibility of putting things right if they were wrong was now at an end. Away then we rattled with eight coolies and four little carriages, leaving the great city behind us, bent upon at least a month of real country life in the interior of Japan.

We started along an excellent road which was then in course of construction. It was being built by the government for military purposes, and is really a most admirable work, five years ago there being but a small mountain trail leading from Kioto in this direction. After a delightful journey of two or three hours we came in sight of Lake Biwa, and soon were running through the busy streets of Otzu, the fishing town at the south end of the lake.

We found the people of Otzu making holiday on the evening of our arrival, and consequently every tea-house in the town was crowded. My friend and I ascended the steep steps of a temple, and enjoyed some exquisite views of the lake, whilst our boy was fighting the landlords, and trying to obtain a room for us. His endeavours met with no success, and in half an hour we got into our jinrikishas again, and trotted along the edge of the lake to another fishing village, lying in a beautiful little creek five miles beyond Otzu. Here we with some difficulty obtained a room, but had little rest, as the night was one of general festivity, drinking and dancing going on on every side. We accordingly left our quarters next morning with little regret, and went on board the steamer which ran to the northern end of the lake. I could hardly reconcile myself to steamboat travelling in the interior of Japan, for it did not seem at all in keeping with one's expectations of novelty and perhaps of adventure. I consoled myself, however, by recalling Sir Rutherford Alcock's wonderful, but no less true story of how, in Nagasaki, a steam engine with tubular boilers was made by the natives, before a steam-vessel or engine had ever been seen by a Japanese—made solely from the plans in a Dutch work.*

Our little lake steamer was built and engined in Japan, but I cannot say much in her praise. She only travelled about six knots, and made a great noise and splutter in accomplishing that. Her cabin was but four feet six high, and the awning above was the same height from the deck. We were accordingly compelled to enjoy the beauties of Lake Biwa in a reclining position, which after six or eight hours

---

* "This engine was not only put together, but made to work a boat, and is one of the crowning testimonies of Japanese enterprise and ingenuity, which leaves all the Chinese have ever attempted far behind." Vide 'Three Years in Japan,' by Sir Rutherford Alcock.

became somewhat wearisome. The lake is, however, of great natural beauty. It is about fifty miles long and ten wide at its broadest part, the shape resembling a Japanese stringed instrument, not unlike a banjo, called a "biwa." After a quiet and uneventful night at Myaharra, the little fishing village at the north end of the lake, we set off at daybreak in four jinrikishas on our overland journey. At what a pace these coolies can run! Down the street we rattled in the early morning, children and dogs and poultry scurrying out of our way, and staring as we passed; bells jingling under the little carriages, and our coolies as fresh and frolicsome as well-bred horses—we only wanted whips to crack, and the experience would have been perfect! At the end of the main street, turning sharply round to the right, we dashed up a muddy hill and out into the country lane without a pause. Such villages as we pass, such hedges on either side of the path, such trees and fields, and in the distance mountains flanking the valley, blue and misty in appearance—what a valley this is that runs to the north of Lake Biwa! I think it is probably as beautiful as any in the world.

Villages and hamlets and farms are scattered about in every direction. Coolies are working in the fields and passing along the road; women coolies, too, doing their share, and working hard with babies strapped upon their backs. Trains of horses pass us from time to time, but horses of burden only; they are fine thickset animals having long manes and tails, and looking very handsome with their arched necks and fanciful trappings. They are all shod with large straw boots, and so make no mark upon the smooth and beautifully-kept pathway. Beasts also pass us in no small numbers, laden and shod like the horses; they are mostly small, short-necked bulls with large heads and thick horns. There is no lack of jinrikishas either upon the road, but they are somewhat clumsy and badly made. The sleepy men or women that are riding in them look curiously up at us as we pass. Everywhere by the road side and in the fields are peasants working, and at each half-mile or so, we pass a village; the Foochow valley in China is not more thickly populated. But what lovely villages these are! Cottages of clean unpainted wood with thickly thatched roofs and neatest little gardens. The hedges between them are often cut square or smoothly round, with a little piece, clipped into some fancy shape, left standing up at intervals. Then at the cottage doors are gay little Japanese children in blue and red, with smaller children on their backs, and round the houses are balconies of polished wood, so bright and shiny that they make you blink. Azaleas are in the gardens, and camellias, and many well-known flowers; nearly always some rock-work also, and a little pond kept fresh by a fountain, the water being led from the higher land in bamboo pipes. Gold-fish, too, where there is water, and as a rule a little miniature rustic bridge across the pond, and tiny paths leading about the garden. The road is nowhere dusty, but smooth and pleasant to travel upon, being only about ten feet wide, and in this district hedged on both sides.

Each village has its trade, its fans to make or lacquered boxes, paper umbrellas, or whatever it may be, and each cottage has its loom and the old lady sitting in the doorway spinning her children's children's frocks. In the houses, if we stop and visit them, everything is found to be orderly and clean. We are offered rice and tea; tea in such china pots and cups as we put into cabinets at home. The people are gay and merry and very glad to see us. Care does not seem as yet to have taken its grim march down that happy valley, and the peasants, if they can get their rice and tea, seem to want nothing more.

Such then are the houses, the villages, the people of that inland valley in Japan. I have seen nothing like it either before or since, such peace and happiness, such simple country life, with Nature smiling kindly everywhere—smiling in the bright sky and warm sun, upon the green and beautiful hills, the well-tilled and ripening fields, the great and glorious trees, the pretty cottages and happy peasants; it was all quite Utopian, and every prospect pleased us and not even man seemed vile.

The tea-houses of this part of Japan were far more interesting resting-places than those of such ports and cities as Nagasaki or Kioto. Here we were treated with the genuine and unspoilt hospitality of the natives. As we entered our hotel that evening, I remember the landlord and lady came out upon the balcony to meet us, prostrating themselves to the very floor, with many and grave "Ohaios," drawing quickly in their breath with a sort of inhaled sigh, which is in Japan a mark of respect. Then came the little tea-house girls, in gaily-coloured dresses, and with rosy cheeks and bright silver ornaments in their black hair. These young ladies bring with them buckets of hot water, in which, after taking off our boots and socks, amidst shrieks of laughter at their strange construction, they carefully wash our feet, drying them on little æsthetic towels, such as one might in England use for chair-backs. Next we are led over polished floors past the public room and kitchen, and along the clean verandahs to the suites of rooms allotted to us. These are walled with sliding paper-screens, and carpeted with thick white mats, all of a given size, and fitting the room exactly. Outside our verandah we find a pretty little garden, with a rockery carefully planted with dwarf azaleas, and a pond containing gold-fish and spanned by a tiny bridge. A little fountain plays by the rockery, and narrow gravel paths run in several directions, on each side of which are small coniferæ clipped into fancy shapes. The whole thing is a carefully laid out pleasure park, and measures about ten yards by twelve! The next thing is tea brought in by the little "moosmees," who always go down upon their knees in our presence, and make us feel like princes of the blood royal at least. Then trays and tables six inches high, and bowls and cups to be used in the consumption of the European meal, now being prepared by our boy. After supper a cigar upon the verandah with an admiring crowd standing around, always staring at us, but always pretending not to do so. Later on great mosquito nets are brought, which entirely fill up our room, being hung from hooks in the four top corners; at last we lie down to sleep upon the clean, but not too soft mats, and know nothing more of Japan or tea-houses, until awakened by the laughing, chattering moosmees, who at daylight ruthlessly pull down our net, and push back the paper screens, turning us out upon the balcony to wash, whether we are lazy and sleepy or not.

We had travelled forty miles the first day of our journey northwards from Lake Biwa, and as I had been once violently pitched out of my jinrikisha at a sharp corner into a hedge, and also had walked up many steep hills, and waded a few streams, I confess to being very sleepy the next morning, but lying in bed was out of all question, so we soon drank our coffee, eat our rice, and were off. That day also we covered forty miles, including an hour's delay caused by the passage, in a ferry-boat, of a large and rapid stream. Towards the close of the second day we approached the hills, and our pleasant valley was left behind, and the smooth well-kept road changed into a mere mountain trail. We had no jinrikisha after this second day, and were glad enough to be really in the mountains, with only our legs to depend upon. The condition of life changed rapidly with the country; we saw no more fine horses, or well-bred bulls of burden, the path would not have admitted of them; no more peaceful hamlets either, or pleasant lanes and hedge-rows.

Life is harder here on the mountain sides, and the men and women are poorer, and wear less brightly-coloured clothes. Even Nature seems no more at peace, but is restless and hard-working, roaring herself hoarse in noisy mountain streams, tearing down her well-grown forests by landslips and falling boulders, leaving nothing at rest; even the trees and shrubs seem to cling to the ground as though for their lives, and the house roofs, no longer of thatch, are made of heavy logs of wood, and held down by great stones. Man shares this feeling and lives hard; he has to toil up the passes with burdens on his back; has to bank up his land into terraces on which to grow his rice, to prop up his house as well as hold it down with stones, and cannot find time to keep his garden in order, but leaves his gate falling from

TOO LATE FOR THE FERRY.

the post, and the weeds springing up amongst the flowers, while he must needs go and turn off the fierce watercourse that threatens to destroy his house and home. I do not, however, think these rougher mountain folk are less happy than their neighbours of the smiling valley. They are not less merry, and if they wear more shabby clothes, and live in ruder cottages, are every whit as hospitable, and bow not a jot less low than their more prosperous neighbours.

It was a long while before I became used to the extreme and indeed almost *abject* politeness of the Japanese, and always felt some bashfulness on seeing gray-haired old veterans on their knees, bending their heads until they touched the floor, to a young stranger of twenty-two summers. It seemed hard to believe that less than ten years before, these self-same venerable Japs were swaggering about the land with double-handed swords, cutting off men's heads for pastime, and thinking little of it! Ten years ago some great daimio was holding sway on these hillsides, and every able peasant was his serf, and had his coat of mail and trusty sword, and woe betide the hapless hostile one who came that way. Far less than ten years ago no foreigner was ever seen, or had been seen, or would be seen again, chanced he to meet but one warlike "samurai" taking his walks abroad. And now both old and young bow themselves to the ground and say "good-day, my friend," and make us strangers as welcome as their own children! We must not underrate this unprecedented revolution: it is absolutely unique in all history.

In Europe, people will think of China and Japan together, and talk of both as though their differences were quite insignificant. Nothing can be more wrong, for the Japanese are almost less like Chinamen than Europeans. It is their writing and modes of drawing that have deceived people. I believe fifty per cent. of the English race believe that the Japanese wear pigtails, and are almost indistinguishable from Chinamen, and yet in these rural districts, amongst the peasant class, one can hardly trace the Mongol, and I have often hoped that the Japanese would some day be shown not to be Mongolian at all, but of Caucasian race, and brothers of the Saxon and the Greek.

These peasants are for all the world such as one sees in Northern Italy or Southern France, brown, weather-beaten men with open faces and bright round eyes. The women, too, are pretty and of fair complexion, with good noses and pretty chins, their mouths also are well formed and small; in fact, were it not for their almond-shaped eyes and the somewhat unintellectual character of their foreheads, they would pass for first-class beauties in any capital of Europe. Both men and women are, however, undoubtedly very small, and everything connected with them seems upon a corresponding scale. Even the coolies, these mighty men who will draw their jinrikishas fifty miles a day, are rarely over five feet, and the farm labourers seldom reach a greater height. They live in little houses, and till little farms. They eat from little dishes with little chop sticks, and drink out of little cups tea drawn from little teapots. Their umbrellas are indeed large, and do not very closely resemble the umbrageous curios so common in Regent Street shop windows, but their fans are little, and their pipes the smallest in the world, only holding as much tobacco as will serve for three little whiffs. So in Japan there is about everything the people possess a quaint minuteness very interesting and novel, making it all seem like doll-land, toy-land.

Amongst these people we travelled, in utmost comfort and with infinite delight, for some weeks, traversing pass after pass and valley after valley on our northward journey. Our path was almost all the time in good repair, and pleasant to walk upon; its direction, moreover, had been arranged with great taste, always having regard to the scenery as well as the gradients and engineering difficulties. We did not find many villages amongst these mountain valleys, but there were way-side inns and little rustic sheds wherever a fine view was obtained.

The forests upon the hillsides along the Nagasendo Road are amongst the most beautiful in Japan; infinite variety is their special feature, lending to them an attractiveness which, in my opinion, no tropical vegetation possesses. All our more familiar English trees are met with here in great perfection. I noticed oaks and elms, and maples of many kinds, including very frequently the beautiful golden one, beeches too, and great horse-chestnut trees in flower, and large pear-trees, and amongst these, scattered with such beauty that one could not help thinking it was like an artificial forest, were the endless and glorious specimens of coniferæ, for which Japan is so celebrated. There were weeping willows also by the mountain streams, and red azaleas one blaze of flower, and honeysuckle, and wild roses, and ferns innumerable.

In about a week after leaving Lake Biwa, we came in sight of Asama-yama (smoky mountain), the most considerable active volcano in Japan. At its foot lay a lake and a large fishing village, through which ran a hot and sulphurous spring. This place, Ohio-waki is as near as I can get to the name, is a favourite watering-place, and the tea-houses were full of people who had come to take the baths. As we walked in at sundown, we found the entire population bathing in front of the house doors. It is the national custom; when the day's work is done, men and women, girls and boys, all repair to the nearest bath and there sit and talk over the day's news, and their own affairs and their neighbours'. The sense of bashfulness amongst women and girls practically does not exist where the foreigner has not much intruded. We saw no sign of it in such districts as this, and I may add that my own short experience enables me to agree entirely with the opinion of all recognised authorities on Japan, that the popular idea concerning the immorality of the people is a fallacy.

From Ohio-waki we crossed a pass which, from the readings of my aneroid, could not have been less than ten thousand feet. It was cold, but exquisitely bracing and delightful at the tea-house upon the summit. Asama-yama was smoking just above us on the west, and our position commanded exceptionally fine views in all directions. We were detained at this place as much as two days, being quite unable to obtain a coolie to carry our baggage. I was frequently, during our passage of the Nagasendo, astonished at the utter indifference with which the peasants looked upon money. In this instance we offered a full week's wages to have our baggage taken to the next stage, but we received the same answer from our boy, "They no wantchee come, no wantchee pay, wantchee plant that paddy-rice."

The labour expended in the production of the rice crops upon these mountains is indeed enormous. The farmers have banked up the hillsides until little terraces have been formed over which the streams are led, or, where no streams are available, water is poured by means of a simple contrivance, closely resembling the "shadoof," so familiar to Nile travellers. The terraces are all made to hold six or eight inches of water, in which the rice is grown, and the labour required to prevent banks bursting and sluice gates getting out of repair, must become a heavy burden to the population, which in these districts is comparatively thin. After several days' walking northwards from Asama-yama, our road

METHOD OF IRRIGATION.

diverged somewhat to the east, and, descending the slope of the central mountain range by a deep and beautiful valley, led us out upon the plains and into an important town called Takasaki, only eighty miles from Tokio.

I have seen no difference so great between any adjacent places, as that which we found when we reached this city on the plains. Japan it still was, truly enough, but dirty and squalid Japan, changed almost out of all recognition from the old beauty and simplicity, with which we now, through weeks of experience, had become so familiar. There was no speciality of manufacture in Takasaki, no pride in ancient art or industry, but shops with leather boots and English looking-glasses, with European umbrellas and Yankee clocks and lamps. No gardens here to the houses, or little fountains and pools for gold-fish, but outside the shops were paraffin lamps, and in the front, panes of bad glass. These people will not have dirty or torn paper panes in their native windows, but when they use glass they do not mind it being cracked and grimy. They will not tread upon their clean white mats with muddy sandals, but leather boots cannot be taken off every time upon entering. These are small things, but they tell their story. The people in such places begin to burn paraffin at night, and lie in bed in the morning. The clean doorstep and polished floor are seen no more, nor the neat pathway and pure stream of water. Even native pottery is no longer in request, but iron and stoneware must be imported from Europe.

These are perhaps the most superficial of the changes wrought by European innovation, but even these are significant enough. They speak of the Western government at Tokio, and the new European mania which is now no longer a local fashion of the treaty ports, but is working its way surely and even rapidly through the very heart of the land. Not only the poetry of Japanese life must disappear, but all that is characteristic and beautiful also. The new rule in Japan has not been a very wise one. These men-of-war and standing armies are surely not the first things needful, indeed every so-called modern improvement hitherto adopted appears to have come before its time. The position of China is exactly reversed in Japan. In China the government is whole decades behind the people, and in the sister kingdom it is generations before them. I hardly know which is the more fatally wrong condition. Progressive movements must be national, not governmental. The revolution of 1868 was indeed well timed, and constitutes perhaps the most interesting fact to be found in any history, but it was enough for a generation or two; there should have been a pause after so great a step. Instead of this, however, the government, without knowing the good work that may be done by repose, has plunged headlong into an absolute intoxication of progress, and madly striven by every means that could be devised, to grasp the wealth of Europe, and lavish it upon Western luxuries and extravagancies. Great piles of brick and stucco, of all and no architectural styles, are being run up in the capital towns to serve as mints or palaces or barracks; the national costume is being abandoned for European slops; foreign food, unsuitable as well for climate as for race, is being introduced, and artificial conditions of every sort and kind have become the rage in New Japan. For my own part I would side with the small conservative party, and would vote for less precipitance in this march of progress, and I will in conclusion quote the views upon this subject of a well-educated native politician, who has in the following lines expressed himself with what I venture to consider great common sense.

"Our country supplies every want which is felt by the population who inhabit it. We are dependent for no single article upon our neighbours, and still are deprived of no necessities of life. With the exception of a few religious mendicants, abject poverty is unknown among us. The great masses of the people are contented and happy. We see no change by which either upper or lower classes can be

T

benefited. We desire nothing that we have not got. It has not yet been proved to us that railroads or electric telegraphs make people happier. We tried the Christian religion once, and it led to the destruction of thousands of our countrymen. We do not think our civilisation would be improved by a knowledge of the latest advancement in gunnery, or the newest inventions for the destruction of our fellow-creatures. We are content with saki, and desire neither rum, gin, brandy, whisky, nor any other spirituous productions of progressive countries. We can bear to be deprived of opium, a luxury the charms of which are as yet unknown to us. There are also a few diseases which do not exist among us, and the importation of which we do not think would increase our general happiness. At present our subjects are peaceable and well conducted, of an honest and simple nature, not given to brawling or quarrelling; from what we have seen of foreigners we do not think this simplicity and tranquillity will be increased by their presence. For these reasons we do not desire to see happy Japan open to the civilisation of the West."*

* I have no memorandum as to the authority for this extract, but, finding it amongst an accumulation of notes and statistics, quote it as it stands.

CHAPTER XX.

NIKKO AND TOKIO.

> " Aloft, the ash and warrior oak
> Cast anchor in the rifted rock;
> And higher yet, the pine-tree hung
> His shattered trunk, and frequent flung,
> Where seemed the cliffs to meet on high,
> His boughs athwart the narrow'd sky.
> Highest of all, where white peaks glanced,
> Where glistening streamers waved and danced,
> The wanderer's eye could barely view
> The summer heaven's delicious blue;
> So wondrous wild, the whole might seem
> The scenery of a fairy dream."—*Scott.*

LEAVING Takasaki of much abuse behind, we struck out once more to the northwards from the Nagasendo road, which pursues its degenerate way across the plains, and through the Europeanised villages between the hills and Tokio.

Our way for many miles lay through what I suppose is the richest silk-producing district of Japan. Silkworm-raising seemed to be the sole employment of the population. One could not wish for any sight more picturesque, and at the same time more animated. In the fields young men and boys were picking the mulberry leaves or carrying them home in deep baskets; in the cottages, women, both old and young, were busy soaking the cocoons, or winding the fine thread upon large spindles. The silk is finally made up into neat skeins, and sent to Tokio to be manufactured, or to Yokohama for exportation. There seemed to be great prosperity and happiness in this silk district, and everywhere we noticed pretty gardens, well-kept cottages

SOAKING AND UNWINDING THE COCOONS.

and neatly trimmed hedges. Our path, however, soon took us out of the plains, and wound by a steep zigzag ascent amongst the hills again. After ten or twelve miles of hard walking, we crossed a magnificent watershed, and descended the north-west slope of the hills into a long and steep valley. This was the most thinly-populated part of the country we had visited. For fifteen miles we did not see a house or a living soul, and our night's lodging that evening was in a lonely homestead in the deepest part of the valley, where lived but one small family, whose business it was to give food and shelter to pilgrims who chose this unfrequented route from Takasaki to Nikko. One more long solitary day's tramp over mountain pass and through long winding valley, brought us to what for the time was our journey's end. Late evening, long after the sun had set behind the mountains and cast the forest-covered ravine in sombre darkness, found us trudging footsore and weary through the streets of the little town of Nikko, where we were given most comfortable rooms by the kind host of one of the best tea-houses in the country.

Nikko is the Canterbury of Japan. No traveller has written of it but in terms of highest admiration, and were I to attempt a detailed description, I should no doubt work myself into an absurdity of enthusiasm. If we take the city itself and its district, which includes the baths of Yumota, it may be safely said that they equal and even surpass all else of interest or beauty in the East. Of the two great temples of Nikko, I shall also say little more than that they are the finest in Japan, and "sui generis" in the world; one indeed is so magnificently wrought in lacquer and gold, that it has been actually boxed up in a colossal pine covering, like a great packing case, to keep it from the influences of the weather. These temples, with all their wealth and marvellous workmanship, did not, however impress me so greatly. They were, after all, only Buddhist temples, and merely so much more rich and curious than others I had seen. It was in their site and surroundings that I found the greatest delight. Nothing elsewhere in Japan approaches the sublime; the attainment of this is not attempted by the inhabitants; they have not even anything of magnificence in the true sense. In architecture certainly not, and therein is greatest scope, in sculpture not, nor indeed in music or literature.

Here at Nikko, however, in what perhaps one may call forest gardening, they have produced by nature's aid a masterpiece both magnificent and sublime. The approach to the temples is through a short but wonderfully perfect avenue, the trees of which are giant cryptomeria two hundred feet high and twenty to thirty feet in girth. They stand back from the roadway, and spring from well-kept and grass-grown terraces. The ascent leading up to the gates consists of a wide flight of stone steps almost black with the rains and dews of many centuries. The scale of everything is grand in the extreme, and I have seen nothing more impressive. Thousands of pilgrims come every year to view these ancient shrines, and look upon the tombs of the old Shoguns which are situated upon the hill behind the temples. Nikko is a show place now, and sharing in the general revolution, can claim no longer to be the head-centre of whatever of a religious system may still remain in Japan. It is, however, the prince of show-places, and as long as its giant trees and time-worn shrines and temple stairs remain, will be the crowning point of interest as well to Japanese as European travellers.

After some days of rest and sightseeing at Nikko, we started for Yumota, a little watering-place high up in the mountains, which is scenically, as Nikko is historically, second to none amongst the sights of Japan. Six thousand feet of climbing were necessary before we reached our destination, and the path for fifteen miles exceeded in its beauties anything I had hitherto seen in this beautiful country. It would be wearisome to recount in detail the features of interest on our journey; suffice it to mention, that these included waterfalls, that would compare with the Handeck in volume or the Staubach in height, and which perhaps surpass either of these in beauty.

Our path wound along the shores of lakes, too, that were clear as crystal, bordered by weeping-willows, and overshadowed by great oaks, their surfaces broken by loveliest islets, that reflected upon the smooth surface a thousand shades of green. Above these lakes were mountains with dark and overhanging crags, their summits shining with snow. After the lakes we came upon a great natural rockery, made by the hand of fire many thousand years ago, and now overgrown with flowers and ferns and moss. A botanist employed by Mr. Veitch, and who had spent his life in tree and flower hunting all the world over, told me in Nikko that this was the richest valley that he had ever seen, and that from it he had obtained dozens of new plants.

We reached the village of Yumota at sundown, and found it to be a mere cluster of tea-houses, which were supported entirely by people who came to take the baths. Right down the centre of the principal street, a row of neatly-built bathing houses had been erected, and these we found on the evening of our arrival to be crowded with people. There were perhaps twenty baths, in size about twelve feet by six, all clean and suitably arranged for bathing. Men, women and children were sitting in them, with the water up to their chins in the very height of enjoyment. They were chattering and gossiping away, like truly jovial holiday-makers, and in some cases tea was being handed round or pipes were being smoked. There was more universal nakedness here than in any place I had visited, the people actually taking off their clothes in their respective tea-houses, and strolling down the streets in parties, without as much covering as a South Sea Islander. The waters issue from the earth at boiling point, and are very strongly impregnated with sulphur. The particular stream that is used for the baths in the main street of the village, is almost identical in composition with the sulphur springs of Manitou in Colorado.

After some delightful days in this neighbourhood, we started from Nikko down the great cryptomeria avenue for

Tokio. The main road to the capital deserves a word or two of notice; it is about ninety miles long, and originally was shaded by an avenue of magnificent trees, extending along the entire length. About fifty miles of these trees still remain. They are from a hundred and fifty to two hundred feet high, and are planted so closely together that their trunks form a wall of timber on either side of the road. The effect is very impressive, especially in the long straight reaches, for on a cloudy day the light is partly excluded, and a sombre and solemn effect is produced. The road, moreover, in many places lies as much as ten or even twenty feet below the surrounding country, and is flanked by steep banks, above which rise the walls of tree trunks.

I was very disgusted to find that this magnificent roadway was in a state of utter and disgraceful neglect. The modern Europeanised Japanese government has not, it seems, money enough to keep its highways in repair, but must build great arsenals and mints, and give gold-laced caps and trousers to its police, and put telegraph wires and stations where no one wants or cares for either. It consequently cannot maintain the public works that it inherits, but leaves this national highway a dismal swamp, so that for many miles we had to be pulled in our little carriages across the fields, upon which our coolies found it easier to travel than the neglected road. The modern government can indeed appreciate the money value of its avenue, and has already, to pay its army tailor's bill, cut down thousands of these royal cryptomeria that botanists have come from Europe to see, but it is too poor to spend a few hundred dollars a year to maintain what in all Japan is the one thing most needed, a really good road.*

---

* The reader may remember the old saying, quoted, among other places, in Kingsley's 'At Last,' "The first step in civilisation is to make roads; the second, to make more roads; and the third, to make more roads still."

On the second day after leaving Nikko, we turned off from what remained of the royal avenue, and crossing an open and rather bleak tract of country, found ourselves in the outskirts of Tokio, the modern capital and home of the existing

WINNOWING RICE.

Europeanised government. Everywhere as we passed along, the signs of innovation and change became more apparent. At times we would see an oldfashioned cottage with the old lady spinning in the doorway, and the labourer winnowing his rice beside the house, or watering his little garden-farm, as we had seen them in the inland districts; but for the most part, as we approached Tokio, we found the nature of both land and people changed. The men wore boots and trousers, or carried European umbrellas, or showed some other sign of the existence of the new régime. Panes of glass, too, might be seen in the cottages, as in Takasaki, and paraffin lamps outside, the people looking more dirty and unnatural every mile we traversed. At length we found the villages connected into one long line of houses, and, passing through thickly-populated suburbs, at last reached our destination in Tokio, the modern capital.

Our stay in the Japanese metropolis was short, and not so full of interest as might be expected. I found it almost European compared with Kioto, and thoroughly prosaic after the inland villages of the Nagasendo. Its streets, however, are full of life and gaiety, and we had some pleasant drives and hours of shopping in the Tori, as the Regent Street of the capital is called. The Temple of Shiba is less beautifully situated than those of Nikko, but has, perhaps, more architectural pretensions than any other temple in Japan. The shrines of the Shoguns (the 2nd, 6th, 12th, and 14th) that are buried there, are also of interest.

I think emphatically the sight of Tokio is what is known as Asakusa. The temples are much as other temples, the Daimio's castles are made utterly unromantic by the addition of modern buildings in red brick, which serve as training colleges or paper money manufactories or embassies or what not; the character of the streets even is lost to a great extent, for in them one sees little monkey-like soldiers in French uniforms, or Japanese dandies in tall hats and frock coats. At Asakusa, however, you are carried back to old Japan, and I was delighted with my day there. The place consists of a temple surrounded by pleasure-grounds beautifully planted and laid out, in which is held a sort of perpetual fair. The whole presents the most extraordinary spectacle of holiday-making and festivity, and every device to attract and obtain money from visitors of all classes, both young and old, is to be met with at this pleasure place.

Of the temple of Kuanon, which is the nucleus of all this congregation, I saw nothing and cared less, but spent my time amongst the stalls and shooting galleries, indeed no city clerk at the Derby could have found more to amuse him.

Finding a theatre amongst the many attractions, I looked in for an hour, and derived the greatest amusement from what fragment of the play I was able to witness in that time. Aided by my boy's very indifferent translation, I gathered that some such tragedy as the following was being enacted. The father of the heroine wants his daughter to be married to a wealthy merchant from whom she has been receiving considerable attention. After much discussion the faithless merchant refuses to comply with this desire. The father, however, being determined to make something out of the affair, asks for the loan of a thousand yen. The wealthy merchant, feeling he has behaved rather badly, in a weak moment lends the money. In the next act he is heartily sorry for what he has done, remembering that it will soon become generally known, and that he will be pestered for loans of money from all sides: this act of weakness must not, therefore, be allowed to get abroad. Dead men tell no tales. He accordingly puts some poison in his victim's rice, which results in the father of the lovely heroine dying in agonies upon the stage. Next act; Enter with great pomp and ceremony, ten blood and thunder two-sworded ruffians with enormous beards. They view the corpse. They jabber and stamp about, and pull their flowing beards and roll their eyes horribly. The lovely girl becomes much agitated, and finally faints. The rich villain is so overcome by her charms when in this interesting condition that he repents of his foul deed, and marries her. The bloodthirsty ruffians, like the gentleman on the campstool at Mr. Winkle's duel, feel that some one ought to have satisfaction, and are very anxious to use their swords, until at last pacified by a bribe from the happy bridegroom. This little tragedy was a mere fragment of the entire play, of which it would have taken a long time to obtain so much as a bare conception.

From Tokio we travelled by railroad to Yokohama, the journey occupying about an hour. After a few days of visiting and shopping and packing, my friend sailed in the *City of Tokio* for San Francisco, and I, having some more sightseeing before me in the Southern Hemisphere, started in the old wooden paddle-boat *China* for Hong Kong, en route for the Torres Straits and Australia, after over three months of the most delightful experience and unalloyed pleasure in the Far East.

The following statistics, furnished by the Japanese Commissioners at the Melbourne International Exhibition 1880, may be of interest.

The Empire of Japan comprises four principal, and an immense number of small islands, with an area of 160,000 square miles, and a population of 34,338,404 inhabitants, of which 17,419,785 are males and 16,918,619 females.

It is divided into 85 provinces and 717 districts, which contain 63,510 villages and 12,276 towns. There are five towns (Tokio, Osaka, Kioto, Nagoya, and Kanazawa) with a population of upwards of 100,000, and a hundred with that of 10,000. Of the 34,338,404 inhabitants, 37 belong to the Imperial family, 2,965, to the hereditary nobility, and 1,894,784 to the samurai or gentry class. Over 90 per cent. of the public officers, professional men and others who occupy prominent positions in society, belong to the samurai class, which indeed constitutes the backbone of the Empire.

The number of deaths from unnatural causes is about 3,500 per annum, of which 1,600 are by accident and 1,900 by suicide.

The criminals amount to about 22 per 1000, of which $\frac{1}{3}$ are convicted of gambling, $\frac{1}{3}$ of larceny, and $\frac{1}{3}$ of miscellaneous crimes: 4·37 per cent. of the criminals are females.

The farmers of Japan raise, perhaps, the heaviest crops known to the world, and the superior productiveness of the small lots of land held by peasant proprietors will be acknowledged from the fact, that with but 11 million acres of cultivated land, $34\frac{1}{2}$ million people are fed and clothed for the greater part, and are still able to export 25 million lbs. of tea, 3 million lbs. of raw silk, and 35 million lbs. of rice.

PART IV.

SPANISH AMERICA.

. . . . "There is a law above all the enactments of human codes—the same throughout the world, the same in all times—such as it was before the daring genius of Columbus pierced the night of ages, and opened to one world the sources of power, wealth, and knowledge, and to another all unutterable woes—such as it is at this day."—*Lord Brougham.*

CHAPTER XXI.

CENTRAL AMERICA.

> .... "And ye know, my masters, that wherever Spain hath ruled she hath wither'd all beneath her. Look at the New World—a paradise made Hell."—'*Queen Mary.*'

THERE is attached to Spanish America a certain romantic interest which does not, I think, belong to any other part of the world to the same extent. It is not an interest born of schoolbooks, for that surely would savour but little of romance; nor is it connected with bygone arts or mysteries of legendary lore; it is not quite anything that one experiences with regard to Europe or the East; it seems indeed to be the peculiar offspring of such books as 'Robinson Crusoe' and 'Westward Ho'—it is the interest of adventure and romance. We must not, however, omit to speak of Prescott in this matter, for the romance of Spanish America is historical. What a charm is there in those two histories of Peru and Mexico! The hardships of Marco Polo or Cook or Stanley seem quite insignificant as compared with the adventures of Cortez, Pizarro or Amyas Leigh. I dare say we should not have read Pizarro's journal, had he known how to write and had left us one—it would doubtless have been as tedious as Livingstone's—yet what a story his conquest is as told by the New England historian!

It is my purpose here to write a short chapter or two on the Spanish America of to-day, thinking that perhaps some of my readers may care to know a little more about the modern ports and larger cities of that great continent, in which we have all at one time or another been so keenly interested. My spying out of the land was neither exhaustive nor prolonged, for I merely passed along its coasts as a visitor seeking for new sights and experiences, and propose now simply to write down such things as I saw.

We steamed into the harbour of Mazatlan, in Northwestern Mexico, on the very brightest and most dazzling of spring mornings, and, steering past some rugged and igneous rocks, over which the blue sea was lashing itself into a wilderness of snow-white foam, dropped our anchor in any number of fathoms of smooth water about two miles from the town. The general view of the little strip of Mexico now before us was certainly not very promising, resembling nothing so much as the shores of the Red Sea, or the country behind Aden; high mountains lay away at the back of the harbour, rose-coloured and purple, looking, however, parched up and sun-scorched as they undoubtedly are.

The invariable boats soon came off in the invariable manner, and a crowd of shouting, large-hatted Mexicans in blue blouses and red sashes, for all the world like Neapolitan fishermen, were soon vociferating round the ship in what, no doubt, was horribly corrupt Spanish. Having delivered ourselves into the hands of these enthusiastic natives, we were pulled rapidly ashore and landed on a desolate and broken-down quay, where a dismal tramcar drawn by one wooden-legged mule was waiting to take us up to the city.

But a very few moments sufficed to dispel any fondly cherished expectations we may have had with respect to Mexican cities, for one always has cherished expectations of places of this sort be one never so often disappointed.

Mazatlan as one may see it to-day is indeed as little interesting a spot as any sight-surfeited traveller could expect. The streets are paved with glaring and almost red-hot flags, the houses, built of similarly hot and glaring blocks of stone, are low, plastered, whitewashed, one-storied strongholds, heavily barred as to windows and doors, and seemingly more adapted to withstand a siege than to house a citizen. The plaza—I am almost frightened to think of the times I shall have to call attention to the plaza in my description of South American cities—is bare, dazzling, deserted. A number of seats, out of all proportion even to the inhabitants of the town, much less to the probable occupants, are standing in a state of dusty simmer, under the leafless and sun-scorched trees. Surely this is not the very centre and pride of the second city in Mexico?

We pull up at a vast oldfashioned Italian sort of hotel, standing at the top of the square, just where in fourth-rate Italian towns the hotel always does stand; we tramp in along the stone-paved corridor, papered with gaudy frescoes, and up the dismal staircase to the "salon," seeking shade and comfort but finding none. What a lifeless wilderness of a place! the very marble-topped tables and seedy little broken-down cruet-stands, might have come over with Cortez, and been left unmoved from his day to this. The meanest conceivable breakfast is given us for a dollar and a half, and there is no fruit although we are in the tropics. We wander again into the streets later on in the day, and gaze distressfully at the little white and pink houses, with their pale green shutters and low stone doorways. Lazy and sunburnt half-castes are lolling about the streets, or lying asleep in the shade, their hats, certainly the most interesting thing about them, being made of thick heavy felt, with an inch or more of silver braid round the brim, and measuring two feet or a yard in diameter. Of women we saw but few, and these with black shawls over their heads like nuns in France; we had the fortune to meet several in "mantillas," but these only served to make the whole town more desolate when they had passed hurriedly by. In a smaller plaza a mile away we did indeed discover some pretty little stalls with flowers and white curtains, wherein were sold sundry sweet and syrup-like drinks by dark lemon-coloured girls; it was quite an oasis in the desert of Mazatlan, and we went on our way almost rejoicing. No, there is nothing to see, nothing to praise in this our first Mexican city, and I buried my visions of gold-spurred caballeros and dark-eyed señoritas and bloodthirsty brigands from the hills, away where many another bright expectation has been buried in the course of my wanderings.

The ports along the coast lower down are in no way to be compared even with Mazatlan in interest, for their united population I think would not amount to 10,000. Manzanillo possesses a few green hills and picturesque wooden houses, which the almost entirely Indian population prefer to those of glaring stone or stucco. Acapulco can boast of a very magnificent harbour where several men-of-war of one or another nationality are generally lying, but beyond this there is indeed nothing to record.

Of Acapulco I had expected great things, for is it not familiar to all from the histories, and geography books? What a ruin of a town it is in these latter days! a town of perhaps only four hundred inhabitants, and in which no civilised mortal could so much as obtain a decent luncheon! The only interesting remembrance I have of the place is that we there met an Austrian gentleman of fallen fortunes, who had been in Maximilian's body-guard, and was full of Mexican information of very varied interest. He had for some unaccountable reason come down by the road to Acapulco from the City of Mexico, thus exposing himself to a danger which seemed very unnecessary; it was, I fancy, his having quite nothing but his life to lose that made him take so perilous a journey, the high roads of Mexico being in as deplorable a condition as those of Greece.

This gentleman told me a story of his late and ever to be lamented master, which so well illustrates the state of Mexico, that I relate it here, although it may not be new to some of my readers.

A cabinet meeting was being held at the palace in the City of Mexico, but a few years before the death of the unhappy Archduke: none were present but the ministers themselves and the small body-guard of which our newly-arrived passenger was a member. Maximilian looking up from his seat at his ministers around the table, says very gravely,

"Gentlemen, I had but now a gold pencil case of, to me, great value, for it has been an heirloom in our family for many years. The pencil case you all know; a minute since I was writing with it, and now it is gone. I would on no account cast a suspicion on my honourable cabinet, but I propose for a moment to lower the lights in the room, and upon the lights being restored I am persuaded that the pencil will again be found where I, a minute ago, laid it. Officer, take away for a moment these candles."

When the lights were restored, the pencil lay there, and the business of the meeting was resumed as though nothing had happened.

Many were the stories our new companion told us as we paced the deck on fine clear nights, and great indeed was his admiration for the unhappy prince, his late master.

It is terrible to contemplate the debasement of everything

Mexican since the restoration of the republic; in those three short years whilst Maximilian reigned, the only signs of light can be found that have shone upon the dark history of Mexico. The republican government has, since 1867, gone from bad to worse; the slight impetus given of late years by the adoption of a progress policy, the introduction of railroads, telegraphs, &c., has been but the feeblest flicker, with no visible result save addition to the nation's liabilities; revolution still rages throughout the land with the appalling frequency of about one outbreak a year. All the public works are in a state of neglect and decay, and more than three-fourths of the people can neither read nor write. The debt is over sixty-three millions, on no part of which a cent of interest has been paid for many years, and in addition to this the expenditure is almost invariably in excess of the revenue.

"Nothing with us is organised except robbery," say the observant Mexicans, and the latest authority on the subject concludes his account of the country in these words: "Through this deplorable state of things, one of the richest lands in the world has been reduced to a nation of mendicants, and not only the central government, but those also of the several states have succeeded in exposing themselves to a universal obloquy."

Mexico in its earliest days of independence stood at the very top of the tree of ancient civilisation in the New World: the Tezcucans and the Aztecs in many ways surpassed even the Incas of Peru in their advancement. Again, Mexico in the early days of colonisation was the most magnificent of all the Spanish possessions. It has now fallen to the very lowest place among nations, and has become an actual byeword "with none so poor to do it reverence." As I think of this I am tempted to quote a few lines from the works of one of the old kings of this land, a monarch who reigned many years before Columbus discovered the West Indies, and who was the most high-minded and enlightened perhaps of all barbaric potentates. In his old age, this king, Nezahualcoyotl the Tezcucan, retiring from the government of his country to pursue his literary inclination, perhaps anticipating the downfall of his great empire, wrote as follows:

"All things on earth have their term, and, in the most joyous career of their vanity and splendour, their strength fails, and they sink into the dust. . . . The great, the wise, the valiant, the beautiful, alas! where are they now? They are all mingled with the clod; and that which has befallen them shall happen to us and to those which come after us. Yet let us take courage, illustrious nobles and chieftains, true friends and loyal subjects, let us aspire to that heaven where all is eternal and corruption cannot come. The horrors of the tomb are but the cradle of the sun, and the dark shadows of death as brilliant lights for the stars." I fear there are few modern Mexicans with either the wisdom or the religion of this old royal philosopher.

We steamed away from Acapulco, our last port of call on the Mexican coast, with no great feelings of regret, and made an uneventful run of about two days down to San José de Guatemala, which port lies on an open coast where no break of any kind is offered to the great rollers of the Pacific, which come sweeping up over thousands and thousands of miles, and hurl themselves with a noise like thunder upon the hard shelving beach.

No boats of any kind can be used on the coast of Guatemala, and a long light iron pier has been erected by an English company, at the end of which it is possible to land. The vegetation here is very beautiful as far as eye can reach, and the little bamboo huts of the village of San José look most picturesque under the shade of the great palm-trees. Guatemala, the capital, is fifty miles or so from the sea, but the duration of our stay was too short to enable us to undertake the journey. In a few hours we were again under weigh, steaming down the coast and catching occasional glimpses of the great volcanoes, for which Guatemala is justly celebrated.

Our next republic was San Salvador, of which we were also unable to see anything, as our stay at the port, La Libertad, was but for a few hours. The same system of landing cargo and passengers is in force here; the scenery, too, is of the same most beautiful order, the hills at the back being clothed in the richest of tropical garments.

At Punta Arenas, the port of Costa Rica, where we arrived a day or so later, there is a very lovely harbour surrounded by picturesque hills, and where, in the language of many a harbour description that I have read, all the navies of the world might lie at anchor. We had a pleasant day on shore at this strange little place; the streets are very wide, quite unpaved, and lined with huts built of thin poles placed side by side with a small opening between each; the roofs are of thick thatch which keeps off the sun, the dwellings thus being very cool and comfortable in such a climate. A few stores of Manchester goods, a fruit market and several hundreds of these huts constitute the town. I should not omit, however, a large barn-like cathedral where we saw mass going on, a military band in dirty scarlet playing a fast and monotonous waltz in one of the transepts. A dozen soldiers, unshod, and in raggedest blue uniforms, with fixed bayonets, and, I dare say, loaded rifles, were drawn up down the nave. Fifty women were kneeling on one side, and twenty men on the other, whilst the most criminal-looking priest in vestments which had once been white was officiating. This constituted high mass in the Punta Arenas cathedral on that Sunday morning!

I am afraid the republic of Costa Rica is in no very flourishing state if the following report of the Minister of Justice a year or two back may count for anything: he says:

"We have reached such a degree of corruption as to be compelled for the sake of our honour to conceal the statistics of crime amongst the population, else we should lose the good repute we have hitherto been held in amongst nations."

We sailed from Costa Rica with good wishes for the place, for it is very pretty and the people merry and kind, and two days later we brought our long voyage from San Francisco to an end, by dropping anchor off the islands of Taboga in Panama Bay, seven or eight miles from the town. We pulled slowly across the wide bay soon after we had anchored, and were glad enough to see the last of the cheerless American steamer, in which we had spent nearly three weeks of great discomfort.

Panama at a distance is somewhat picturesque; there is an ivy-mantled appearance about its walls, and a fortified, mediæval aspect generally pervading the city, but when you set foot on shore it proves to be the most ghastly of ruins. We landed at a ruined quay, and toiled laboriously up a ruined street to a ruined square where the grass is a foot high; it is the dreariest of spectacles. A cathedral stands on one side with two tumble-down, pretentious-looking towers; on another side is a shabby, but once gaudy hotel. This latter we enter, and obtain earthy and dungeon-like rooms, here also we dine in a melancholy, marble-paved vault. Ruin and decay stare at us from all sides. A revolution took place but two days before and twenty-five people were killed in the grass-grown square under our windows; there will have to be another revolution next week if the average is to be maintained.

The day after our arrival we took the train across the isthmus to Aspinwall, returning in the afternoon in time for another dinner in the marble-paved vault. It is a very pretty journey, and the railway is a thoroughly good one, although the service of trains may well be complained of. We had thirty large goods waggons on our train, which occasioned an amount of jolting not easily to be forgotten. I should call the character of the country "lumpy," the hills being at no point high, but very numerous: the greatest elevation attained by the railway is two hundred and fifty feet. The line runs for the entire distance through a rich tropical jungle, which is the cause, taken of course in connection with the climate, of the great prevalence of fever.

To an ordinary visitor the difficulties in the way of constructing a canal at this point upon the isthmus seem almost insurmountable. Yet M. de Lesseps is sanguine, and people will hesitate before they again cast ridicule upon an enterprise undertaken by that great engineer. The Nicaragua scheme appears to the uninitiated by far the most feasible, for in that country white men as well as Chinese can live, and the formation of the land seems more suitable for the construction of a canal.

The villages we pass on the road are exceedingly picturesque and quaint, and the cottages, with their exceedingly steep roofs, closely resemble those of Fiji. The natives are of a beautiful copper-bronze colour and finely made, the women wearing a droll little short-sleeved chemise and a print petticoat.

I think Aspinwall of all places I have visited is the most essentially *mean*; a long row of tumble-down houses, over an arcade of shops like those of a fourth-rate seaport town, constitutes the entire settlement. In an out-of-the-way place where no one would be likely to see it, we literally ran up against a statue of Columbus. There is a lurking inclination amongst both travellers and geographers to call the place Colon, which perhaps this statue may in some way account for.

The day after our excursion across the isthmus, we started in the most comfortable of steamers belonging to the Pacific Steam Navigation Co.,—than whose steamers in all my wanderings I have found none more admirably managed in every detail—on our voyage down the coast of South America.

Our first port of call was Buenaventura, which lies twenty miles up a very lovely river, where we found about thirty little Columbian huts such as those upon the isthmus. In front of these was a large tract of pestilential mud, across which we were on landing "sleighed" as it were, by barefooted natives, who drew the flat-bottomed canoes along over the slimy surface at a great rate. There being nothing to see on shore whatever, and no cargo to speak of for our steamer, we were glad to be able to steam away in but a few hours.

The next day we put into a still more beautiful, although but little more inviting place called Tumaco, also in Columbia. The natural luxuriance surpassed anything I had hitherto seen, the place being simply one vast tropical garden; there were some exquisite meadows by the river, scattered over with large trees as in an English park, and owned by a German settler. We found here quite different houses from those of Northern Columbia; these were almost flat-roofed and of two stories, presenting a very picturesque appearance, and looking almost like Swiss chalets in amongst the palm-tree shadows. The natives, too, are of a different Indian tribe, being lighter and of finer features, resembling indeed very strikingly the Bishareeyah Arabs of Upper Egypt. I was surprised at there being no native industries whatever at any of these ports; the people depend absolutely on natural products, and not a thing can be bought but fruit or vegetables.

Of the republic itself I could learn very little; it rejoices in the well-sounding name of The United States of Columbia, having entirely abandoned its old style of New Granada. It consists of nine states of which Panama is the most important, and with an area of half a million square miles, its population is only three-quarters of that of London!

Before I close this chapter I must say a few words about Guayaquil, the capital of Ecuador, although neither that republic nor Columbia belong properly to Central America.

Guayaquil is quite the most interesting place of its kind that I visited on that coast. It lies probably as much as a hundred and twenty miles up the Guayas River, although that stream is so wide at its mouth one can hardly say where the sea ends and the river begins. We took a pilot on board at the river's mouth, and steamed for several hours up just such a stream as one sees in travellers' pictures of the Upper Amazon. At last, and just as the sun went down blood red behind the rich, forest-covered hills, we came in sight of the town and let go our anchor in mid-stream. The quay is now well lighted with gas, and the effect was very pretty by night, the long, brilliant reflections quivering in the fast-running water.

We wandered about Guayaquil all the next day, and

enjoyed it very much, for there was a world of novelty in the
quaint tumble-down place. The houses are all built of wood
and painted blue and pink and white; there are arcades
along the main street which runs parallel to the river, and
natives of every colour selling fruit and vegetables along
the pavement. There is a large and dilapidated bull-fight
amphitheatre, and a gaudy wooden cathedral, everything

GUAYAQUIL CATHEDRAL.

looking somehow like theatrical scenery by daylight. The
people, too, had a stage-like appearance, such of Spanish
extraction as we saw wearing either the very shortest
or the very longest of dresses, and being always mounted
on high-heeled boots, and covered as to the face with chalk
and rouge. The pure Indians wear as nearly nothing as
possible, and are picturesque and of most beautiful colour.
Hammocks and Panama hats are the two specialities here,

both very good and both very expensive; the former are the universal beds of the natives. Some idea of the extent to which hats are made in Ecuador may be gathered from the fact that from the little port of Manta, some miles north of Guayaquil, 24,000 dozen, or about £45,000 worth, are exported annually.

Perhaps the most interesting political feature of the republic of Ecuador is the relation of its church to the state. Up to the year 1875 the republic had at its head a Clerical President, and although he was assassinated in that year, the Jesuit element is still absolute throughout the state. The Board of Trade refuses admission into the country of everything that is not sanctioned by the brethren of the order, and the entire educational system of the state is in the same hands. The very army is styled the "Army of the Sacred Heart of Jesus," and is split up into the following four divisions:

1. Division of the Son of God.
2. Division of the Holy Lancers of Death.
3. Division of the Good Shepherd.
4. Division of the Holy Virgin.

It seems on the whole, however, to be generally admitted that the despotic sacerdotal rule of the Jesuits is more conducive to the general well-being of the community than the anarchy of the other small American republics.

At a point a few miles to the south of the Guayas river, the entire nature of the coast changes with astonishing abruptness. The richly tropical character of the country ceases, and gives place, for the next two thousand miles, to a barren wilderness of sand and hills, unsurpassed in desolation by any portion of the world's surface.

CHAPTER XXII.

PERU.

> " Nor tree, nor shrub, nor plant, nor flower,
> Nor aught of vegetative power,
> The weary eye can scan."

I FEEL more inclined, in writing this chapter on Peru, to launch out into violent invectives against the Spanish nation in general, and Pizarro and the "Conquerors" in particular, than to calmly draw a sketch of the country as I found it on my visit in 1879. The Incaland, if such an expression may be used, as described by the Spanish conquerors, and more especially by Las Casas, whose life has been recently written most admirably by Señor Fabié,* is such a Utopia, such a model of prosperity and, after its kind, wise government, one can but cry, "Ichabod, Ichabod" over the wreck of to-day, and turn again and vilify those intruders who have brought about such a woeful change. I have stood on a vantage point in the Andes and tried to picture to myself those by-gone days, the royal Inca, King, High Priest, Supreme Judge, "himself the State," proceeding along the great highway, from palace to palace, with all the pomp of a western Solomon. The three great divisions of land were clearly marked out upon the plain, this for the Sun, that for the Inca, the other for the people, that last, the people's land, looking like some vast chessboard with its

* 'Vida de Bartholomé de Las Casas,' 2 vols., Señor Fabié, Madrid, 1879.

"per capita" divisions. In the centres of each section the great stone-built storehouses in which the Inca, with a Joseph's wisdom, had stored the surplus of good years to be used during bad; and across the whole plain the broad, stone-paved highway with its viaducts, embankments, galleries, bridges.* What a country it was! No one but the decrepit or sick in Incaland were permitted to remain in idleness, for that was a crime in the eye of the law severely punishable. Industry was publicly commended and stimulated by rewards. No man could be poor, moreover, none a spendthrift nor an impoverished speculator—ambition, avarice, love of change, morbid excitement, all absent in old Peru. "Not poetical," you say; " Not enviable; " yet surely a most model empire? Shades of Atahualpa, how the mighty are fallen! here is the modern republic of Peru only rivalled by Mexico in precedence of poverty and degradation.

It was a perfect morning some days before my abovementioned reveries that our cable rushed with familiar rattle into the calm blue bay of Callao. We had called at a few ports, Payta and Pimmentel amongst others, on our way down the coast; but I hesitate to write of them lest I should exhaust my abomination and desolation epithets.

Callao had a somewhat special interest to me in memory of a hundred yarns from hyperbole-inclined ancient mariners. It was a sorry enough place that we found answering to the name upon landing—this the Callao of Liverpool sailing-ship captains? Why it is but another Guayaquil devoid of that city's picturesqueness!

There is a railway, there are indeed two railways, running

* " The roads of the Incas are amongst the most useful and stupendous works ever executed by man."—*Humboldt.*

up to Lima, so shaking the very plentiful dust from our feet, we hurried to the capital, the city of the Viceroys, the home of Pizarro and the Conquerors.

Truly Lima is well worth seeing. I stood in the Plaza with a feeling that here was a city indeed out of which Mr. Murray might even have made a handbook. Here is the Cathedral, and here the Palace; the Chamber of Deputies lies yonder, and churches to half the saints on the other side of the sun are sprinkled about with almost Venetian profusion. Maria was selling fruit on the kerb-stone and José lay asleep in the shade—it all seemed familiar to me, and yet it was a familiarity seasoned with novelty. The Cathedral of Lima is very different from those to which we are accustomed in Europe, and indeed there is about everything in the city, down to the very street Arabs, a freshness which is thoroughly interesting and enjoyable. Large and covered-in balconies project from every house, Egyptian in form though less elaborately wrought than the beautiful casements of Cairo; there is grateful shade too in the roadway, for the streets are narrow and oldfashioned, as they always should be where the sun pours down so fiercely. Ladies are to be seen not unfrequently, always using the "manta," and gentlemen, howsoever richly dressed, carrying if not wearing, the universal poncho; most noticeable of all, however, are the little boys in dismal rags crying out the news; I can hear now in my mind's ear—if the mind have an ear as well as an eye—their shrill cry of "El Patria—cinque centavo!"

Lottery tickets are being sold by men and boys at every corner; they are a government institution, and a prize was drawn for on the night of our arrival worth twenty thousand "soles." The currency everywhere is paper—the most utterly disreputable paper in the world. There has been a

x

silver coinage in past years, and one sees a coin or so now and then at the coast ports; the people, however, know of no silver in Lima, and two or three men, whom I offered to pay in that metal, did not know in the least what it meant, and gladly took half its value in the dirtiest of paper! The "sole" of Peru, originally equal in value to a United States dollar, was worth eighteen pence when I was in Lima, with every prospect of an immediate reduction to fourteen pence.

What money must have been squandered here! the riches of the country are well nigh incalculable, and minerals are undoubtedly very plentiful; but it is the guano islands and nitre beds that have brought such incredible sums into the treasury, and one cannot help asking what has become of all the money?* The great dock and harbour works of Callao are in ruins, though but half completed, and one of the most amusing instances of misgovernment I have come across is, that no steamers are allowed to moor at the dock wharfs until the passengers have been landed from twenty yards outside the end of the quay—so strong is the waterman interest in this republican cabinet!

On Sunday evening we went to the leading theatre, a thoroughly good one, and saw the performance of an historic drama of some interest. The piece had reference to the old days of the Revolution, previous to the final overthrow of the Spanish yoke. The interest shown by the audience was intense, the applause being always given to the sentiment of the text, and not to the acting, and yet the end was most

* "The Chinca Islands, which we passed two days before landing, have produced an equivalent of a hundred millions sterling. An officer told me when I was at Chicla, that he had himself discovered a fountain of pure petroleum in the Andes; national wealth such as this, however, seems to evaporate in Peru, where money is stolen by every official, and where there is more "pocket-lining" than in Egypt.

unsatisfactory, for the hero, with whom we all sympathised, was shot dead by the Imperial officers in the last act, and the women, his friends, who moved us all to pity, were reduced to hysterical despair. The villain, against whom was the strongest resentment expressed in hisses and groans, accomplished the consummation of his ambition, and the dear old Spanish general, whom we admired, only sent in his pardon to the hero as the fatal shot was fired. At the climax of this accumulation of reverses the curtain fell, and we were all left with an uncomfortable sense of justice having been defeated, and vice remaining triumphant.

To the Cathedral of Lima some few words are, perhaps due: it is in design a truly noble structure, standing on a broad open Plaza, where are fountains and trees and seats. From each of the two high towers, there projects a gibbet, whereon, from time to time, are suspended the most notorious disturbers of the public peace, for the edification of the citizens.

Upon the interior one can bestow but little praise; it is bare and uninteresting, a whitewashed and barn-like appearance prevailing. The great square columns are hung from base to summit with rich crimson velvet, which helps somewhat to make the place look comfortable, but all the rest of the building, including the roof, has been given over to the whitewasher. The only point of real interest is the carving at the back of the stalls, representing fifty scenes from biblical history, and deserving more than the dusty neglect to which it is now consigned. Only a small side chapel is in present use, the main body of the building being entirely deserted, neither cleaned nor cared for. The glory of the great cathedral like that of the whole country has, seemingly for evermore, departed.

I have nothing to say of the hundreds of minor churches;

they are in the lowest style of vulgarly ornate decoration, and abound in sensational wax figures and tinsel ornament; the horror chamber in Baker Street would soothe the feelings after a visit to some of these shrines.

We were not fortunate enough to see a bull-fight in Lima, a whole series of such entertainments having been brought to an end the day before our arrival. The amphitheatre, I understand, is equal to any in Spain, and we spent an afternoon at the place, whilst the "modus operandi" of the exhibition was explained to us. It is truly a fearful sport, and has a terrible hold on the people. Sixteen thousand persons can witness the fight in this arena; it must be a grand and awful sight on a field-day.

On another occasion we visited the cemetery, where are arranged numerous galleries of sepulchres above the ground, into which the coffins are placed and hermetically cemented, the end being closed by a marble slab. The general arrangement resembles that of the Campo Santa at Genoa. There are a few monuments besides, but of utterly execrable quality. I remember seeing nowhere before any works so utterly devoid of artistic merit, and they reminded me of an unlucky statue marked number I. at South Kensington, against which Mr. Ruskin has recently been declaiming.*

There are large and pretentious public gardens in Lima, which people implore you to on no account fail to visit. But little can be said in their praise, for Nature is here over-

---

* "There I saw the most perfectly and roundly ill-done thing which, as yet, in my life, I ever saw produced by art. . . . It was very right, the South Kensington people having been good enough to number it " I.," the thing itself being almost incredible in its oneness; and indeed such a punctual accent over the iota of miscreation—so absolutely and exquisitely miscreant—that I am not myself capable of conceiving a number II. or III., or any rivalship or association with it whatever."—*Fors Clavigera*.

powered by the obtrusive would-be beauty of gaudy and vulgar arbours, alcoves, temples, and the like. An elaborately stuccoed and ornamented building stands in the middle of the gardens, where exhibitions have in more prosperous times been held. Both buildings and gardens seem to belong to a past age, for all look forsaken and in ill-repute. Not more than a dozen people were making use of this pleasure place, and of these few I could see none but strangers or visitors like ourselves. Maria was not here, nor José, nor the children, neither did we see Don Alphonso's carriage come sweeping down the drive; no, the seats were dust-covered and forsaken, and weeds were growing on the road. The sun had been more powerful than the gardener, and there was neglect and ruin written on every object. The ladies of Lima seem to love their balconies more than their gardens, and indeed, both in habit and morals, are more Eastern in their ways than European.

At our hotel we heard nothing but complaints from all sides; it was the government and the war and the overtaxation and the "pocket lining," that people spoke to us of, and the Frenchman, our host, though struggling bravely to make his house of entertainment comfortable, swore with many "sacrés," blue and otherwise, that it was the most uphill work.

We started after a few days for a trip up the celebrated Andes railway, which is indeed by far the greatest sight in Peru, and more notable than anything in either city or citizens that we could discover. I should perhaps before leaving the capital have said something of the old viceregal palace, and the house where Pizarro was slain, and of other such historic monuments, but that work savours too much of guide-books, and I am inclined to think my readers will thank me for sparing them such a dreary catalogue.

We have palaces enough surely in Europe, and as to bloodstained pavements and scenes of tragedy, I fancy for such we need hardly venture beyond our own shores; but Andes railways we have not, nor indeed any railways soever that can compare, in daring enterprise and brilliancy of engineering conception, with this which I am now about to describe.

Our time in Lima being limited, and there being but one train every other day on the mountain railway, we succeeded in obtaining a small saloon carriage and special engine to take us up and down in the twelve hours; this saloon is kept by the company for such trips as ours, and being completely open on all sides enabled us to enjoy every view to the greatest advantage.

The line is the commencement of a great scheme for establishing communication between the watershed of the Amazon and the Pacific Ocean; it rejoices in the well-sounding name of the "Grand Trans-Andian Railroad," but as there is no immediate prospect of its reaching any point beyond Oroya, which is situated on the eastern side of the highest range of the Andes, it is commonly known as the "Oroya Railroad." The line is now open to a place called Chicla, eighty-six miles from Lima, and twelve thousand two hundred feet above the sea.

For the first fifty miles we ran along a gently rising and narrow valley, down which might be traced a strip of fertile soil lying on either bank of the Rimac river. The hills on both sides are utterly barren, arid, desolate, sun-scorched; the scene may be compared with the Valley of the Tombs of the Kings at Thebes on a large scale, for it is a perfect Inferno of sand and rocks. On reaching the head of this valley, the ascent in real earnest begins, and from here to the top continues with unbroken precipitance. A slight lichen now appears on the hills, and higher still a stunted mountain grass, but this does in reality little to destroy the utter desolation, and weirdly unnatural character of the scenery. The grades are here exceedingly steep, one in twenty-five prevailing for tangents, and one in thirty to thirty-five upon the curves. The zigzag principle is adopted in many instances, and so by tunnels and bridges, and Vs and double Vs, we mount steadily up the great Andes range. There are forty tunnels in the thirty miles of actual ascent now opened, and before the line is completed to Oroya there will be many more. The bridges are no less wonderful than the tunnels, and we stopped from time to time to examine them. At one point the line runs through a long tunnel, and right out across a chasm to which I know of no parallel; the rocks on either side are absolutely perpendicular, and the line, crossing the gorge with a single span, enters the face of the opposite rock by another tunnel, the bridge, many hundred feet above the stream, being simply suspended between the two tunnel mouths.

I must avoid the temptation of rushing into figures and measurements, and therefore will only call attention to one great bridge which I believe claims the pre-eminence attached to the highest viaduct in the world. It also stretches across a vast chasm, but is supported from beneath upon light wrought-iron and beautifully-constructed piers. Its height is 252 feet and its length 575 feet; it is withal a marvellously strong structure for its weight. The line itself is of the common English gauge, and thoroughly well laid throughout. The work is, as far as the engineering difficulties are concerned, all but completed for another twenty miles beyond Chicla, and the enormous and unprecedented height of 15,722 feet, or only eight feet less than the altitude of Mont Blanc has been reached.*

The scenery throughout the whole ascent is simply tremendous, and nothing more grand or awful could be conceived. The crags and precipices and peaks are those of nightmares and dreams, the whole terror and awful magnificence of the Andes being laid open to the spectator. The wildest hyperbole of the most enthusiastic traveller could not do more than justice to these mighty Cordilleras, and the idea of building a railway here was as daring and presumptuous as it was impolitic and unnecessary. The undertaking is of course excelled in magnitude by many others, but as a piece of bold and skilful engineering, it undoubtedly stands foremost among the works of man. To what extent it may in the future succeed it is impossible to say; it will certainly, when finished tap, as it were, a great and rich tract of country, to which at present there is no access save by three thousand miles of fever-stricken river-way. At

* The following are some of the altitudes upon the Oroya Road:—

ALTORAS DEL FERROCARRIL DE LA OROYA, SOBRE EL NIVEL DEL MAR.

Kils.	Miles.	Estaciones.	Metros.	Ft.
..	..	Callao.	3·0	10
14·3	8·9	Lima.	157·5	517
53·8	33·4	Chosica.	863·5	2832
72·4	45·0	Cocachacra.	1427·0	4682
75·8	47·1	San Bartolomé (V).	1508·5	4949
85·4	53·0	Cuesta Blanca.	1843·5	6048
111·8	69·5	Tambo di Visa (VV).	2703·7	8870
119·1	74·0	Tamboraque (V).	2994·5	9825
121·4	75·4	Arurl (V).	3076·7	10,094
129·3	80·3	Cacray (VV).	3330·0	11,089
139·2	86·5	Chicla (VV).	3724·8	12,220
151·1	93·9	Casapalca (VV).	4218·3	13,340
168·9	104·9	Tunel en la Cima.	4792·5	15,722
181·9	113·0	Rumichaca (VV).	4490·0	14,731
200·2	124·4	Pachachaca.	3995·0	13,107
218·6	135·8	OROYA.	3736·0	12,257

present the whole scheme is at a standstill, and the railway itself seemed as dismal a failure as everything else connected with this unhappy country.

There was one feature of the valley scenery more interesting to me than any other. The sides of the mountains for many many miles at a time are covered with the irrigation works of the old Inca race. These works are in the form of terraces—smaller than the rice terraces of China and Japan, being in places mere horizontal ledges but a few feet wide, yet admirably adapted to the growth of corn. The work that these terraces represent, scattered as they are over miles and miles of hillside, and reaching to incredible heights, is so stupendous, that it is, in my opinion, a no less wonderful specimen of human capability than the railway itself.

No one can travel in Peru without a feeling of wonder at that vast organism the Inca empire: it is only with the temples of Egypt and of Nineveh that such works as these of the Incas can be compared. I have always felt most keenly the contrast between those past and these present days; it is ever upon the field of the greatest human works of the past that the most despicable human conditions of the present are to be found. In the Nile valley and amongst the ruins of Syria; at poor modern Tunis, or amongst the hovels on the plain of Smyrna, turn where you will to seek monuments of the past, and the very Pariahs of modern races shall you find. And if the lowest of Eastern peoples are to be found at Thebes and Carthage and Ephesus and Nineveh, the same fact is no less observable in the new world, where the Tezcucans and Aztecs have been supplanted by the lawless Mexicans, and the royal land of the Incas has given place to poverty-stricken Peru.

Returning to Callao after our peep at the Andes and our visit to Lima, we resumed our journey down the coast, still enjoying the comforts of the most admirable boats of the Pacific Steam Navigation Company. It is no less strange than true, that the west coast of South America, although furnishing a class of passengers to whom, as a whole, it would be absurd to apply any less mild term than beastly, is supplied with the most comfortable steamers that have ever been run by a public company. So persistent indeed are the directors in their desire to maintain this state of things, that they have been the first to introduce in ocean navigation the two greatest modern improvements in ships—namely, the use of steel in the construction of the hull, and electricity in the lighting of the saloon.

On our way down the coast we called at many ports, varying but little from each other in their general appearance, and all bearing the same dried-up, desolate, tumbledown character. Within miles and miles of some of these ports, there is not a blade of grass or drop of water; the wretched mules are kept alive by imported grain and hay, and condensers and long aqueducts from the hills supply the people with water; at some ports they are even for this latter necessity dependent entirely on steamers, which bring them their water with their mails!

Mollendo is a little port of some importance where we spent a few hours on shore: the place was fairly riddled by Chileno cannon balls, which a few days before were whizzing through the town; the holes were very clean and neatly bored, running right through the blocks of wooden houses, but having done little harm; it is when shot are sent smashing into massive stonework that the real trouble begins, this bombardment of Mollendo causing little more destruction than the bullets that pass through the paper targets at Wimbledon.

From Mollendo runs another great railroad, second only to the Oroya line at Lima. This also penetrates far into the Andes, and attains an enormous elevation (14,600 feet). The distance to Puno or Lake Titicaca is two hundred and seventy-seven miles, and I was greatly disappointed at finding the delay that the run up would involve was greater than I could spare, there being a train only each alternate day. Lake Titicaca has necessarily a great attraction for travellers, it being the highest lake of any magnitude in the world, and also *the* historic spot " par excellence" of South America. It is over twelve thousand feet above the sea, but has never been frozen over, owing perhaps to its great depth and extent.

Upon the island of Titicaca, the largest upon the lake, Manco Capac, the Romulus of the Inca race, is supposed to have been born. From here he set forth to discover and found his great kingdom, the nucleus of which he formed by building the city of Cuzco. The spot is still held in great veneration, there being many ruins of temples of high interest; treasure-seekers may also be found grubbing among the mounds upon the island.

Arica, a town situated a hundred and thirty miles farther south, is of rather more importance than any at which we had hitherto called. It is the port of Tacna, a provincial capital, to which place there is a railway, forty-two miles long. A great bluff stands boldly up to the south of the town with five hundred feet of sheer rock wall; here the Peruvians had mounted some guns, and were sanguine about giving the Chileno fleet a warm reception. The war spirit was strong at all these coast ports, and we experienced often great difficulties in landing.

Arica is chiefly notable as being a victim to earthquakes and tidal waves. Here have been the most terrible of natural phenomena, the whole town having repeatedly been entirely demolished. Here the United States' frigate

Wateree, was carried three-quarters of a mile inland in 1868, and was floated down again and stranded on the beach, a few years later. We saw her lying there at the time of our visit still in great measure intact. There are caves in the bluff, many of very respectable dimensions, and with highly coloured roofs and walls. An Inca burial ground is also within a mile or so of the town, in which many relics have been found. It is undoubted that the Incas fortified this bluff at Arica, and many a primitive encounter must have taken place here, between the shore natives and the great "balsas" which plied up and down the coast.

I regret that I can say nothing of Iquiqui, which is, with the exception of Callao, the most important port in Peru. It was in a state of blockade at the time of our visit, and we were not allowed even to drop our anchor, but were instantly taken in hand by a Chileno gun-boat. H.M.S. *Turquoise* took our mails and gave us despatches with which we at once proceeded on our voyage south. The Chileno fleet lying in front of the town, looked not unformidable; all the ships had steam up, and were lying to wire rope cables, ready for any emergency.

Our next call was at Antafogasta, the great nitrate port, and the real initial cause of the present disastrous war between Chili and Peru. It is but a sorry-looking place, burnt up and desolate like its neighbours, but the great chimneys which stand up here and there indicate the presence of modern civilisation and English capital.

The sums invested out here in nitrate works have indeed been prodigious. The nitre deposits are seventy to eighty miles inland, and a railway runs up to the fields. It is found from ten to twenty feet below the surface, and is loosened by blasting, and then thrown into the trucks by navvies. The labour is mostly Chileno, wages averaging £8 a month.

There being a large salt water lagoon near here, the very simple method of roofing a portion of it in with glass, like a forcing-bed has been adopted for condensing purposes. The whole of the glass is on a slight incline and the various channels are led into one main pipe, from which flows from six to seven thousand gallons of fresh water a day, according to the strength of the sun's rays. The water of the lagoon is four times as salt as ordinary sea water, and there are about three acres of glass. It is estimated that a square metre of glass will condense a gallon a day.

But a few weeks before my visit, this, financially the most valuable port on the coast, was taken by the Chilenos, not with great difficulty, indeed, since the whole of the working portion of the community consisted of emigrants from Chile.

So we passed out of Peru with the Chileno flag flying over one of her most valuable districts, and an expensive and disastrous war raging along her whole coast line; with Callao in a state of perpetual alarm at the reported advent of the Chileno fleet, and Lima in the now almost chronic throes of revolution and anarchy. There seems to be a judgment upon these Spanish Americans for that great crime at Caxamalca, when the ransomed Inca was burnt in the great square, and the honour of Spain and the fair name of Christianity were dragged in the very dust. That murder perpetrated by Pizarro three hundred and fifty years ago is, perhaps, the foulest crime in the long black list of wickedness that history can show: it seems that his own assassination in Lima was not punishment enough; it seems that the fall of his race and at last of the whole line of Viceroys was not enough; it seems that the crimes of those bloodthirsty Conquerors are still bearing their punishment even unto these last generations of those that have hated Him.

CHAPTER XXIII.

CHILE.

> "Around about you see what endless feasts
> The Spring and Summer bountifully cast;
> 'A vale of tears,' ye cry; if ye were wise,
> The earth itself would change to Paradise."
>
> *The Legend of Oran.*

ALTHOUGH now fairly within the territory of the Republic of Chile we found no perceptible difference whatever in the nature of the country. Still the great mountain wall standing out of the Pacific, a giant cliff five thousand feet high, still the dried-up valleys running down to the sea and splitting open this giant cliff, still the scorched and dusty ports, still no sign of tree or grass or shrub or flower.

We stayed at Caldera, the port of Copiapo, for two days, and stumbled out on to the desert for exercise, and lay down in the sand under the shade of a weird boulder of rock, and fancied that surely we must hear the cry of "backsheesh Hawajii" and that yonder sandy rise must hide an Egyptian temple. It is for all the world like the Nile desert, yellow and glaring and desolate, but there is no narrow strip of green, no smoothly flowing river, there are no palm-trees or graceful sails, and the eye positively aches with the monotony of desolation.

A railroad, grim and gaunt, striking rigidly across the sandy plain, with old iron rails for telegraph posts, runs up to Copiapo, but we had seen too many of these cheerless towns to care to make the journey. We were glad to be at sea again; the blue water seemed restful and pleasant to the eye, its motion spoke of life, its colour was akin to green, and we had seen nothing of that colour since leaving Ecuador; here, indeed, must be people living and dying and never so much as seeing one green tree or a dozen blades of grass. There is a story told of this port or another, that our English consul in a moment of thoughtlessness had his yard palings painted green; to everyone's surprise and wonder the palings were in the morning nowhere to be found, but it was at last suggested that the mules must have eaten them!

Cocquimbo and Yacan are ports of more importance than Caldera: they are the great centres of the copper-mine districts. I was surprised to find in both places a great number of English and other Europeans. Engineers, mechanics, miners fill the streets. These ports really deserve the name of manufacturing towns, for they abound in sights and sounds such as one would expect to find in Lancashire or Northumberland, rather than on the west coast of South America.

At last we reach Valparaiso, the chief city and port of the west coast. Valparaiso is in a very beautiful position upon a very beautiful bay. It is built on the side of a steep hill like Hong Kong; it is spread out in the arc of a fine bay like Wellington in New Zealand. It is in short a very fine attractive and busy place. No mean, paltry collection of wooden houses and narrow streets, but as Anglo-Indians say a "pucka" city. In its harbour lie a fleet of steamers and sailing vessels that any European port might be proud of, and I counted ninety-eight ocean-going ships at their moorings on the morning of my arrival. The hills at the back are high, and the great snow-capped Andes with Aconcagua above them all, stretch away in the far background, forming a very pleasing picture. Undoubtedly the most attractive feature of the scene to any one coming from the north is that it has colour; it is like a water-colour drawing after a wearisome gallery of crayons. How pleasant is the green upon the hills, how pleasant are the few trees in the square, how delightful the grass in the villa gardens! —one needs to go through two thousand miles of wilderness to properly appreciate these things.

The Chilenos are vigorous business men, and the streets are full of life and energy. Great office buildings line the quay, and men with the unmistakable mercantile air are hurrying through the streets. The Custom House and bonded warehouses are the most conspicuous buildings in Valparaiso, for it is a commercial city, and not one of parks and palaces. A tramway company has complete command of the streets, which are narrow but well-paved, and the tramcar seems to come down them like a train in a tunnel. At the back of the business part of the town are rows of pleasant houses built on terraces on the hillside, and above them again are villas and many a pretty homelike house. It was surprising to find that whole rows of these houses are English, and there are three English churches and a large English school. Little fair-haired children might be seen playing in the gardens, and there, too, was an unmistakable Mary cleaning a window. I almost thought myself in an English colony, so general were the signs of our countrymen.

There is quite nothing to see in Valparaiso itself, so I am spared the writing of any further description. It is merely, as I have said, a place of business, a pretty place of business truly, and one where doubtless is much pleasure also, for did we not see theatres? and were we not entertained at the club? still in the main it is a city of commerce, and as such sufficiently uninteresting.

Let us hurry then over the hills to Santiago, the Paris, or lest my friends of the east coast should think me partial, let me say the Brussels of South America.

A railway—it seems one can go anywhere in South America by railway—runs up to the capital, crossing the western range of the Andes, properly called the Cordilleras. The journey occupies from four to five hours, and is as beautiful a railway ride as one need wish to take. A few miles from Valparaiso is Viña del Mar, a pleasant suburb, and like all the little wayside places, prim, neat, and pretty, with smart-looking cottages of brick and stucco. Fruit and flowers are as plentiful as our most sanguine expectations had led us to hope, and I bought two enormous bouquets for ten cents; they were both very tastefully arranged, and were sold by dark-eyed Spanish girls who cried their flowers with a musical intonation.

For the last two hours the scenery becomes grand in the extreme, the great snow-capped Andes are brought into full view, then the flat, broad plain between them and the Cordilleras, and at last Santiago de Chile itself.

At the station are the most lumbersome and villainous of carriages, in which we are driven roughly up to the hotel, the best hotel in South America—one that would be a credit to any European town; a building of architectural pretensions, with great balconies and a dome, and occupying the whole of one side of the Grand Plaza.

A somewhat detailed account must be given of Santiago, the capital of the republic, for it is the most enjoyable place in South America, and has all the comforts of an European city with a great deal that is strange, interesting, and attractive. Its situation is, I suppose, quite incomparable. It lies in a great amphitheatre; the level plain, with the river

Y

Mapoche meandering across it, is the arena around which stand up tier upon tier of Andes and Cordillera ranges.

SANTIAGO DE CHILE.

There is upon the plain a curious rock some 300 feet high, of which the Romans would have made another Capitol, and where Valdivia with his hundred and fifty Conquerors three centuries ago, halted and set up his standard. The city lies all round this rock of Santa Lucia, and the Chilenos of to-day have turned it into a quaint kind of pleasure place. It has been embanked, planted, and built upon, and ornamented with fountains, statues, and sham fortifications. It is like an artificial rockery at Rosherville or some such place, on a very large scale. It is all paths and steps, and bridges, and platforms, and seats, and goodness knows what not. Strange statues and monuments in bronze and stucco are to be seen on all sides, and toy battlements, baby castles, and miniature forts frown from diminutive precipices here, there, and everywhere.

It is a great city, this Santiago, lying three hundred feet below us; we can overlook it from the summit of the rock with such thoughts as those of Teufelsdröckh, as he watched from his high perch that wasp-nest or bee-hive of Weissnichtwo, "and witness their wax-laying, and honey-making, and poison-brewing, and choking by sulphur. From the Palace esplanade, where music plays while Serene Highness is pleased to eat his victuals, down to the low lane, where in her door-sill the aged widow, knitting for a thin livelihood, sits to feel the afternoon sun, I see it all. . . . Couriers arrive bestrapped and bebooted, bearing Joy and Sorrow bagged-up in pouches of leather: there, topladen, and with four swift horses, rolls-in the county Baron and his household; here, on timber-leg the lamed Soldier hops painfully along, begging alms: a thousand carriages, and wains, and cars, come tumbling-in with Food, with young Rusticity and other Raw Produce, inanimate or animate, and go tumbling out again with Produce manufactured."

Away the city stretches upon the plain far and wide; the house roofs of dull red tiles are nearly flat and have no chimneys; the buildings are all built with a view to their appearance from the street—a grand façade of stucco and stone, and at the back a low one-storied building surrounding a quadrangle. There are several good squares, well planted with trees, and there, a beautiful green stripe, stretching right across the city, is the universal Alameda, here more than usually broad and beautiful. The trees which are fine and well grown, form a complete archway over the wide footpaths, and almost meet over the carriage and tramway roads as well; they are planted in four, six, and even eight rows, constituting the grandest avenues of their kind anywhere to be seen.

A nearer view of the city takes nothing from our admiration; the squares and streets have the gayest and most pleasant appearance. There are also two arcades of very considerable merit, the larger one suggesting even a comparison with that of Milan. We took a drive into the Park, where was a grand review, and all the beauty and fashion of the capital assembled. Closed carriages and broughams are the Chileno ladies' delight, and I fancy the open air and broad daylight is rather wisely avoided by these made-up and painted beauties. Both in the Park and at the Botanical Gardens there was no lack of visitors, and the streets also were gay with carriages, and mounted caballeros with massive trappings, and officers in gorgeous uniforms. The war interest is at its height, of course, just now in Santiago, and the scarlet fever rages furiously.

The cathedral of Santiago is a large one, but not beautiful; it may however claim the peculiarity of being actually *used*. We were present one morning at high mass which was held in the nave, and the whole building was comfortably filled, although the occasion, if I remember rightly, was not one of any great importance. All the women wear the "manta," and in the churches, where they form so great a majority, the effect is weird and mysterious. The front of the cathedral is not finished, nor is the tower, and it has never been the intention of the architect for there to be more than a grand façade facing the Plaza; the main portion of the building is designedly long and low, and is intended to be hidden amongst the surrounding houses. This, I may add, is an almost universal feature in Spanish American architecture.

At the back of the cathedral is a small square, and in the centre the statue that commemorates the most tragic

MONUMENT ON SITE OF OLD JESUIT CHURCH, SANTIAGO.

episode in Santiago history, namely, the burning of the old Jesuit church.

It was the feast of the Virgin, and during a crowded service the fire broke out—the story is too well known to repeat—two thousand persons, "mas o menos," were burnt to death. The monument is of bronze, a well-wrought female figure with outstretched arms, as though crying to heaven one of those half complaining, half supplicating songs of the Psalmist—a very beautiful, very pathetic work of art, and in no way in ill taste, which can but rarely be said of any American monument.

We left Santiago very reluctantly, the view from our rooms was so exquisite. Where again shall we see sky so blue and giant peaks so purely white, their serrated crests breaking into snowy foam, and flinging themselves as though in a wild ecstasy, high into the deep blue peaceful sky? There is indeed no range of mountain peaks that can quite compare with the Cordilleras of the Andes.

Our route from Santiago lay southwards along the wide valley between the two Andes ranges, for several hundred miles. There is a pleasant easy-going continental sort of railway down the plain. The country everywhere reminds one of Belgium and North-western France: long rows of poplars stretching out in all directions; open and but indefinitely-divided fields; cattle grazing quietly; large thick-wheeled bullock carts plodding along slowly; dingy tumble-down old homesteads with small vineyards and orchards and dirty-white, red-tiled walls; rough peasants, too, in wide hats, walking in the fields, always in many-coloured ponchos, as they have ever been since old Bolivar so clothed his army. Dull, sleepy peasant men and women at their cottage doors, all as one sees it in France, and as is described for us in half a hundred books of travel. The stations, too, are the same, and the lazy train the same, stopping and going on, with all the eccentric unreason of an European "petite vitesse,"—so we jog slowly down this fertile land of Chile, to the little town of Talca.

Talca is a square, dirty, dismal, whitewashed city of the parallelogrammatic genus. The houses all look as though the backdoors faced the streets, which are ankle deep in brown and sloppy mud. It rains fast as we drive along in a most seedy carriage, and I have seen no more dismal place than this in the lessening evening light. The length of that one Talca street, shall I ever forget it? a length only equalled by its unloveliness. It was of Wimpole street, I think, that Sydney Smith declared there was no ending; whether the street of Talca has ending or no, I did not learn, for at last we turned off into the square, where in due course we found the usual cathedral and hotel. The cathedral stared at us dismally from the Plaza, large, unfinished, bleak and dreary. Its red brick front is, I believe, some day to be stuccoed, but it seems as though all-destroying Time will have done his work of ruin long ere the fulfilment of that consummation, devoutly to be wished.

We resumed our journey in the morning, and passed more fields, and time-worn homesteads, and bullock carts, and ponchoed peasants; more old wooden ploughs, and women burning twitch, and lazy men at cottage doorways, and children playing. At the stations women selling fruit and flowers, and idle loungers staring at the train. Beyond again more rows of poplars, and whitewashed red-tiled walls, and women hooded with the "manta," and men on horseback with huge spurs and more huge stirrups, or driving oxen in the plough, or leading teams along the road, or smoking at their cottage doors; always in ponchos and wide hats, brown and sunburnt, slow, prosperous, contented.

I like this peaceful Chile with its plodding peasants and pleasant little farms; the restless fiery Spanish blood seems to have settled down to rustic homely life; these peasants are like those of northern Europe, and the fiery warriors and daring pioneers from Spain are of a past age in Chile.

Great open rivers cross and recross the plain, laying waste acres of good land, and bearing down bridges and roadways in their headlong course, just as one sees them in New Zealand and Japan, and wheresoever else a high mountain range starts up abruptly from a plain. We had at times to climb across the broken bridges, leaving our train behind, as I have often had to do in similar places; then we take another train and jog slowly on our way again. We get to the end of this tract of country at last, and find ourselves hedged in by hills once more. Here is the Rio Bio Bio, winding almost Rhinelike among the hills; the scenery is wonderfully pretty, as we run smoothly round and along the green hillsides, now getting glimpses of long reaches of river, now of land-locked lakes, the autumn light painting the hills a brilliant yellow-green, and the cloud-shadows chasing each other up and down. At last, after a journey of four hundred and fifty miles, we reach the city of Concepcion.

Concepcion is a gay town, famed for its pretty women and pleasant social life. It has fifteen thousand inhabitants, and spacious shops and Plazas and Alamedas; it has a wall of green hills at the back and a broad shining river in front, the whole aspect of the place being cheerful, clean, and prosperous.

We climbed a hill behind the town as the autumn sun went down, and saw the rose and orange tints upon the mirror-like river, and saw the white prim blocks of houses and the green squares and the long dark Alameda: saw, too, the hills beyond the river, with high lights upon their grass-grown sides, and the islands away at the river's mouth, and the great Pacific a faint streak in the far-west—it was a scene for the easel, all too varied and beautiful for prose and pen and ink.

Our visit to Concepcion was but a flying one, so I can write nothing of the pretty ladies or pleasant social life.

The picture from the hill I must always remember with pleasure as I saw it on that lovely autumn evening, and, if I may state so wide an opposite, the pleasant dinner in the excellent hotel. Beyond these things I had no time to go, but had to hurry on to Coronel to catch the homeward-bound steamer.

In the early morning then, we started to drive across to Coronel, which is the great coaling port of Chile, and where the steamers mostly call, both on the outward and homeward voyage.

The country below Concepcion is poorer than on the fertile plain to the north, and the people, too, are poorer and the houses poorer. After a tedious hour or more, drifting about the river in a punt, trying to find our way across through a white cold fog, we started in the crisp morning air, leaving fog and damp behind with the river, over the hills to Coronel. We see on our way fine open grazing country, which will some day be under cultivation no doubt, and large trees, and green grass, and cottages, poor and dilapidated, if such a word can be fitly applied to structures of mud-plastered sticks, and thatched over with leaves. We see also peasants carrying loads, or driving creaking old carts with Dutch-cheese-like wheels, drawn by thick-set bullocks with their noses on the ground; flocks of sheep also, and lazy, ragged-looking horses, and naked children, and ponchoed caballeros with huge stirrups and spurs—it is the same kind of country, though less prosperous-looking, as elsewhere in Chile. Coronel is the sorriest of villages; dirty, noisy, wooden, smoky and inhospitable; we spent there one of the most miserable of nights, sleeping in the back room of a whisky store, and shivering all night with the cold. A long ramble over the hills in the morning revived us a little. There are pretty views from the high lands round the bay, notwithstanding the coal mines in all directions, and the chimneys vomiting almost solid smoke.*

Yonder, at Lota, on the other side of the wide bay, are the great Consiño Copper Smelting Works and coal mines, that until lately supplied three-fourths of all the copper used in Europe. The place is in every way very perfect, and Madam Cousiño's house and grounds are quite *the* thing to see in Southern Chile.

In four days after sailing from Coronel Bay, four days of cold stormy weather, we ran in under the great rocks of Cape Pillar, the entrance to the Straits of Magellan. Nothing more wild or tremendous in natural scenery can be conceived than the western portion of the Straits. High mountains stand up from the narrow channel like great battlements; the dark and snow-pregnant clouds scud wildly across the white peaks, now shrouding the hills almost to the water's edge, now streaming off to leeward in great angry wisps. The mountains when we see them are of a deep cold purple, with slightly-whitened crests; it is the autumn season, and the snow is at its least. The whole scene is a fit end to that mighty range of the Andes, which starts under the fiery tropical sun and stretching through four thousand miles of varying climates, here loses itself in broken rocks and storm-beaten crags and lonely peaks, battered and rent by the frosts and gales of the cold southern seas.

By the light of a clear bright moon we steamed through the so-called Crooked Reach and Long Reach, the mountains towering above us as in some wild dream, the dark

---

* The coal is considered about equal to second Welsh, its price being twelve shillings a ton, sevenpence of which is the cost of loading. The seams average about five feet thick, and run under the sea only a yard or two beneath the harbour bed. The engineers are mostly English, and receive high salaries.

smooth sea rushing past our great ship's side. I think there is nothing with which to compare these Straits: one must go himself there to conceive the weird grandeur of those vast glaciers, and ravines, and mountain walls rising sheer from the black water.

We reached Punta Arenas, the little Chileno settlement in the Straits, as the first streak of dawn shot across the horizon; it is a mean little place of no interest, beyond that attached to the chance of obtaining skins, and of seeing some of the Patagonians. A few prisoners are still kept here, although as a convict station it has been practically abandoned. Some hopeful adventurers have made this out-of-the-world spot their home, and are, as I heard, doing fairly well. The whole country is forbidding, desolate and cold, and yet, as the temperature of the water never falls below F. 40°, it is believed by many that sheep will some day be extensively introduced. To the east of the port of Punta Arenas the whole nature of the land changes, and the mountains and rocks give place to rich alluvial plains, on which good grass is growing, and where great herds of guanaco are to be found.

Two or three Frenchmen have quite recently settled near the Atlantic entrance, and were when last visited by Sir George Nares in the *Alert*, very contented and hopeful. This somewhat adventurous enterprise is looked upon with considerable interest, and hopes are entertained that they will be able to open up a fine sheep-growing country. The Indians of the mainland are peaceful and harmless, differing altogether from their warlike cousins on "Fireland" and the adjacent islands.

The passage through the eastern part of the Straits is of no great interest, and after straining our eyes for sometime, in hopes of seeing guanaco or Indians, we took shelter below, from the cold biting winds, and in the evening of that day, or after about thirty steaming hours from the time of leaving the Pacific, were once more rolling heavily in an open sea, with our ship's bow pointed northwards, on our voyage to the River Plate.

CHILIAN PEASANT GIRL.

CHAPTER XXIV.

MONTE VIDEO AND THE ARGENTINE REPUBLIC.

> " And one a full-fed river winding slow
> By herds upon an endless plain,
> The ragged rims of thunder brooding low
> With shadow-streaks of rain."—*Tennyson.*

I HAVE always held that great rivers are a fraud. One thinks of them as majestic, broad-bosomed, imposing, even beautiful; they make a good figure on the map, and we read with awe in our geography books of the great Amazon and the great Mississippi.

I found out the Mississippi some years ago, seeing in it but a muddy "snag"-abounding, uninteresting wilderness of running water, and my faith in great rivers was shaken. The Rio de la Plata, however, has a fair-sounding name, and is more than usually conspicuous on the map—then perhaps it is an exception? I was soon disappointed in any hopes and confirmed in any suspicions I may have had, when coming on deck one most beautiful morning I found our vessel at anchor off Monte Video. We were lying out in the yellow, unlovely stream, five miles from the shore, and a fair city was shining prettily between us and the rising sun. This appeared as a great mass of churches, houses, and uneven structures of all shapes and sizes, indefinite, truly, in the distance, but singularly light and aerial as the morning sun flashed upon it a thousand tints of crimson and orange and gold. To the left of the city is to be seen the

Emerald Hill, 450 feet high, with a low fortress on the top; perhaps the only hill whatever for half a thousand miles. There is, moreover, no timber to be seen, and very evidently we must look for other than natural attractions in this land of the Plata.

Large sailing boats are beating up to and around us, pitching most horribly; very broad and shallow and buoyant are these sailing boats, and in them we must, I fear, go ashore. The river is lumpy as well as muddy, and everything afloat seems bobbing up and down in a manner animated and vivacious, but not reassuring to indifferent sailors. A large fleet of ships lies between us and the shore, increasing in numbers and decreasing in size as we get nearer the landing place.

In their main points of interest, as are all these South American cities, so is any one of them; there are somewhat finer shops here, a larger cathedral there, better paved streets in this city, more substantially built houses in that. I am reduced, therefore, to pointing out only such things as strike me as exceptional in these the later halting-places on my journey. The hotel appears to us as exceptional immediately on our entrance; it is quite a palatial building, with marble courts and staircases, and cheerful rooms and French waiters. There is a French air about all we see, as we first land on this east coast. Old Spain seems to belong to Chili and Peru; all is modern here and European. The square is large and open, with bright green trees and pleasant fountains. The cathedral is new-looking and clean, it also is more French in appearance than Spanish. The ladies here seem quite European to us from the west coast, the "mantas" are seldom seen, and in all directions we notice bonnets, an article of dress absolutely unheard of in a Trans-Andian city. Less black, too, is noticeable in the dresses of the women—less of that mysterious conventual air to which we have become accustomed in all the churches of the other coast from Mazatlan to Concepcion. In the streets are good shops and good houses, of the one-storied court-yard genus as usual; the windows are all strongly barred, needfully enough in this land of revolutions.

We drove out into the suburbs later on in the day, and had a glimpse of the cattle-raising plains of the Banda Oriental, or Uruguay as it is called on the maps. Our way lay through long dreary third-rate streets; surely the poor streets here are even more incomprehensible than those of our own cities. Such a melancholy semblance of respectability as they have! Such a sad failure as are their efforts to look other than the wretched homes that they are!

A flat and dreary, although green country, is this round Monte Video. It is open, treeless and desolate, yet green, and in a way prosperous-looking. The streets run far out into the "Camp"—which term is used in exactly the sense of the Australian word "Bush"—and gas lamps and kerbstones are to be found wandering away into the open country. We soon found ourselves in the region of the "Quintas," which we were assured, and justly, would surprise us. Of all the extraordinary houses in the world of wonders, surely these are supreme. Moorish, Turkish, Italian, Chinese, Swiss, German, Gingerbread, Theatrical, Nursery-book, whatsoever architecture you will, here you may have it, not done by halves, but to the very extremity of folly, foolish. Such a thing as comfort never seems to have been for a moment considered, but only passionate eccentricity and preposterous display. The gardens of the "Quintas" are hardly any better than the houses, but it is winter time and we must not criticise them too closely. One great monument of folly is there in this suburb that I must not neglect to mention; one estate so far beyond all the rest in its magnificent absurdity, that it seems to me to be the most absolute and complete example of snobbery extant. This estate is many miles broad and long, and contains a model farm, model park, model cottages and lodges, a model avenue, and goodness knows what not else. For miles we drove along a road with a wall of brick and stucco and an iron railing on either side. Upon each pillar of this outrageous wall there had stood, and even then, in dismal and maimed mutilation was to be seen an iron female statue clothed in a torn and ragged vestment of white paint. The model buildings were like children's broken toys, and the roads and fences and fountains and gardens a mere chaos of dilapidation and decay. We drove back from the suburb of "Quintas" in the twilight, the sky being flushed with a strange and brilliant crimson after-glow such as one sees in Upper Egypt—back through the streets, now lighted with a thousand gas lamps and looking more French-like than ever—back to our grand hotel and a comfortable dinner.

After but a short stay in Monte Video we sailed in one of the river steamers for Buenos Ayres. They are good steamers, these of the river Plate, in almost all respects resembling the river boats of the United States. A most elaborate dinner was served in the saloon, of which the passengers partook with the same appetite and rapidity that one notices on the Hudson or Mississippi; a dozen times I felt as though I must be in the United States.

Early on the following morning we found ourselves off Buenos Ayres. The experience of landing at this port is, I think, absolutely unique. Suppose you come out from England in an ocean-going steamer, after steaming for many hours up the river, quite out of sight of land you feel the engines stop, and soon become aware that the vessel is at anchor. You are told that your journey is at an end, and boats will shortly be out to take you ashore. You look anxiously around—ashore? Buenos Ayres? There must be some mistake! Not at all. Away on the far horizon may be seen a dozen tiny specks; these are the spires and domes of the city, and you are at anchor in five fathoms of water fourteen miles from the quay.

The surface of this great shallow expanse of river is generally choppy and agitated, and not unfrequently so rough that people who have come all the way from England, are compelled to give up their pretensions to being good sailors, during the steam-launch passage from the steamer to the shore. The Inner Roads have ten or twelve feet of water, and here lies a fleet of light-draught vessels, inside of which again are innumerable small craft of every kind. At some seasons a rowing boat even cannot approach to within a mile of the shore, and at all seasons carts on high wheels are driving about off the ends of the two long piers, taking loads from the launches to the shore. There was just sufficient water to enable us, with some bumping, to reach the pier end and clamber up the slippery wooden stairway; we were glad to be off that shallow and restless river and to feel a firm footing beneath us.

Vast enterprises, such as the construction of piers, docks, and other expedients have been proposed, by which to make Buenos Ayres a decent port, but so far every proposition has fallen though, and with the exception of a small branch of the river, known as the "Boca," there is no reasonably good discharging place for ships at the Argentine Republic capital. A deepening of this "Boca" will, we may hope, ultimately be resolved upon, and fairly good docks thus be thrown open. There is great opposition, however, even to this scheme; the lighter interest, backed by many of the most wealthy citizens, is against it; the shipowning interest, which, finds that unloading into lighters is in many ways a great deal more economical than the expensive quay-side system in contemplation; the waterman interest, which, as we have seen in Callao, can be vastly influential in a republican cabinet; thus there can, in the face of all this, be no very immediate improvement in the landing facilities at Buenos Ayres.

There is in front of the city and along the river side, a railroad ingeniously hidden by a garden and small avenue. Behind this garden, which converts a quay-side railroad into quite a pleasant feature in the aspect of the place, lies the business part of the town, and behind that again the Plaza and fashionable streets are situated.

The Plaza Victoria is a large open square of the true South American type. The cathedral, as usual, stands on one side of the square, and a most imposing building it is, resplendent in elaborately moulded stucco. Other large buildings, such as the great theatre and the general post office, are also situated in the Plaza Victoria, and the whole effect is very striking. The city is laid out in blocks of houses a hundred and forty yards square, and Philadelphia itself is not more strictly parallelogrammatic. The streets are even more cobbly and ill-paved than is usual in South America, and all things considered, Buenos Ayres will not compare at all favourably with the beautiful Santiago de Chile. The lack of pleasant suburbs accounts for the very splendid town mansions which adorn the principal streets. We gaze longingly in at the open doorways of these palaces, where a vista of "patios," or shrub-planted quadrangles, may be seen, which run back from the street in charming perspective, their white marble grandeur being increased

by a distant statue and alcove, in front of which are flowers
and fountains playing. The exterior, too, of these mansions
is no less magnificent, often resplendent in coloured marbles
and elaborate relief carving. One could indeed hardly be
more royally lodged anywhere than in the Park Lane of
Buenos Ayres.

We drove about the city on a most pleasant afternoon, and
saw many handsome carriages and pretty faces. The tramway lines, like those in the United States, play sad havoc
with carriage wheels, and to a great extent spoil the appearance of the streets. We visited a "Borraca" being in a
sightseeing mood, where the wool is received from the
"camp," and sorted and packed in bales; and very dirty and
odoriferous wool it is, being always shipped "in the grease;"
most of it is sent to Antwerp, where it undergoes various
scouring and cleaning processes. We passed a large Foundling Hospital on our way, where the "panier" system is in
vogue and much patronised. The babies are farmed out by
the week, and there were over five hundred little un-
fortunates undergoing that interesting process at the time
of our visit.

We started, after but a rapid inspection of Buenos Ayres,
up the country to get a glimpse of the great plains and one
or two of the inland cities. Our road lay first across the
delta of the Paraná to a little river port called Compaña,
thence by steamer to Rosario. The line lies along a perfectly level plain, green and pleasant looking, where horses
and cattle were feeding now in large droves, now in small
companies. A small but comfortable steamer awaited us at
Compaña, and took us swiftly along the smooth broad waters
of the Paraná. The banks are low, and with the exception
of grass have but little vegetation. During the whole time
of our journey a wonderful calmness prevailed, and the sur-

face of the river was like a sheet of glass. We plashed and snorted on through the whole night and into the bright fresh morning, no change whatever being noticeable until within an hour or so of Rosario, when the western bank became high, and a few trees were observable.

Rosario is a stiff, square, white and yellow city, with the tramways and the Plaza, and the cathedral, and the hotel, and the shops, and the ponchoed natives, exactly as in the small towns of Chile and elsewhere in Spanish America. We were surprised to find a pleasant club in Rosario, and a small colony of English, from bankers and merchants down to railway guards and shunters.

There was quite nothing to see in this inland town, but we had to satisfy ourselves that there was nothing, and so wandered about the streets and out in the universal tramway to a wretched little garden, where was the skeleton of a band-stand and other relics of past festivity. Later on we made one or two calls, and were most kindly entertained until the time came for another start on our up-country journey.

A railway runs from Rosario to Cordova, and indeed beyond that again to Tucuman. On this railway we are soon travelling in a long American car with seats down the sides, and a dozen or so Argentine Spaniards, and a child or two, and much tobacco, and poncho, and tall hat and swagger. The country is quite unvaried; still flat, absolutely flat, and boundless, and tame, and green, and treeless. Cattle as before, and small farms, and but little more imposing " estancias—"a strange land this to come sight-seeing in. Mile after mile absolutely unchanging, like a great smooth sea of grass. The night closes in and we pass dozens and dozens of little stations, all like little back-country stations in North America or anywhere else. It is now bitterly cold, and the frost settles down on the broad plain, and the south wind blows like a veritable northeaster, and we roll ourselves up in our warm guanaco rugs and settle down to sleep.

Cordova, where we find ourselves at daylight, is quite a sacred city in its way, with a cathedral of no mean architectural pretensions, with a beautiful Jesuit Church, two

monasteries, several convents, and half a dozen other places of worship, scattered round the town. Here is an observatory which is in many re-

CORDOVA CATHEDRAL.

spects the finest in the Southern Hemisphere, and here also is the best university in South America. But for the plain-weary Argentines Cordova has an attraction beyond all churches or universities, in that, lying far away to the west, and standing out beautifully against the deep blue sky, there is to be seen the great Andes range, most refreshing of sights to the inhabitants of the lower country.

It is not necessary to weary my readers with a guide-book account of the churches, university, and observatory; it is sufficient to say that they are all good of their kind, but possess little peculiarity. The university was founded in 1622, which surely entitles it to veneration in this New World. The churches are bare and empty, both out of repair and out of patronage. The Jesuit Church is the most interesting of them all, having a splendid roof of native cedar, built in circular ribs, and both curious in construction and effective in appearance. From the top of our hotel is a really fine view, comprising the numerous churches with their fantastic spires and towers cutting the sky; beyond, the low wall of hills round the city; and last of all, to the west, the great Andes range. We walked to the station in the evening, having exhausted the sights of Cordova, and once more settled ourselves in the long American car, and prepared for another cold night on our way back to Rosario.

I must here write down a word about a habit of these South Americans. One speaks at times of the people of the United States, and their habit of chewing and spitting, and I had thought that there could perhaps be nothing on earth more disgusting than that; but nowhere have I seen or heard of anything to compare in outrageous exaggeration of nastiness, with the Spanish American habit of spitting. It is a worse exhibition of the practice by far than that of the tobacco-chewers of the States, and can indeed be compared to nothing whatever, being absolutely unique in its exquisite filthiness.

In our carriage that night we saw more of it than we had ever done before, although from Mexico to Chile the same horror had been present with us, and it is no exaggeration to say that the society of hogs in a hovel would be preferable, on the whole and generally, to that of Spanish Americans in a railway car. Ladies were present, but that made no difference whatever, for the smoking continued until the atmosphere in the carriage was suffocating and the state of it defied all description. No carpet, indeed, is too clean, no church chancel too sacred, no circumstance too delicate, to prevent these republicans from spitting beastfully, and the only satisfaction we had during the journey was when one individual became so fatigued, and withal so exasperated at having no place to lie down upon, that he was obliged to curl himself up and sleep on the spittoon of a floor that he and his friends had created.

On our return from the up-country towns we stayed a few days in the capital, and were fortunate enough to witness an especially good operatic performance. The piece was Aida, given in the Colon Theatre, a large and beautiful house. The citizens of Buenos Ayres are great patrons of music; we found two opera companies in full swing, and the tenor we heard was receiving two thousand francs a night. The institution known as the "Cazuela," so universal in South American theatres, is in every respect an admirable one. It consists of an entire tier—the one above the grand tier—being given up to ladies only. There is a separate entrance by a side door in the street, and young girls and unattended ladies of all classes can go there with the utmost comfort and propriety. The theatre was crammed to the doors on the night of our visit, and presented a really grand spectacle. What señoras and señoritas! What dress and powder, and finery and magnificence! What dark flashing eyes behind large black fans! The men here are far behind the ladies in what may be called style, dress clothes even being quite the exception.

I have no more to say about Buenos Ayres in this rough sketch of my visit, for I have an aversion to enlarging upon public buildings and municipal statistics; besides, all this is done by quite another class of writers. The passing traveller must not attempt to compete with the authors of such books as "Twenty Years in the South American Camp," or "A Life of Adventure on the River Plate." Such books may not indeed exist, but I find, that wherever I may go, all the real hard, dry, uninteresting facts of the country have already been written down, and all that is left in such a case as my own is briefly to record personal experiences.

There are two unpleasant sights which I ought here to describe; and having no tales of blood or murder on the plains with which to make this chapter delightfully interesting, I may perhaps be forgiven for mentioning these, as the nearest thing I can do in the way of stories of slaughter and bloodshed. The first is nothing either more or less romantic than a cock fight!

The old Spanish entertainment of bull-fighting has passed out of repute in the Argentine Republic, although it is still patronised and allowed in the Banda Oriental on the opposite side of the river. Its place has been taken by the once English national sport of cock-fighting, and we were accordingly taken one afternoon to the leading ring in Buenos Ayres. It is an amphitheatre, resembling a coliseum on a very small scale. A box is set apart in the most prominent place for the judge and officers of the ring. The former, a venerable and respectable white-haired gentleman, is seated at a little table whereon is a small silver bell. The amphitheatre is crowded with well-dressed men, mostly of a fast air and sporting appearance. A main has just been fought, and a new one is about to commence. Two young men enter with dismal-looking cocks, and in the presence of the judge solemnly affix the silver steel-tipped spurs. The judge weighs the combatants with a small brass steelyard, and the "game" then begins.

At first the onslaught is terrific, and at each rush of the birds their respective backers call the odds. The betting varies very rapidly, as at every peck the knowing ones change the odds, watching the effect with the closest attention. At last, after what seems to us a long time, the poor wretches become fairly used up, but still peck at each other dismally and blindly. At times one hides under his opponent's wing and must be detached by his owner. The contest continues until one bird makes three decisive sets at the other without provoking a retaliation. He is then pronounced the conqueror, and borne triumphantly out amidst some cheering.

It is a most horrible sight, and but poor sport surely; indeed it appears to be essentially brutal and brutalising in every way, and yet it is, amongst a very large class of the people, the most favourite sport in South America. In connection with the place was a bar, cigar shop, &c. Well-dressed men of all ages were lounging about, some dressing and washing the wounds of their birds, some discussing the points of the last main. The most singular thing was that it was not at all particularly the rowdy or low-bred people that were there, but sober and respectable citizens whom one could not but feel ought to have known better, as the phrase is.

The other experience of a somewhat objectionable kind which I have to describe, is of a very different nature. The subject to which I refer is a branch of the main River Plate industry called the "Saladero." We went one bright morning to see one of these great cattle-slaying places, and it will be a long while before I forget the subtle and terrible odour with which the whole expedition is associated. The place, which was a few miles from Monte Video, looked like a great factory as we approached, with its large chimneys, and sheds, and shops, and a tramway running down to the river wharf.

We were first taken to a small stockyard, where what would in Australia be called a "mob" of cattle was penned. A man on a low wall flings his lasso into the mob, and a couple of mules attached to the end of the lasso, are ridden violently up a small path, dragging by the horns as they go the entrapped and struggling beast. On a seat above the pulley through which the lasso runs, the butcher sits with a small knife; this he most leisurely and with great ease pushes into the back of the beast's neck, upon which the animal immediately drops stone dead on to a sort of trolly placed ready to receive the carcass. The work is most perfectly done, without effort, causing neither struggle nor pain. When the lasso has been taken off the horns, and handed up to the man on the wall, the dead beast is pulled onwards from under the butcher's seat, and run out into the first large shed. Here it is seized upon by a blood-stained ruffian, who skins and quarters it with the most marvellous dexterity, its various parts being instantly passed on to other men who severally separate the bones, head, etc., which go to the boiling-down shed, to be used as fuel or ground into bone ash; cut off the hoofs, and send them to the glue department; hang up the hides to be dried, and sent with the horns to England; cut out the tongues, which are dried and salted; clear away the fat, which is boiled down for animal oil and tallow, and lastly cut up the lean meat into thin slabs, which are salted, dried, and piled up into huge stacks with salt. This last production figures in the market as "carne tasajo," and is largely consumed by the negroes in Brazil and the West Indies, also being used in small quantities by the Gauchos of the Argentine and Banda Oriental plains.

The man with the knife, seated on his bridge, asked for a cigar, and afterwards told us that he kills from sixty to seventy head of cattle an hour; we also heard from the manager, that when in full swing and working night and day, they slaughter and entirely dispose of as many as 1500 beasts in the twenty-four hours!

A few weeks after our visit to the Saladero we embarked from Monte Video, and in four days found ourselves steaming into the harbour of Rio de Janeiro.

CHAPTER XXV.

BRAZIL.

... " Every form, every shade, so completely surpasses in magnificence all that the European has ever beheld in his own country, that he knows not how to express his feelings."—*Darwin*.

It is the calmest, stillest night in all the year, the loud rattle of our cable chain has just ceased, and we are at anchor in the bay of Rio de Janeiro. Across the harbour lies the great city, shining with a hundred thousand lights; here dotted among the hills, and there in long even rows down by the water's edge. Mountains loom vaguely in the starlight, blotting out a hundred constellations; there is a hushed rippling sound upon the water, and the lights shoot across its surface, now in bright spangles, now in waving lines towards us from the shore. We are on the eve of a great experience—the experience of beholding Nature's fairest handiwork.

The sun rises gloriously some hours later, and we are on deck again to catch the first glimpses of Rio's bay. What can I say of it in the early morning's sunlight as it breaks upon me? How beautiful a scene it is! Its rich green hills, its barren rugged peaks, its thickly clustered houses! What peaks! where are any else so fanciful? What hills! where are such slopes of green, so rich and varied? What groups of villas! hundreds and hundreds of them glistening amongst the green, now in great masses, now wandering away amongst the hills. See, away above the

town, the strangely-shaped peaks and precipices one behind
another. See again, amongst the islands of the bay, the
same strange peaks and rocks. See once more, far off there
in the west, that great wall of Organ Mountains, with their
serrated crests, like organ pipes, cutting the blue sky. See
near again, less striking hills and islands, but all as green;
and forts and piers and palm-filled gardens, and low and
fern-hung rocks. See, nearer still, the blue smooth water,
and a hundred boats swarming around us, as all the world
over, so at Rio. I recall memories of Sydney Bay, and
Smyrna, and Stockholm, and Stambool, the Min river,
too, in China, and the harbours at Hobart Town and
Wellington, and San Francisco's Golden Gate, and Turkey's
Bosphorus and Naples' Bay. Enough surely there is in
those of the beautiful in land and town and bay, but I can
recall, charm I never so wisely, no bay like this Brazilian
Rio, far or near. There are here the little coves and bays of
Sydney, and green hills of that far east, and all the glories
of the tropics, and the blue water of the Bosphorus, and the
rugged peaks of Smyrna, and the quaint church domes
and castle battlements of Genoa, and the broad open amphitheatre of hill walls of Wellington; but the magnificent
completeness of no other place, for none other is there so
exquisitely perfect. It is the monarch of all scenery, the
greatest combination imaginable of Nature's wildest glories,
this peerless bay of Rio in Brazil. There is such variety, as
I have tried to say, the utter peacefulness at sunrise of the
western end, where one might dream of paradise, and endless
summer days, and lotus-eating lives and perfect rest. The
grand and boisterous glory of the entrance, with Sugar Loaf
and Gavia and Corcovado looming near, and affording
endless temptation to mountain-climbing minds; the noisy,
hurry-scurry wonders of the great city itself, from every

street of which one has a view worth crossing Europe for; the less distracting suburb scenery all round the town; the great broad-spreading views from mountain ridge a dozen, twenty miles away; what have you not in Rio to delight the eye, where all of Nature's grandest works seem to converge in one sublime and mighty whole?

A quaint city we find here, as we land some hours later at the quay. A city of forts and barracks, and custom house and battlements and monastery. No new broad city of to-day, but one of narrow streets, and tall ruined-looking blue stone buildings, and quaint old walls and dingy churches. A city where great business firms have musty offices up dirty lanes; where ugly sign-boards stretch across the streets, and uglier sounds come piercing through dark doorways and strike unpleasantly upon our ears as we pass by. A city with high and narrow windows, too, above the streets, and strange and shaggy heads thereat, and linen drying, and rags and paper everywhere. A city without pavements, but such as form the street, and equally belong to man and horse. A city of teeming citizens, busy and hurried, flocking here and everywhere, across and down and up the narrow streets. A city not too clean or free from smells down by the custom house and quay, not too decent in some respects, not too bright or cheerful as one casts glances down side streets. Papers for sale, and fruit and fish, and what you will, by dusky boys or crippled men, or gorgeous negro women in loose dazzling coloured dresses. In the market and in the square and at the street corners, and indeed everywhere, these splendid negroes in brilliant prints, and gay red ribands, and curly heads; always the same, so bright and happy, so fond of finery, so vain, so kind-hearted and big and strong, their merry sable faces a sure cure for the blues!

There is the widest difference between this Brazilian city with its Portuguese inhabitants, and those Spanish cities of the south and west. Here is an air of energy and life and business. Here are anxious men hurrying to their work as in London or Liverpool. The change is absolute from Spanish to Portuguese America. I saw no sight in Rio proper, went over no public buildings, visited no churches or institutions. The streets are the greatest attraction, and the market-place so full of wondrous birds and splendid fruit and monkeys, and parrots without end, and laughing negro women everywhere. There are fine shops in the Rua do Ouvidor, where you can get photographs, and the most perfect feather flowers, and fans ornamented with humming birds, and trinkets made of beetles' wings. It seemed almost like being in the East again, there was so much to see and buy. Tramways, as always in the New World, run along the streets, and as the evening closes in, we think of making our way to the suburbs, for Rio is not too safe a place to sleep in. The tramways are of the best, the cars, clean and well-kept, being drawn by strong mules. No animals in the world seem so suited for this purpose as mules, their strength and hardiness serving them in such good stead. Perhaps the Rio tramways pay better than any other enterprise of the kind: their shares stand at 400 per cent., and the patronage they receive is universal.

From the terminus of the tramway line, we took a carriage and four mules, and rattled away at a fine pace up the hills to the suburb of Tijuca. It was a lovely drive, the road being of the very best, lined with tree-ferns and rich foliage and lovely flowers. A strong, moss-grown stone wall runs along the outer edge. Our team of mules worked willingly, and we were soon at the summit of the little pass, and galloping down the hill again to the village of Tijuca, where we pulled up at White's Hotel,—clean, cool and comfortable.

One must be excused for using strong superlatives in such a country as Brazil; the whole country is superlative, superlatively rich, and green, and beautiful. We rode some distance the next day, crossing the hills at a different point from the road of the night before, and, sending our horses back, walked down the range, and into the town by another route. The head of this pass is called the Chinese View, on account of some Chinamen being employed upon the road. It is thought to be the finest view near Rio, and certainly appeared to us quite unsurpassable.

> "When for a mile or two we thus had gone,
>   The mountains opened wide on either hand,
> And lo, amid those labyrinths of stone
>   The sea had got entangled in the land,
> And turned and twisted, struggling to get free,
> And be once more the immeasurable sea."

Our way thence lay along the foot of the hills, and past the Botanical Gardens, which are more beautiful even than those of Sydney. The main attraction there is the great avenue of palms, of which there are forty pairs planted in most exact symmetry, and all of equal height and size, like columns in an Egyptian temple, as some one has said. The base of each palm is surrounded by a neat little circle of green grass, the whole effect being most imposing, and quite novel.

From the gardens we ran into Rio by tramway, a pleasant ride of about seven miles, passing through the nearer suburbs and along the shores of Botafogo Bay. Here are boulevards and avenues and city gardens; it is the modern quarter of Rio, and quite Parisian. Above us hangs the great Gavia Peak like an iceberg summit, and near to it stands the Corcovado, 2,300 feet high.

Another day we started for a short expedition up the country, beyond the Organ Mountains, and into some of the

THE "CHINESE VIEW," RIO DE JANEIRO.

coffee-growing districts. Our route lay across the harbour to a little station called Mana, whence a short line runs to the foot of the hills. The sail down the harbour was very pleasant, and the views were those of dream and fairy land. We passed the great island of Gubernador, as large as Jersey, and a score of other green-clad rocks and islands. Our steamer was very clean and comfortable, and we came to the conclusion that the Portuguese Brazilians are cleanlier than their cousins of the Spanish republics. After landing at Mana, and making a short run of twenty minutes by rail over a jungle-grown plain to the foot of the mountains, we took a carriage and commenced the ascent. I had thought the Tijuca road a splendid work, but this is even finer. It is in places cut right into the perpendicular wall of rock, and would have done Napoleon no discredit. The hills, when they will hold it, are covered with most luxuriant vegetation, but often the rocks are too steep for more than moss and fern. Here is another great peak like the Gavia, and to our right are the so-called Organ Pipes, the strangest of crests, as eccentric in form as anything in the Rocky Mountains near Colorado Springs. The view of the bay below is of course magnificent, and, on account of our distance away, more comprehensive than anything we had as yet seen.

We reached Petropolis in the evening after the most delightful drive, and were very comfortably lodged at quite a pretentious hotel. Petropolis is the royal suburb. Here the Emperor flies from the summer of Rio. Here also the diplomatic people have their hot-weather houses. The air is keen and bracing, and the scenery in every direction superb. It is 2,600 feet above the sea, and the nights are cold, and even frosty. The town is most German in appearance, having, indeed, been founded by emigrants of that nationality; a stream runs down the centre of the main street, and trees are planted along its banks, and here and there a garden is laid out. Fuchsias sixty feet high, and the universal tree-fern, and poinsettias a foot in diameter, however, remind us we are in Brazil. The Germans have given up settling in any numbers in this part of the country, but to the south, in the Rio Grande district, there is still a very large annual immigration from Bremen, Hamburg, &c.

We started, literally at the first streak of dawn on the following morning, in a real old English coach drawn by four splendid mules, to drive along the great high road to Entre Rios. Our way lay through a very hilly country, not mountainous, but simply covered, if one may use such an expression, with hills all wonderfully alike. The road winds in and out amongst the valleys, and a capital road it is, comparable with any in Europe or elsewhere. We made the journey, seemingly with great ease, of forty-five miles in five hours, employing six teams. We were often as many as twelve outside, and yet the mules were always up to their work.

Coffee, coffee everywhere; whole forests cleared away to make place for coffee, whole hills close shorn for coffee; coffee above on the right, and again below on the left; coffee along the valley, and on the hill-brow, and down the slope, and up the rise; coffee drying in the sun on flat open floors in front of peasants' houses; coffee in little piles near the cottage doors, or in sacks ready for carting; waggon-loads of coffee being drawn toilfully along towards the railway; coffee too in little cups on the counters of the wayside inns; in fact, everywhere coffee! It is deplorable to see the awful destruction of vegetable life in the production of this berry. The virgin forest is burnt and the hill-side disfigured with smouldering logs and stumps. The lovely valleys are stripped clean, and coffee reigns supreme over hill and dale. "Agassiz convinced himself that this rich country had been swept by glacial action, and that the most successful coffee plantations were found exactly where the movements of ice had most enriched the soil by transportation and mixture of its compound elements." The glaciers surely then worked to some purpose. The production of coffee in Brazil has now reached twelve millions sterling worth a year. Half the supply of the entire world comes from these hills, which are said to produce no less than 260,000 tons per annum.*

---

* An able-bodied man can cultivate 2000 coffee-trees, on an area of five acres: these will give him an average crop of 6000 lbs., worth about £80. With slave labour the produce is reckoned at £60 per head.

Pleasant hamlets line the road at intervals, and prosperity is generally observable. Now a village school, where are clean and neat children; now some rich planter's villa, large and barrack-looking; now, shaking off the coffee for a mile, we catch a glimpse of the old primeval forest glory, with some fine crag or bold hillside, untouched or even untouchable by the planter's destroying hand.

We took the railway when our coaching was done, and ran through more coffee country, and then changed on to the main line, known as the Pedro Segundo railroad, and commenced our journey over the mountains and back to the western side of Rio. This crossing of the "serra" is a great engineering work, abounding in sharp curves, steep gradients, tunnels, high bridges, and the like. We passed through quite indescribable marvels of forest scenery, ferns, shrubs, and trees, flowers and creepers, all mixed in wildest entanglement. Great open views, too, may be had from the Organ Mountains' crest, across the lower hills, beyond and away to the broad Atlantic. With such delights to while away the time, we seemed, all too quickly, to reach the suburbs of Rio.

My stay in Rio being unavoidably limited, I was in a few days at sea again, with the great harbour for evermore consigned to the land of memories. Three days later we steamed into the Bay of Bahia.

Bahia is the old capital of Brazil. It enjoyed that privilege for two hundred and fourteen years, after which, in 1763, the government was removed to Rio de Janeiro. The chief feature of the place is its wealth of churches, of which there are sixty, some being very costly, built of marble brought from Europe. It has not a population of half a million souls like Rio, but it is a great city, lying on the north-east shore of a wide bay. It hangs in a curious sort of way on the side of a steep wall of hills; half of it has succeeded in establishing itself on the top, but the rest lies grovelling by the water's edge, or clinging to the wall at various elevations. The houses are high and built of stone, and full of small windows like factories. On shore we find the same delightful medley of sights as at Rio. The negro women, again, are very picturesque, and bigger than ever; they are said to be the largest human beings extant! In the market, fruit and monkeys and birds. In the naturalists' shops, birds. In warehouses on the quay, birds, and birds at street corners on stalls like sweetmeats. Birds for exportation, thousands and thousands of them; gaudy and tasteless sometimes, seeming to have gone altogether too far in the brilliancy and daring combinations of their colouring.

We ascended to the upper town in an elevator. It is a dingy, greasy lift, two hundred feet high, that pulls you up as though with difficulty, groaning mournfully the while. From the top is a grand view over the bay, the great tropical foliage on the hillside below us, then the busy, dirty, lower town, and busier, dirtier quay; then the bay and ships with the low blue hills lying beyond in the far distance. The streets are wider and cleaner in the upper part of Bahia, but the houses are still like factories. Churches crop up everywhere, and seem as numerous as public-houses in a seaport town.

We have a most dismal account given us by the English merchants here. Three of the best European houses have stopped payment this year; trade is everywhere at a standstill, and the recklessness of the administration is complained of; it is, in short, the worst of bad times. The climate seems much like that of Singapore, a damp and heavy heat, with rain continually all the year round. There is a great trade in tobacco, which is largely exported, whole shiploads going to Hamburg to be made into Havannah cigars.

We called at Pernambuco a few days after leaving Bahia, but it was in a gale of wind, and we could only land and take off the mails, and this with difficulty. I should like to have gone ashore and seen the curious coral breakwater and something of the town, which contains ninety thousand souls and looks imposing from the roadstead. There was no chance of landing, however, in such a sea, and so we steamed away for Lisbon with a last good-bye to Brazil and the shores of South America, after a coasting voyage of fourteen thousand miles from San Francisco to Cape San Roque.

Perhaps no fourteen thousand miles of travelling could present a more varied list of experiences than this along the coast of Spanish America. Looking forward to it as we sailed out of the Golden Gates of San Francisco, that April morning months ago, it seemed an interminable journey and one that no amount of interest could make worth the trouble, and yet now, looking back, I feel rewarded a hundred times over, and would maintain its worthiness against all comers. The hopeless stagnation of the Central American republics and the weary desolation of Peru formed but a cheerless opening to the voyage. Yet Lima was worth seeing surely, and the Andes railway was cheap at any price. Then to the south, rewards fell thick and fast. I was enchanted with Chile, which, indeed, I look upon as the foremost state of Spanish America, the one that is healthy and will advance. Santiago is worth going anywhere to see, for it is the most brilliant and attractive city in the Southern Hemisphere. With the river Plate countries I was the least interested; they are sadly commonplace, and my detestation of the genus "gaucho," not to add the Señor of America, culminated in the Argentine Republic. But then came Brazil which set aside every antipathy, and crowned the whole cruise with glorious success. No description can do more than convey a faint idea of the loveliness of that country.

If the introduction of such a subject in so purely a book of travel as this may be permitted, I will say that the imperial government of Brazil asserts its superiority over the miserable administration of the republics in every detail, from the moment of one's setting foot on shore. In the republican states it is adventurers who rule the land, and I fear that too often the biggest villain has the longest reign. The resources of such a country as the Argentine Republic are simply infinite, and had the English settled there, that country would have been at this day another, perhaps even a richer Australia. In the whole history of the world there is no so forlorn a spectacle as ruined and degraded Peru. There is nothing of which that country was not capable, for where she possessed fertile soil it was of the richest—the watershed of the greatest river in the world, and where there were mountains they abounded in the most valuable metals; where she possessed deserts they were covered feet thick with nitrates with which to revive the impoverished lands of Europe, and even her off-lying islands were covered with twenty to a hundred feet of guano, which had but to be tilted into ships and sent to England. And this is the land the republicans have led to beggary! I say nothing of the Viceroys, for their ill government only stamped out one of the great wealth fountains of the land, and this, the great Inca Empire which they inherited, is not included in the list of Peru's original resources.

Why speak of Mexico, the parallel to Peru in degradation and disgrace? It is simply appalling to think of what this republican anarchy has produced. Time was, indeed, when there seemed some hope for Mexico; in those few years of imperial rule, not a feature in the country's constitution but showed incipient sign of recovery and healthful progress; it was only a short-lived flutter, and the last state of that land is worse than the first.

I like to think that Brazil is struggling manfully in her youth. The country is too vast and unwieldy as yet to make a great figure, but still it moves onwards and upwards, and is at any rate *governed*, which surely is the one thing needful in the youth of a country, no less than of an individual.

One can have no faith in such a spendthrift rake as Peru; one may well despair of fallen Mexico and of those quarrelling dishonest children in Central America; one cannot expect much yet either of that great overgrown baby Argentina; but of slow and steady, although far from faultless Chile, and of strong and rightminded Brazil, all who know them will have great expectations, and will wish them every form of prosperity, and, having visited them will say good-bye regretfully, with the conviction that they are the best hopes yet visible for the future of that great Iberian America.

INDEX.

A.

Acapulco, 292
Aconcagua, 319
Adelaide, 28
———, climate of, 10
———, public gardens, 22
Admiralty Islands, 123
Albany Passage, 3
Altitudes on Oroya railroad, 312
Amazon, river, 333
Ambrym, 124
Amoy, 223
Anecdote of Maximilian, 293
Andes, 29, 303, 330
Antafogasta, 316
Api, 124
Aragh (Pentecost), 124
Arapura Sea, 2
Argentine Republic, 359
Arica, 315
Art, Chinese, 225
——, Japanese, 249
Asakusa, 282
Asama-yama, 269
Ashinoyo, 255
Aspinwall (Colon), 299
Astronomy at Santa Cruz, 152
Atahualpa, 304
Auckland, 47
Aurora (Maewo), 120
Australian Colonies, 26
——————, jealousy amongst, 16
Australian Colonies, future of, 27, 29,
——————, ignorance concerning, 30
Australian blacks, 5
———— climate, 10
———— emigration, 29
———— explorers, 20
———— sports, 25
———— townships, 9
Avava (Torres Islands), 141
Aztecs, the, 294

B.

Bad weather at sea, 190
Bahia, 356
Banks Islands, 136
Banyan Tree, 127
Bartering with natives, 125, 176
Basalisk, H.M.S. 149
Baw Baw, Mount, 24
Bice, Rev. C. 132
Big Bell of Japan, 249
Big Hell, 256
Biwa, Lake, 251, 260
Blacks, potting, 5, 6
Blacks' Spur, 24
Blue Mountains, 7, 18
Bluff, the N. Z., 31
——, Yokohama, 251
Boating in Fiji, 68
Boca, the, 337
Booby Island, 2
Borraca, 339

Botafogo Bay, 353
Bottle Tree, 8
Bounty Mutiny, 51, 136
Brazil, 348, 360
Brisbane, 6
Buddhist fanatic, a, 237
Buenaventura, 299
Buenos Ayres, 336, 339, 343
———————— Colon Theatre, 343
———————— Foundling Hospital, 339
————, Patios, 338
Bugotu, 183
———— natives, 187
Bushmen, Australian, 19

C.

Caldera, 318
Callao, 304, 306
Camp, the, 335
Cannibalism in Fiji, 74
Canterbury Plains, 31, 35
Cape York, 2
Carne Tasajo, 347
Carteret, 147
Caxamalca, 317
Cazuela, 343
Chicla, 311
Chile, 318
———— Agricultural district of, 326
———— future of, 360
Chincha Islands, 306
China Sea, 219
Chinese Art, 225
———————— children, 220
———————— country girls, 234
———————— dockyards, 229
———————— house boats, 238
———————— irrigation, 234
———————— review, 223
———————— sampans, 219
———————— shops, 220
———————— snobs, 222
———————— view, Rio, 352
Chiomin, temple of, 248

Christchurch, 35
Climate of Adelaide, 10
———————— Bahia, 357
———————— Darling Downs, 9
———————— Fiji, 78
———————— Hobart Town, 10
———————— Melbourne, 10
———————— Solomon Islands, 78
———————— Sydney, 10
Club-life in South Sea Islands, 130
Coal mines, Chile, 330
Cock-sparrow Point, 139
Cockatoos at Bugotu, 187
Cock-fight, Buenos Ayres, 345
Cocquimbo, 319
Coffee in Brazil, 355, 356
———— Fiji, 84
Colonial Sugar Company, 80
Colon (Aspinwall), 299
Columbia, United States of, 300
Commodore, Australian Station, 207
Compaña, 339
Concepcion, 328
Congregation, native, 181
Conclusion, 359
Conquerors, Spanish, 303, 317
Cook, Captain, 113
Cook, Mount, 37
Cooktown, 4
Coolangbangara, 205
Copiapo, 318
Copper Mines, Chile, 330
Coral reefs, 64, 151
Corcovado, 349, 353
Cordilleras, 312, 321
Cordova, 341, 342
———— Cathedral, 341
———— Observatory, 341
———— University, 342
Coronel, 329
Corruption by traders, 171, 173
Cortez, 289
Costa Rica, 296, 297
Cousiño, Madam, 330
Crooked Reach, 330

Crossing to Noumea, 195
Cryptomeria Avenue, 280

D.

Darling Downs, 7
——————— climate of, 9
——————— station on, 12
Dinornis, the, 35
Disease amongst South Sea Islanders, 143
Dunedin, 32, 34

E.

Earrings of South Sea Islanders, 166
Ecuador, 302
Emigration to Australia, 28
————— South America, 354
d'Entrecasteaux, 147
Entre Rios, 347
Eruptions, Tambora, 1
————— Mauna Loa, 105, 106
Eucalyptus, 8, 18, 199

F.

Famine in China, 226
Fan making, 222
Ferguson, Captain, 148
Fiji, 63
—— agriculture in, 79
—— climate of, 78
—— missionaries in, 86
—— safety of English in, 85
Fijian doctor, 73
—— houses, 70
—— negroes, 67
—— pottery, 82
—— school, 74
Fireland, 331
Flores Sea, 2
Florida Island, 179
—— beauties, 181
Flowers, Chile, 321

Flowers, Maewo, 129
Foochow, 230
——— arsenal, 229
——— at night, 235
——— bridge, 231
French at Nengone, 193
——— colonists, 199
——— hatred of, at Nengone, 194
Fuzyama, 255

G.

Gaeta, 180, 206
——— pleasant evening at, 180
——— centipedes at, 182
Gaucho, 343
Gavia, 349, 353
Gold rush, 4, 38
Goodenough, Commodore, 147, 157, 160
Government buildings, Honolulu, 90
Government-House, Fiji, 67, 82
Government of Brazil, 348
——————— Mexico, 294
——————— Peru, 306
Govet's Leap, 19
Great Barrier Reef, 4
Great rivers, 333
Greymouth, 38
Guadalcanar, 179
——————— superstitions concerning, 179
Gubernador Island, 353
Guatemala, 295
Guayaquil, 300, 301
Guayas river, 300, 302

H.

Hailey, chief, 205, 206
——————— letter from, 206
Hakone, 254, 255
——— Pass, 256, 257, 258
Haleakala, 94, 95
Hamilton, 47

Happy Valley, 221
Harry Smith's, 80
Havannah Harbour, 122
—————————— missionary station, 123
Havannah Passage, 195
Hawaii, Island of, 97
Hawaiian, liquor law, 100
—————— missionary work, 115
—————— sugar, 96
Hawkesbury river, 18
Head hunters, 184
High Commissioner of Western Pacific, 207
Hill fortresses, 184, 186
Hiogo (Kobe), 244, 245
Hobart Town, 23
—————— climate of, 10
Hokitiki, 37
Hong Kong, 219, 220
Honolulu, 89

I.

Illiberal government, an, 227
Ill-treatment of natives, 210, 214
Indispensable Strait, 179
Inca, the burning of, 317
Incas, the, 29, 303, 304, 315, 316, 317
—————— irrigation works of, 313
—————— government of, 304
Inland Sea, 243
Inner Roads, Buenos Ayres, 337
Institutions, Honolulu, 117
Iquiqui, 316
Island of Nou, 198
—————— convict station, 198

J.

Jackson, Port, 17, 26
Japan, 240
Japanese art, 249
—————— cleanly habits, 270

Japanese cottages, 263
—————— country life, 262, 263, 281
—————— forests, 269
—————— irrigation, 270, 271
—————— peasants, 263, 266, 282
—————— politeness, 267
—————— politician's views, 274
—————— revolution, the, 267, 272, 273
—————— silk districts, 276
—————— smallness of the, 268
—————— statistics, 286
—————— tea houses, 264, 268
—————— theatre, 283, 284
—————— villages, 262
Java sea, 2
Johnson, white trader, 134
Jones, Rev. Mr. 121, 192

K.

Kalakaua, king, 91, 92
Kangaroo, a big, 13
—————— driving, 13
—————— four-in-hand after, 15
—————— hunting, 12
Kanaka divers, 3
Kango riding, 252, 253
Kava drinking, 71
Kealakeakua Bay, 113, 114
Kiga, 254
Kilauea, 99
——————, descent into, 101, 102
King country, 48
Kingstown, New Zealand, 32
Kioto, 248, 251
Kobe (Hiogo), 244, 245
Kuanon, temple of, 283
Kumara, 38
Kushan, monastry, 235, 236

L.

Labour Trade, 203
—————— abuse of, 211

Labour Trade, state of, 204
Lake of fire, 103, 104
La Libertad, 296
Landing at Nitendi, 161
———— Norfolk Island, 52
La Perouse, 148
Las Casas, 303
Legend, native, 139
Lelouova, 157
Letter of Mr. Neilson, 210
Levuka, 64, 65
———— street life, 65, 66
———— village near, 67
Lima, 305, 306
———— cathedral at, 307
———— cemetery, 308
———— gardens at, 309
List of South Sea massacres, 207
———————— white outrages, 210
Lo, Island of, 141
Long Reach, 330
Lord Howe's Island, 51
Lota, 330
Loyalty Islands, 120, 191, 192
———————— natives, 194
Lucia, Santa, 322
Lyttleton, 35

M.

Macwo, 126
———— graves at, 132
———— terraces at, 123
———— village at, 128
Magellan Straits, 330, 331
Malanta, 175, 179, 190
Malays, the, 218
Malicolo, 124
Mana, 353
Manco Capac, 315
Manta, the, 305
Manzanillo, 292
Maori curiosities, 39
———— war dance, 42
Maoris, condition of, 47, 48

Mapoche, 321
Maré (Nengone), 120
Marriage customs, S. Sea Islands, 189
Masterton, 39
Mattiana, 187
Maui, 93, 126
Mauna Loa, 99, 105, 107
Maximilian, 293, 294
Mazatlan, 290, 291, 292
Mbau Island, 69, 73
Melbourne, 21
———— climate of, 10
———— club, 24
———— position of, 21
———— public gardens, 21
Melanesian Mission, 59, 60, 61
Mendaña, 145
Men-of-war, 205
Merelava, 136
Mesa, 161, 162
Mexico, 289
———— condition of, 294, 360
———— boatmen of, 290
Min River, the, 229
Mint at Osaka, 246
Miranda, H.M.S., 134
Missionary work, 115, 116, 117, 118, 194
Mississippi, 333
Mitsui-Bishi S.S. Co., 241
Moa, the, 35
Mollendo, 314
Molokai, 96
Money, curious, 131
Mont d'Or, 196
Monte Video, 333, 334
———— suburbs of, 335, 336
Moosmees, 265
Mota, Island of, 137
Mota Lava, 137
Mount Baw Baw, 24
Mount Cork, 37
Murder of Lieutenant Bower, 182, 205
Murderers, punishment of, 206, 207

Murray, river, 26
Murrumbidgee, river, 26
Myanoshita, 253

N.

Nagasaki, 241
———— harbour, 241
———— tea-houses, 242
Nagasendo, the, 259
Naiselene, death of, 121
Negroes at Rio, 350
———— at Bahia, 356
Nelson, New Zealand, 39
Nengone (Maré), 120, 192
———— natives of, 194
New Caledonia, 196
———————— area of, 196
———————— coast of, 196
———————— convicts, 198
———————— mineral resources, 196
———————— native houses, 200
———————— natives, 201
Newcastle, N.S.W., 27
New Japan, 267, 272, 273, 274, 281
New South Wales, 16
New Year's Day at Lyttleton, 36
New Zealand, 31
———————— South Island of, 31
———————— North Island of, 39
Nezahualcoyotl, 295
Nicaragua, 298
Nikko, 277, 278
———— temples, 277
Nitendi, Santa Cruz, 148
Norfolk Island, 50, 119
———————— burial ground, 56
———————— prisoners at, 55
———————— scenery upon, 57
———————— Town, 54
Norfolkers, the, 54
Nobbs, Rev. G. N. 58
Noumea, 192, 197, 198
———— business at, 201
———— country round, 199

Nufiluli, 149
Nukapu, 147, 166
Nupani, 167

O.

Oahu, 89
Odawarra, 252
Ohinemutu, 46
Ohiowaki, 269
Opa (Lepers' Island), 133, 134
Orakei Korako, 41
Organ mountains, 349
Oroya railroad, 310, 311, 312
———————— altitudes upon, 312
Osaka, 246
———— bronze work, 247
Otago, 31
Otira Gorge, 37
Otzu, 260

P.

Pagoda anchorage, 229
Pali, the, 92
Panama, 297, 298
———— canal, 298
———— hats, 302
———— railroad, 298
Paraná, river, 339
Patagonians, 331
Patteson, Bishop, 59
Payta, 304
Pearl fisheries, 2
Peasants of Chile, 326
Pedro Segundo railroad, 356
Penang, 217, 218
Penny, Rev. A. 180
Pentecost (Aragh) 124
Pernambuco, 358
Peru, 303, 359
———— coast of, 314
———— condition of, 309, 317
Petropolis, 354
Pileni, 149
Pimmentel, 304

Pinus Cookii, 120
Pitcairn's Island, 50, 51
Pizarro, 289, 303, 309, 317
Plata, Rio de la, 333
Platform houses, 180
Poi, 111
Pokefullum, 221
Poncho, 305
Port Jackson, 17, 26
Port Mackay, 142
Postage to Australia, 30
Pululaä, 175
——— curious custom, 177
——— feast at, 176
Puno, 315
Punta Arenas, 296, 331

Q.

Queensland, 2, 9
Queenstown, New Zealand, 32
Quintas, Monte Video, 335

R.

Rapids near Kioto, 250
Reception at Club-house, Santa Cruz, 163
Reef Islands, the, 149
Reefs, New Caledonia, 195, 196
——— South Sea Islands, 202
Religious War, Nengone, 193
Rewa River, 77
——————— delta of, 78
——————— sugar mills, 80
Rimac River, 310
Rio Bio Bio, 328
Rio de la Plata, 333
Rio de Janeiro, 348
——————— Bay, 348, 349
Rosario, H.M.S., 166
Rosario, South America, 340
Rotomahana, 44
Rotorua, 46
Rua do Ovidor, 356

S.

Saä, 175
Saladero, 346, 347
Sampans, 220
San Christoval, 179, 190
Sandal-wood, English, 142
Sandwich Islands, 89
——————— natives of, 110, 111
San José de Guatemala, 295
San Salvador, 296
Santa Cruz Islands, 147
——————— canoes, 153
——————— head rests, 165
——————— landing at, 149
——————— natives, 158
——————— pupil, 165
——————— weapons, 159
Santa Maria, 138
Santa Ysabel, 183
Santiago, 321
——— Alameda, 324
——— cathedral, 324
——— Jesuit Church, 325
——— situation of, 321, 322
Savo, Island of, 182
——— chief of, 183
Selwyn, Bishop, 129, 141, 160
Shanghai, 224
——— curio shops, 225
——— native city, 224
——— tea-houses, 252
Sharp Peak, 229
Sheba, temple of, 281
Sheep-farming, Patagonia, 331
Shimonoséki, 243, 244,
Shoguns, tombs of, 278
Sinter Terraces, 44
Singapore, 1, 219
Sole, Peruvian, 306
Solomon Islands, 146, 168
——————— beauties, 189
——————— bowls, 174
——————— canoes, 170, 187
——————— feasts, 177

Solomon Islands, marriage customs, 189
——————— money, 188
——————— natives, 169
——————— spears, 178
Somerset, 3
South Australia, 28
Spanish America, 289
——— Conquerors, 303, 317
Southern Cross, 119
Squall, caught in a, 135
Station life, 12, 13, 15
Steamer, Hawaiian, 93
——— Japanese, 260
Street theatre, 222
Sugar, Hawaiian, 93
——— Fiji, 80, 84
——— Port Mackay, 142
Sugar Loaf, Rio de Janeiro, 319
Suva, Fiji, 83
Swatow, 221, 222
Sydney, 16, 20
——— climate of, 10
——— clubs, 20
——— harbour, 16
——— public gardens, 22
——— suburbs of, 18

T.

Taboga, islands of, 297
Tahau, 42
Takasaki, 272, 275
Takua, Florida chief, 189
Talca, 326
Tambora, volcano, 1
Tanoa, King, Fiji, 86
Tapua, Island of, 148
Tasmania, 23
Tattooing, Solomon Islands, 190
Taupo, lake, 40
Tea, 233
— farmers, 233
— gardens, 232

Tea girls, 233, 245, 265
— houses, 264, 265
— preparation of, 233
Te Kooti, 42
Temples, Chiomin, 248
——— Kioto, 281
——— Kushan, 237
——— Nikko, 277, 278
Teramakau, river, 39
Terraces, Maewo, 133
———, Rotomahana, 44
Terra del Fuego, 331
Teufelsdröckh, 323
Tezcucan philosophy, 295
Thakombau, 69
——— interview with, 75
The Bluff, New Zealand, 31
Thousand Ships' Bay, 183
Thursday Island, 2
Tijuca, 351, 352
Tinakolo, 167
Titicaca, 46, 315
Tokaido, 252, 256, 259
Tokio, 281
Tongariro, 40
Toowoomba, 9
Tori, the, 281
Torres Islands (Avava), 141
——— Straits, 2
Trade, for natives, 204
Traders, Nengone, 195
——— South Sea Islands, 210
Tree ferns, 25
Tree-houses, 184
Trees, Big, Victoria, 24
Tucuman, 340
Tumaco, 299
Tycoon's castle, Osaka, 246

U.

Ulaua, 168
——— disturbance at, 172
Unfriendly natives, 175

V.

Valdivia, 322
Valparaiso, 391, 320
Vanikoro, 148
Vanua Lava, 138
Vaté, 122, 124
Victoria, 16
Victorian politics, 22
Viña del Mar, 321
Visitors' book, Kilauea, 109
Viti Levu, 67

W.

Waikato, 41, 47
Waikjki, 92
Waimakariri, 37
Wairarapa Plains, 40
Wairoa, 44
Wakatipu, 32, 33
Wallaby shooting, 13
Wanganui, 48
Wango, 173
Waterfall, Hiogo, 245
———— Maewo, 126
Weissnichtwo, 323
Wellington, 39
Western Australia, 28
Whitsunday Passage, 4

Y.

Yacan, 319
Yams, buying, 125
Yang-tse-Kiang, 240
Yarra Yarra, 21
Yokohama, 251
Ysabel, Island of, 183
Yumota, 278, 279
———— baths at, 280

LONDON:
PRINTED BY WILLIAM CLOWES AND SONS, Limited,
STAMFORD STREET AND CHARING CROSS

www.ingramcontent.com/pod-product-compliance
Lightning Source LLC
Chambersburg PA
CBHW030426300426
44112CB00009B/870